THE GOON™

VIRTUE
AND THE GRIM CONSEQUENCES THEREOF

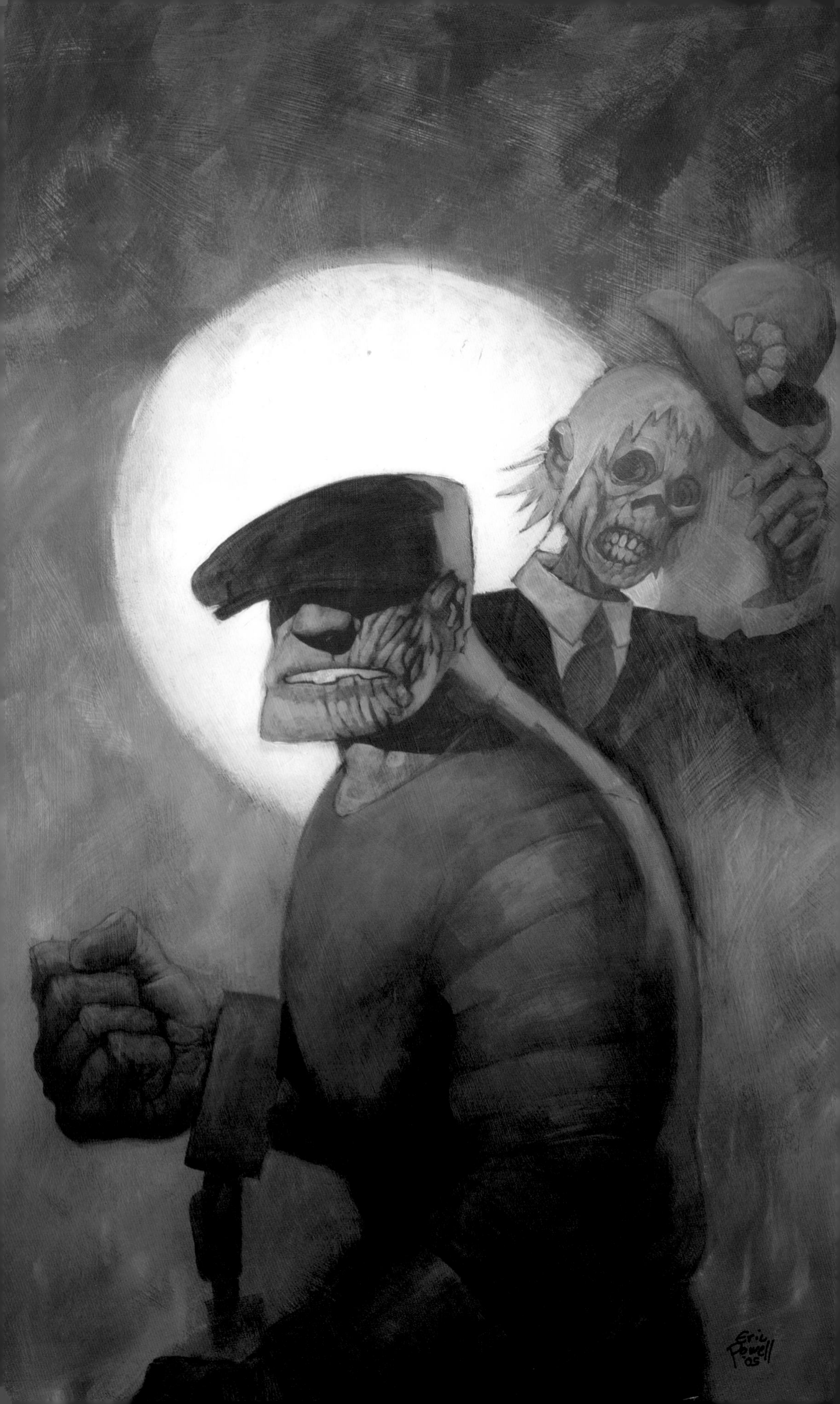

THE GOON ™

VIRTUE AND THE GRIM CONSEQUENCES THEREOF

by Eric Powell

color assists by
Robin Powell

"Jimmy Turtle and the Legendary Boxcar of Well-Made Ladies' Shoes"
written by **Thomas Lennon**

editor | designer
Matt Dryer | **Amy Arendts**

art director | publisher
Lia Ribacchi | **Mike Richardson**

Zombies provided by Jethro & Earl Zombie Wranglerin' Inc.
and The Adopt-A-Zombie Foundation

Ghost of Christmas Presents **Scott Allie**

Dark Horse Books ™

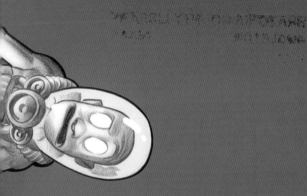

This volume collects issues 9-13 of Dark Horse Comics ongoing series *The Goon*.

Published by
Dark Horse Books
A division of
Dark Horse Comics, Inc.
10956 SE Main Street
Milwaukie, OR 97222

First Edition: February 2006
ISBN: 1-59307-456-5

1 3 5 7 9 10 8 6 4 2
Printed in China

Introduction

Congratulations to you, *The Goon* enthusiast!

You hold in your hand something very special (and expensive! When first released, these five issues would have cost you a total of $14.95. Now they're $16.95). But this volume is well worth the extra dollar or two. It is a landmark in *Goon* history. It could even be … the beginning of the end!

In 2004, Eric Powell received an Eisner Award. One could have been a miscount. But at the 2005 Comic-Con International in San Diego, Mr. Powell received two Eisners. TWO. A pattern is being established. This double-win can only be a harbinger of crap-ola to come for his readers. Now begins Mr. Powell's rocket ride into super-stardom, to that place in the sun that Rush described as: "The Limelight." (Rush, *Moving Pictures*, Mercury Records, 1981.)

The five issues in this volume are from when Mr. Powell was still "nobody"—just a good-natured hillbilly who could draw like Goya. This volume is the last of the P.t.2.W.E.A.s (Pre the Two Will Eisner Awards, pronounced: pri-tchwo-ee-ards). These issues are still the work of an unrecognized genius, whose every pen stroke leaps from the page and punches you right in the face.

From here on in, Powell will be a recognized genius—plodding along on that mangy burro called success.

Yes, there will be more issues of *The Goon*, but the drawings are likely to be slapdash, scribbled between polo matches, art auctions, and Tara Reid's pool parties. Franky's face might have a ring-shaped stain on it, from where the author set down his martini to gaze fondly at his award-laden mantelpiece.

Subsequent issues will be known as the A.t.2.W.E.A.s (pronounced: af-trath-deue-eis-nwärds. Or just say "After the Two Eisner Awards," it's easier than trying to pronounce the abbreviation). In the A.t.2.W.E.A.s, look for appearances by the author's new celebrity friends. Don't be surprised to see Jay-Z or the cast of *The O.C.* sidled up to the bar at Norton's. Perhaps in *Goon* #15, Buzzard will break up Lindsay Lohan's *tete-a-tete* with the Psychic Seal.

Corporate America will hitch their wagon to Powell's triple-Eisner-award-winning ass, too. Look for Peaches Valentine in his poop-filled diaper and brand-new Nike Shox®; perhaps Buzzard will live on the flesh of zombies and Funyuns®!

Authors should only be celebrated after their deaths. Just ask our pal Ernie Hemingway what happens to writers who are declared to be brilliant during their lifetimes: they end up sponge-painting the walls with a twelve-gauge shotgun and their own brain.

Perhaps Mr. Powell can escape the fate of the "genius comic auteur," but that will require the help of you, his readers. Be vigilant. Keep him humble! Keep his feet on the ground! Do not hesitate to write to Mr. Powell and tell him that he sucks donkey balls. If you cross paths with Mr. Powell, toss a can of Mountain Dew at his head and yell: "Yo, Powell, you suck donkey balls!" The words (and the soda can) will sting, and he does not deserve them, but the emotional and physical pain they inflict will be bottled up inside, then come pouring out in the form of his best work ever. Art isn't about awards, it's about pain—and it's up to you to inflict it. You helped put Eric Powell on a pedestal—now, quick, knock it out from under him while he's not looking.

Thomas Lennon
California, U.S.A.
August 2005

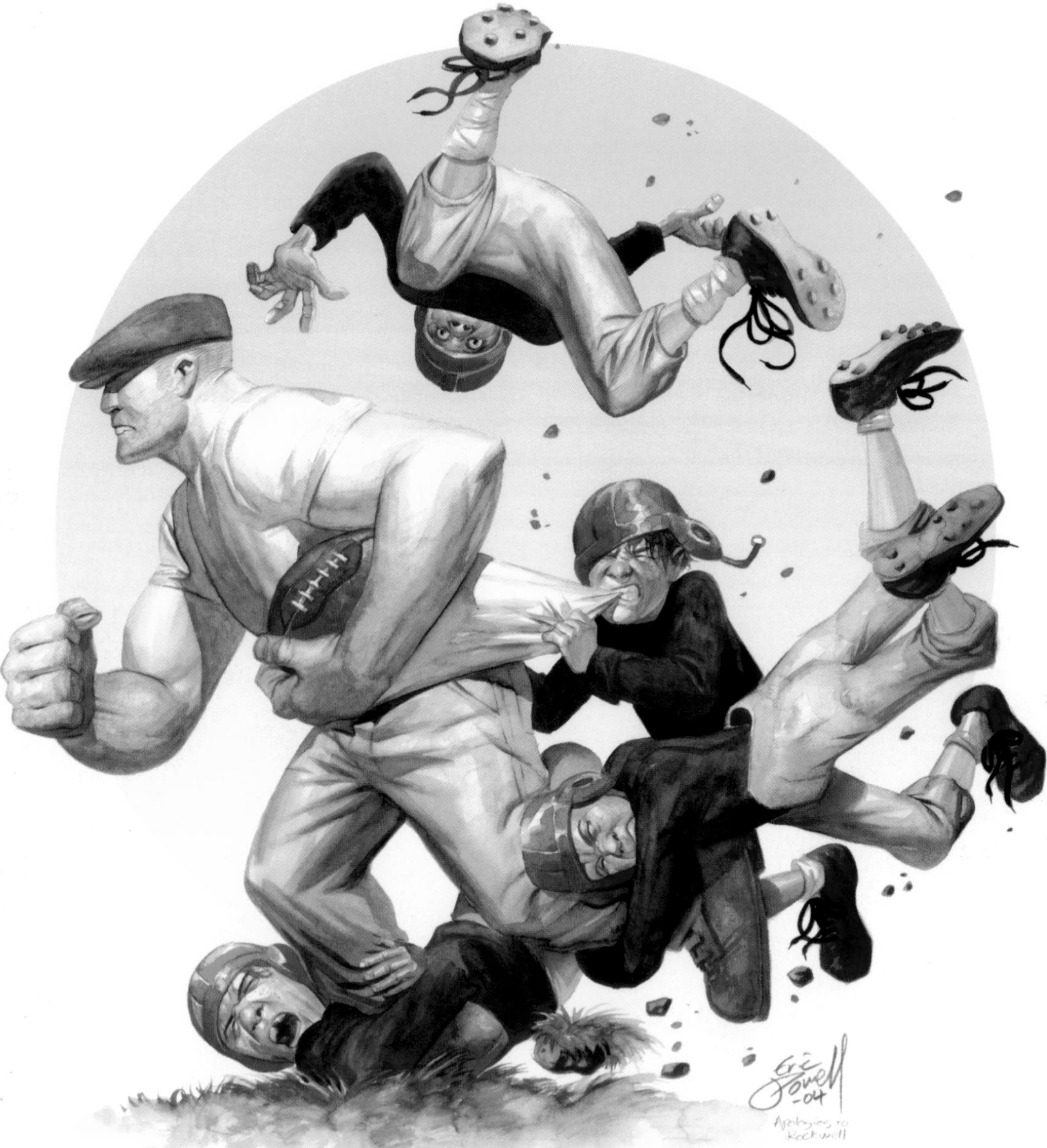
Eric Powell -04
Apologies to Rockwell

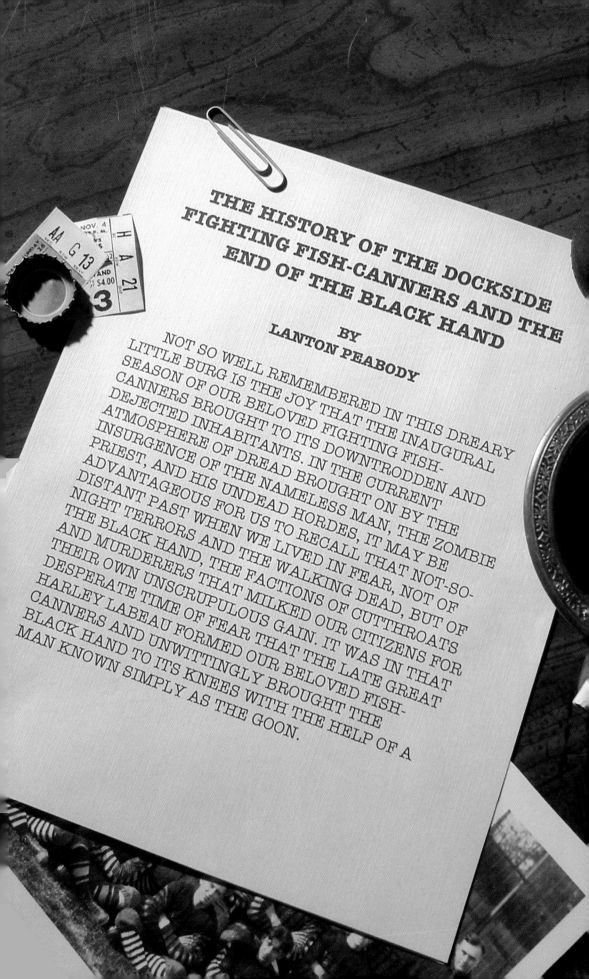

THE HISTORY OF THE DOCKSIDE FIGHTING FISH-CANNERS AND THE END OF THE BLACK HAND

BY
LANTON PEABODY

NOT SO WELL REMEMBERED IN THIS DREARY LITTLE BURG IS THE JOY THAT THE INAUGURAL SEASON OF OUR BELOVED FIGHTING FISH-CANNERS BROUGHT TO ITS DOWNTRODDEN AND DEJECTED INHABITANTS. IN THE CURRENT ATMOSPHERE OF DREAD BROUGHT ON BY THE INSURGENCE OF THE NAMELESS MAN, THE ZOMBIE PRIEST, AND HIS UNDEAD HORDES, IT MAY BE ADVANTAGEOUS FOR US TO RECALL THAT NOT-SO-DISTANT PAST WHEN WE LIVED IN FEAR, NOT OF NIGHT TERRORS AND THE WALKING DEAD, BUT OF THE BLACK HAND, THE FACTIONS OF CUTTHROATS AND MURDERERS THAT MILKED OUR CITIZENS FOR THEIR OWN UNSCRUPULOUS GAIN. IT WAS IN THAT DESPERATE TIME OF FEAR THAT THE LATE GREAT HARLEY LABEAU FORMED OUR BELOVED FISH-CANNERS AND UNWITTINGLY BROUGHT THE BLACK HAND TO ITS KNEES WITH THE HELP OF A MAN KNOWN SIMPLY AS THE GOON.

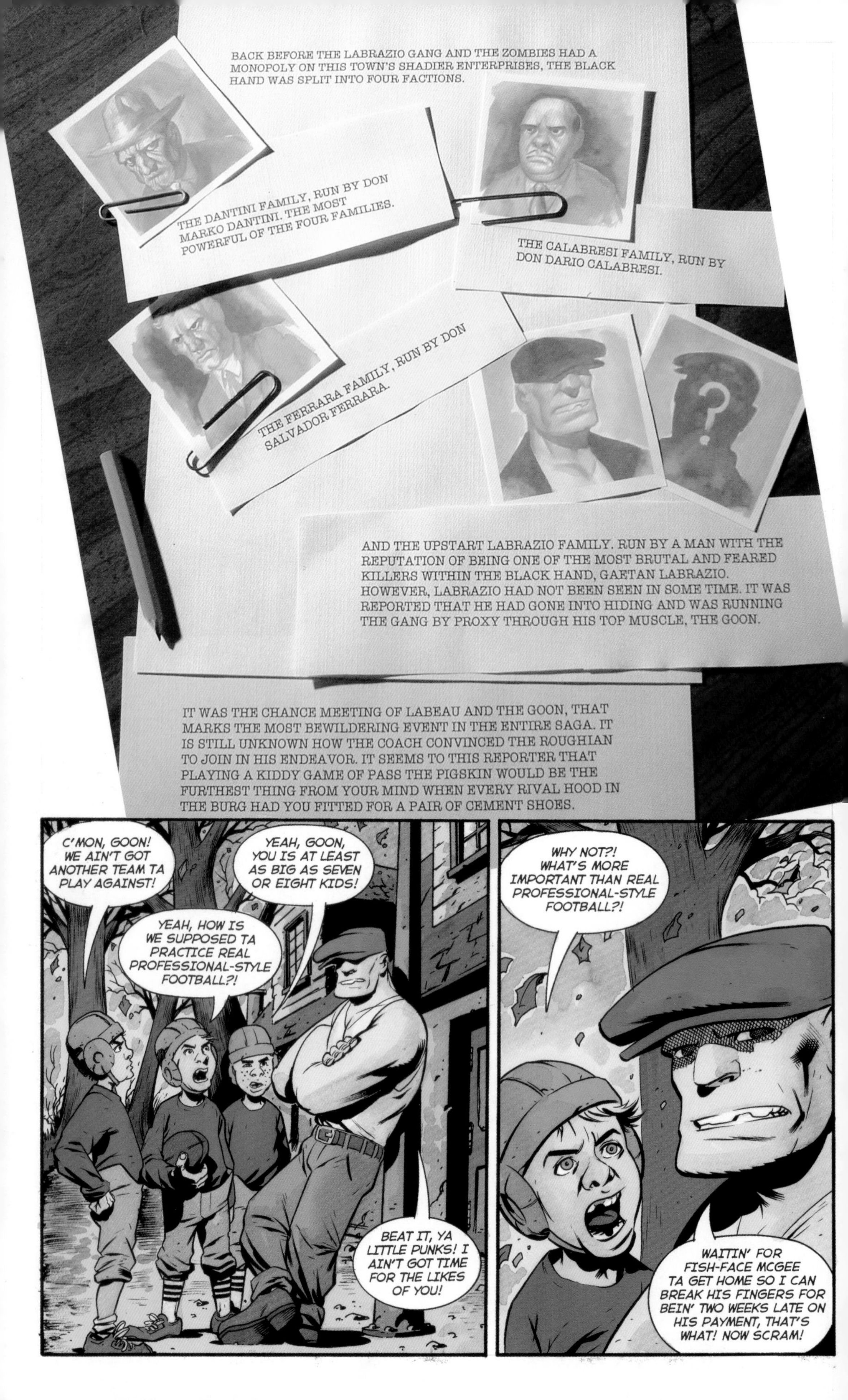

BACK BEFORE THE LABRAZIO GANG AND THE ZOMBIES HAD A MONOPOLY ON THIS TOWN'S SHADIER ENTERPRISES, THE BLACK HAND WAS SPLIT INTO FOUR FACTIONS.
THE DANTINI FAMILY, RUN BY DON MARKO DANTINI. THE MOST POWERFUL OF THE FOUR FAMILIES.
THE CALABRESI FAMILY, RUN BY DON DARIO CALABRESI.
THE FERRARA FAMILY, RUN BY DON SALVADOR FERRARA.
?
AND THE UPSTART LABRAZIO FAMILY. RUN BY A MAN WITH THE REPUTATION OF BEING ONE OF THE MOST BRUTAL AND FEARED KILLERS WITHIN THE BLACK HAND, GAETAN LABRAZIO. HOWEVER, LABRAZIO HAD NOT BEEN SEEN IN SOME TIME. IT WAS REPORTED THAT HE HAD GONE INTO HIDING AND WAS RUNNING THE GANG BY PROXY THROUGH HIS TOP MUSCLE, THE GOON.
IT WAS THE CHANCE MEETING OF LABEAU AND THE GOON, THAT MARKS THE MOST BEWILDERING EVENT IN THE ENTIRE SAGA. IT IS STILL UNKNOWN HOW THE COACH CONVINCED THE ROUGHIAN TO JOIN IN HIS ENDEAVOR. IT SEEMS TO THIS REPORTER THAT PLAYING A KIDDY GAME OF PASS THE PIGSKIN WOULD BE THE FURTHEST THING FROM YOUR MIND WHEN EVERY RIVAL HOOD IN THE BURG HAD YOU FITTED FOR A PAIR OF CEMENT SHOES.
C'MON, GOON! WE AIN'T GOT ANOTHER TEAM TA PLAY AGAINST!
YEAH, GOON, YOU IS AT LEAST AS BIG AS SEVEN OR EIGHT KIDS!
YEAH, HOW IS WE SUPPOSED TA PRACTICE REAL PROFESSIONAL-STYLE FOOTBALL?!
BEAT IT, YA LITTLE PUNKS! I AIN'T GOT TIME FOR THE LIKES OF YOU!
WHY NOT?! WHAT'S MORE IMPORTANT THAN REAL PROFESSIONAL-STYLE FOOTBALL?!
WAITIN' FOR FISH-FACE MCGEE TA GET HOME SO I CAN BREAK HIS FINGERS FOR BEIN' TWO WEEKS LATE ON HIS PAYMENT, THAT'S WHAT! NOW SCRAM!

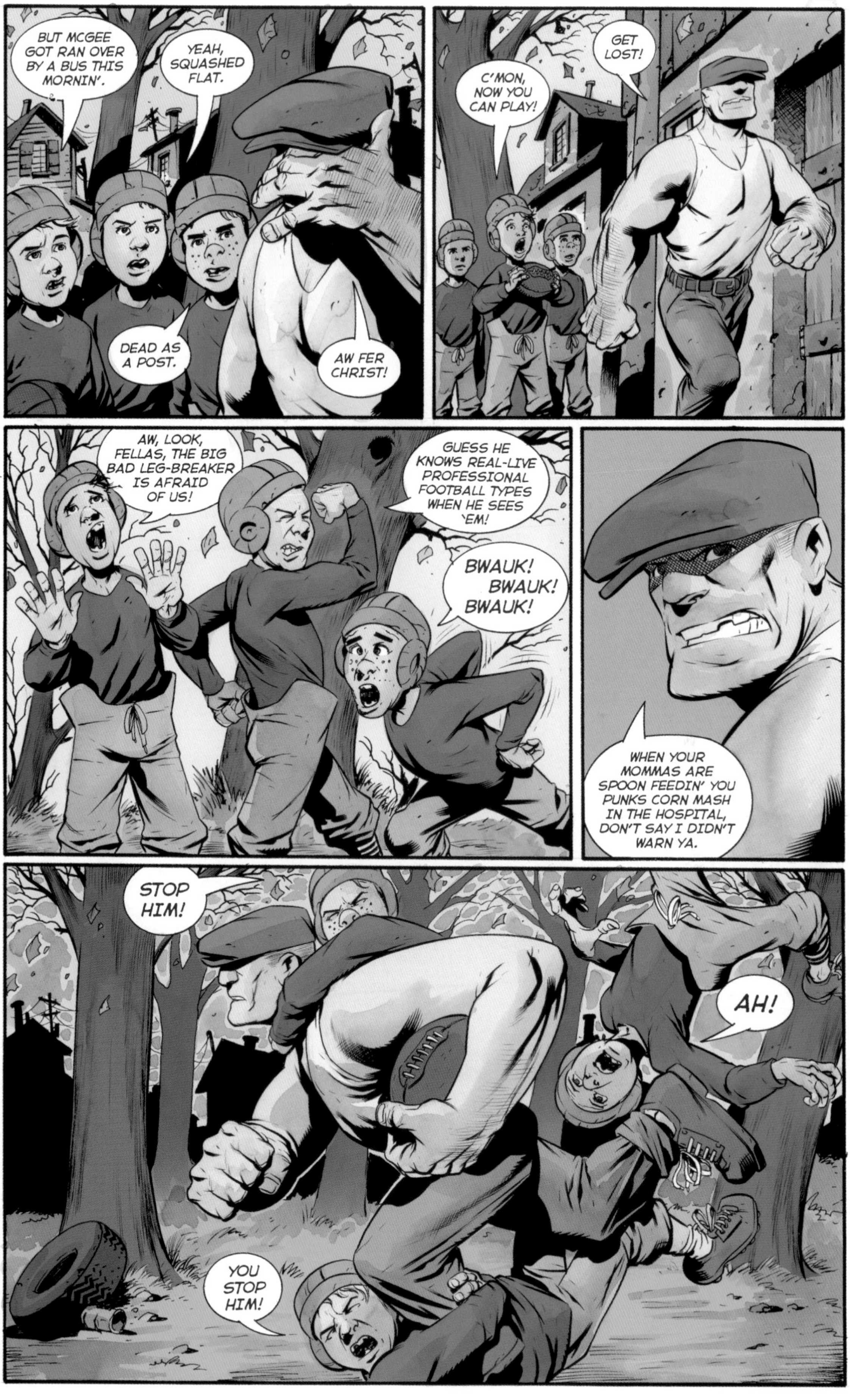

BUT MCGEE GOT RAN OVER BY A BUS THIS MORNIN'.
YEAH, SQUASHED FLAT.
DEAD AS A POST.
AW FER CHRIST!
GET LOST!
C'MON, NOW YOU CAN PLAY!
AW, LOOK, FELLAS, THE BIG BAD LEG-BREAKER IS AFRAID OF US!
GUESS HE KNOWS REAL-LIVE PROFESSIONAL FOOTBALL TYPES WHEN HE SEES 'EM!
BWAUK! BWAUK! BWAUK!
WHEN YOUR MOMMAS ARE SPOON FEEDIN' YOU PUNKS CORN MASH IN THE HOSPITAL, DON'T SAY I DIDN'T WARN YA.
STOP HIM!
AH!
YOU STOP HIM!

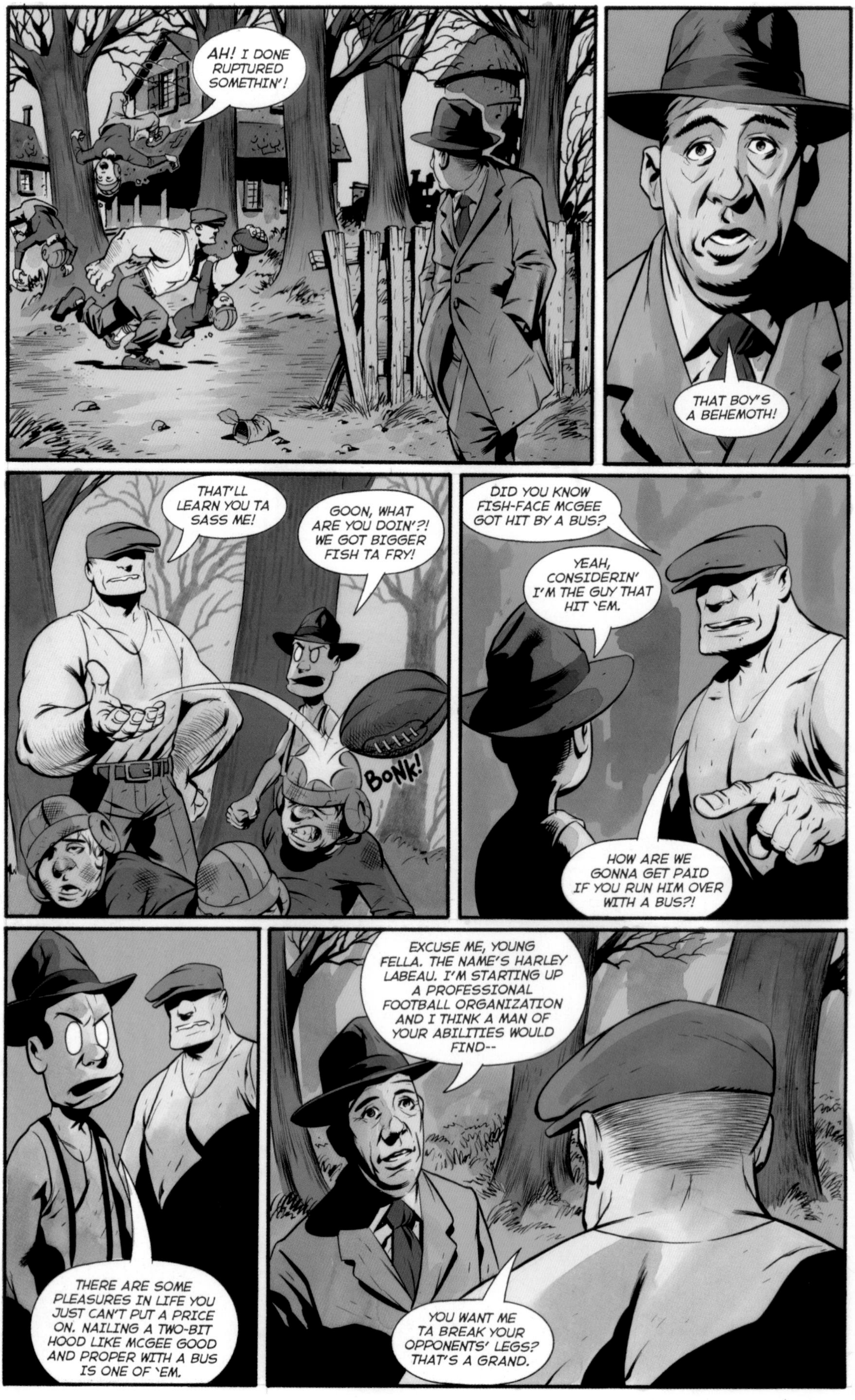
AH! I DONE RUPTURED SOMETHIN'!
THAT BOY'S A BEHEMOTH!
THAT'LL LEARN YOU TA SASS ME!
GOON, WHAT ARE YOU DOIN'?! WE GOT BIGGER FISH TA FRY!
BONK!
DID YOU KNOW FISH-FACE MCGEE GOT HIT BY A BUS?
YEAH, CONSIDERIN' I'M THE GUY THAT HIT 'EM.
HOW ARE WE GONNA GET PAID IF YOU RUN HIM OVER WITH A BUS?!
THERE ARE SOME PLEASURES IN LIFE YOU JUST CAN'T PUT A PRICE ON. NAILING A TWO-BIT HOOD LIKE MCGEE GOOD AND PROPER WITH A BUS IS ONE OF 'EM.
EXCUSE ME, YOUNG FELLA. THE NAME'S HARLEY LABEAU. I'M STARTING UP A PROFESSIONAL FOOTBALL ORGANIZATION AND I THINK A MAN OF YOUR ABILITIES WOULD FIND--
YOU WANT ME TA BREAK YOUR OPPONENTS' LEGS? THAT'S A GRAND.

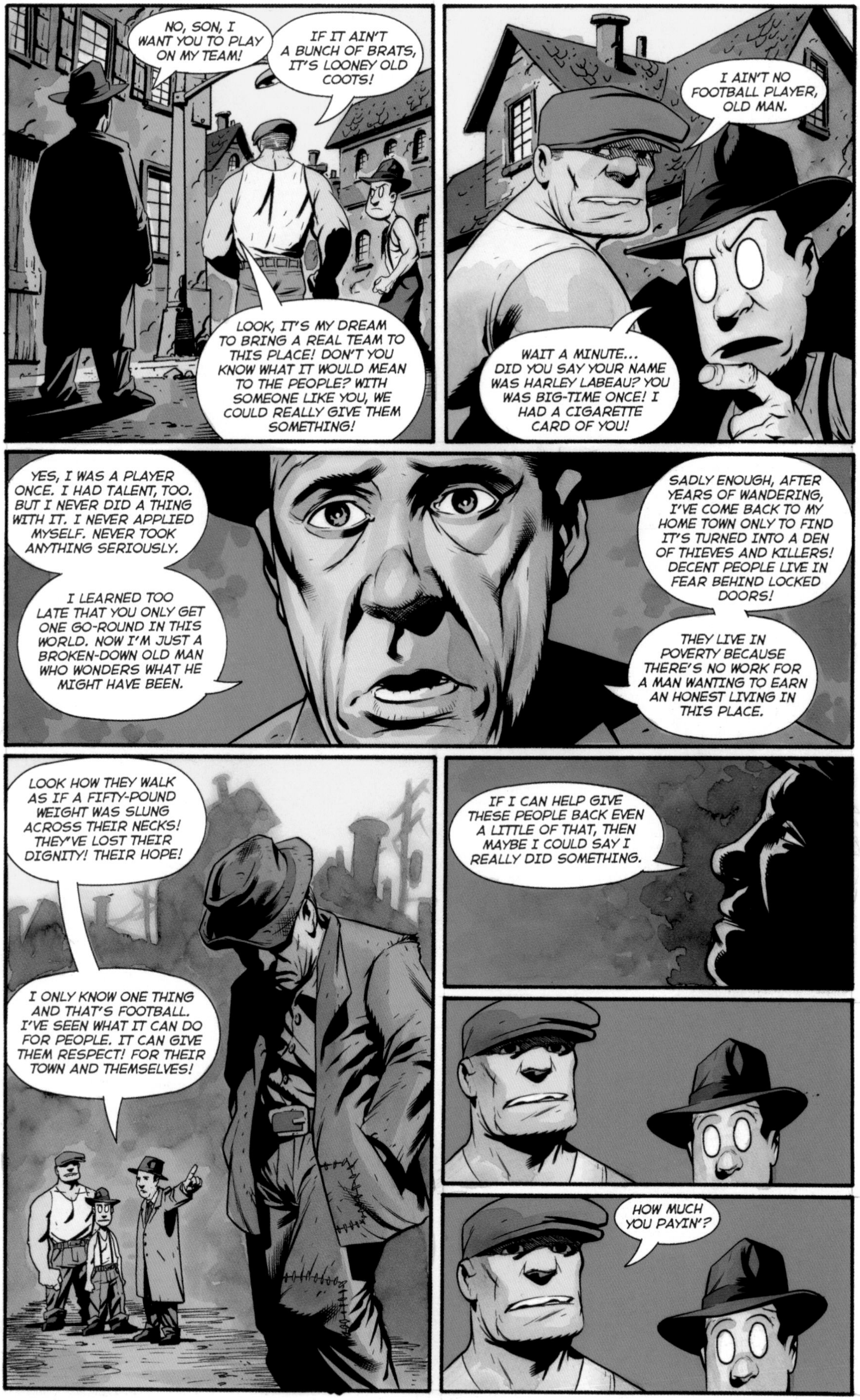
NO, SON, I WANT YOU TO PLAY ON MY TEAM!
IF IT AIN'T A BUNCH OF BRATS, IT'S LOONEY OLD COOTS!
LOOK, IT'S MY DREAM TO BRING A REAL TEAM TO THIS PLACE! DON'T YOU KNOW WHAT IT WOULD MEAN TO THE PEOPLE? WITH SOMEONE LIKE YOU, WE COULD REALLY GIVE THEM SOMETHING!
I AIN'T NO FOOTBALL PLAYER, OLD MAN.
WAIT A MINUTE... DID YOU SAY YOUR NAME WAS HARLEY LABEAU? YOU WAS BIG-TIME ONCE! I HAD A CIGARETTE CARD OF YOU!
YES, I WAS A PLAYER ONCE. I HAD TALENT, TOO. BUT I NEVER DID A THING WITH IT. I NEVER APPLIED MYSELF. NEVER TOOK ANYTHING SERIOUSLY.
I LEARNED TOO LATE THAT YOU ONLY GET ONE GO-ROUND IN THIS WORLD. NOW I'M JUST A BROKEN-DOWN OLD MAN WHO WONDERS WHAT HE MIGHT HAVE BEEN.
SADLY ENOUGH, AFTER YEARS OF WANDERING, I'VE COME BACK TO MY HOME TOWN ONLY TO FIND IT'S TURNED INTO A DEN OF THIEVES AND KILLERS! DECENT PEOPLE LIVE IN FEAR BEHIND LOCKED DOORS!
THEY LIVE IN POVERTY BECAUSE THERE'S NO WORK FOR A MAN WANTING TO EARN AN HONEST LIVING IN THIS PLACE.
LOOK HOW THEY WALK AS IF A FIFTY-POUND WEIGHT WAS SLUNG ACROSS THEIR NECKS! THEY'VE LOST THEIR DIGNITY! THEIR HOPE!
I ONLY KNOW ONE THING AND THAT'S FOOTBALL. I'VE SEEN WHAT IT CAN DO FOR PEOPLE. IT CAN GIVE THEM RESPECT! FOR THEIR TOWN AND THEMSELVES!
IF I CAN HELP GIVE THESE PEOPLE BACK EVEN A LITTLE OF THAT, THEN MAYBE I COULD SAY I REALLY DID SOMETHING.
HOW MUCH YOU PAYIN'?

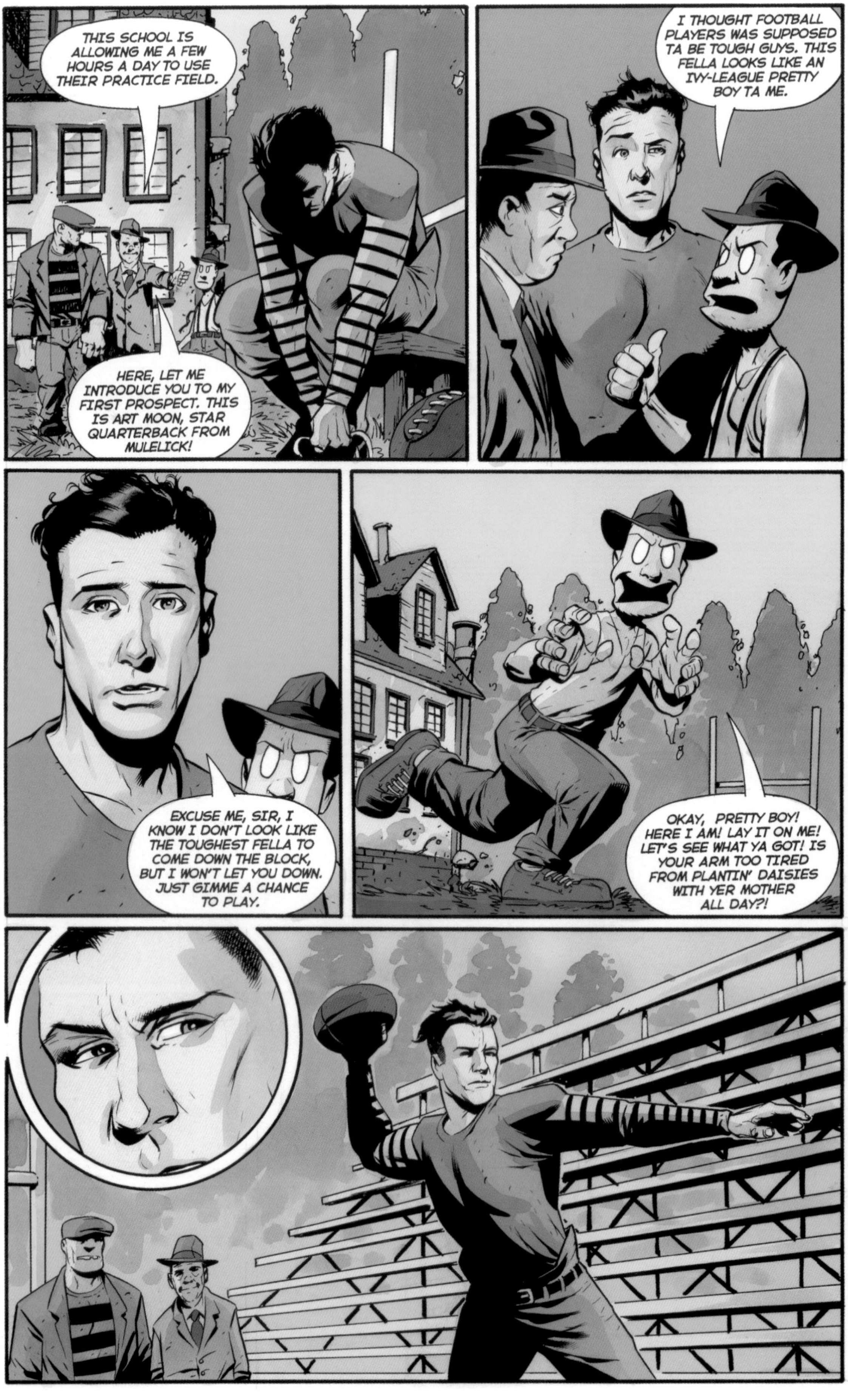
THIS SCHOOL IS ALLOWING ME A FEW HOURS A DAY TO USE THEIR PRACTICE FIELD.
HERE, LET ME INTRODUCE YOU TO MY FIRST PROSPECT. THIS IS ART MOON, STAR QUARTERBACK FROM MULELICK!
I THOUGHT FOOTBALL PLAYERS WAS SUPPOSED TA BE TOUGH GUYS. THIS FELLA LOOKS LIKE AN IVY-LEAGUE PRETTY BOY TA ME.
EXCUSE ME, SIR, I KNOW I DON'T LOOK LIKE THE TOUGHEST FELLA TO COME DOWN THE BLOCK, BUT I WON'T LET YOU DOWN. JUST GIMME A CHANCE TO PLAY.
OKAY, PRETTY BOY! HERE I AM! LAY IT ON ME! LET'S SEE WHAT YA GOT! IS YOUR ARM TOO TIRED FROM PLANTIN' DAISIES WITH YER MOTHER ALL DAY?!

AAA
HH
SNAP!
ARM LIKE A CANNON!
SAY, THAT'S PRETTY GOOD.
C'MON, HARLEY. THIS GUY'LL DO FOR THROWIN' THE BALL AROUND, BUT YOU WANT SOME TOUGH GUYS, I CAN SHOW YA TOUGH GUYS. I KNOW A FELLA THAT'LL BREAK A MAN'S NECK FOR SOME POTATO CAKES.
WHAT ARE WE DOIN' HERE, GOON?!
YEAH, WE DON'T GOT NO BEEF WITH YOU!
WHAT GIVES?!
HURRY THIS UP, WILL YA! IT'S TIME FOR MY MA TA GET HER CORNS RUBBED AND SHE GETS CRANKY WHEN I AIN'T THERE TA DO IT!
GET HIM! DEVOTED SON, OR FREAK WHO LIKES TA HANDLE OLD LADIES' FEET! WHATTA YOU THINK?
I THINK HIS MOTHER LIVES DOWN MY BLOCK AND I'VE SEEN SEXIER HOOVES ON A PIG.

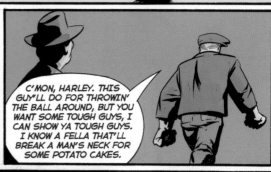

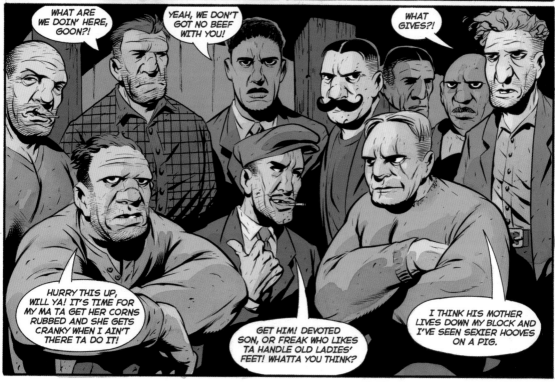

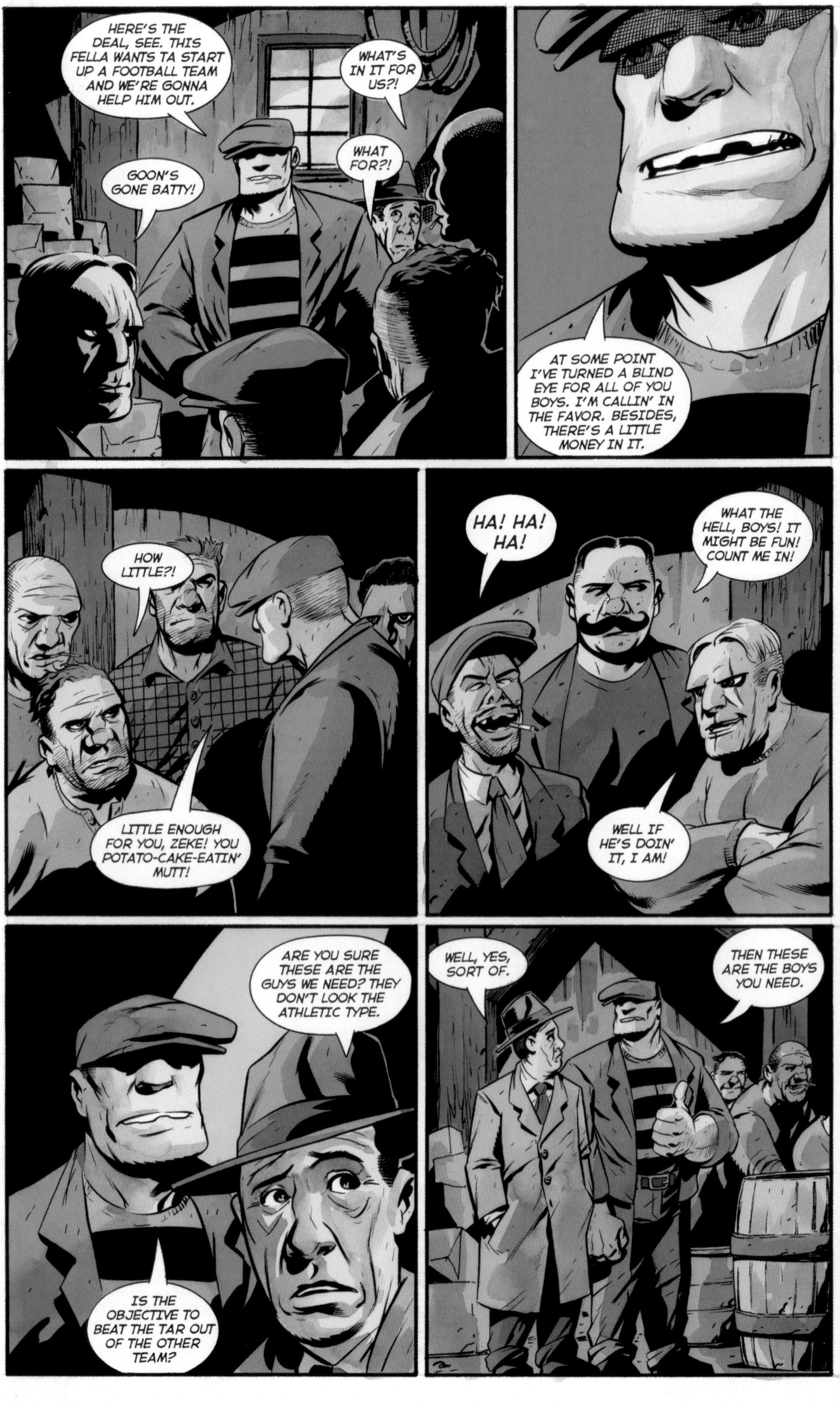
HERE'S THE DEAL, SEE. THIS FELLA WANTS TA START UP A FOOTBALL TEAM AND WE'RE GONNA HELP HIM OUT.
WHAT'S IN IT FOR US?!
GOON'S GONE BATTY!
WHAT FOR?!
AT SOME POINT I'VE TURNED A BLIND EYE FOR ALL OF YOU BOYS. I'M CALLIN' IN THE FAVOR. BESIDES, THERE'S A LITTLE MONEY IN IT.
HOW LITTLE?!
LITTLE ENOUGH FOR YOU, ZEKE! YOU POTATO-CAKE-EATIN' MUTT!
HA! HA! HA!
WHAT THE HELL, BOYS! IT MIGHT BE FUN! COUNT ME IN!
WELL IF HE'S DOIN' IT, I AM!
ARE YOU SURE THESE ARE THE GUYS WE NEED? THEY DON'T LOOK THE ATHLETIC TYPE.
IS THE OBJECTIVE TO BEAT THE TAR OUT OF THE OTHER TEAM?
WELL, YES, SORT OF.
THEN THESE ARE THE BOYS YOU NEED.

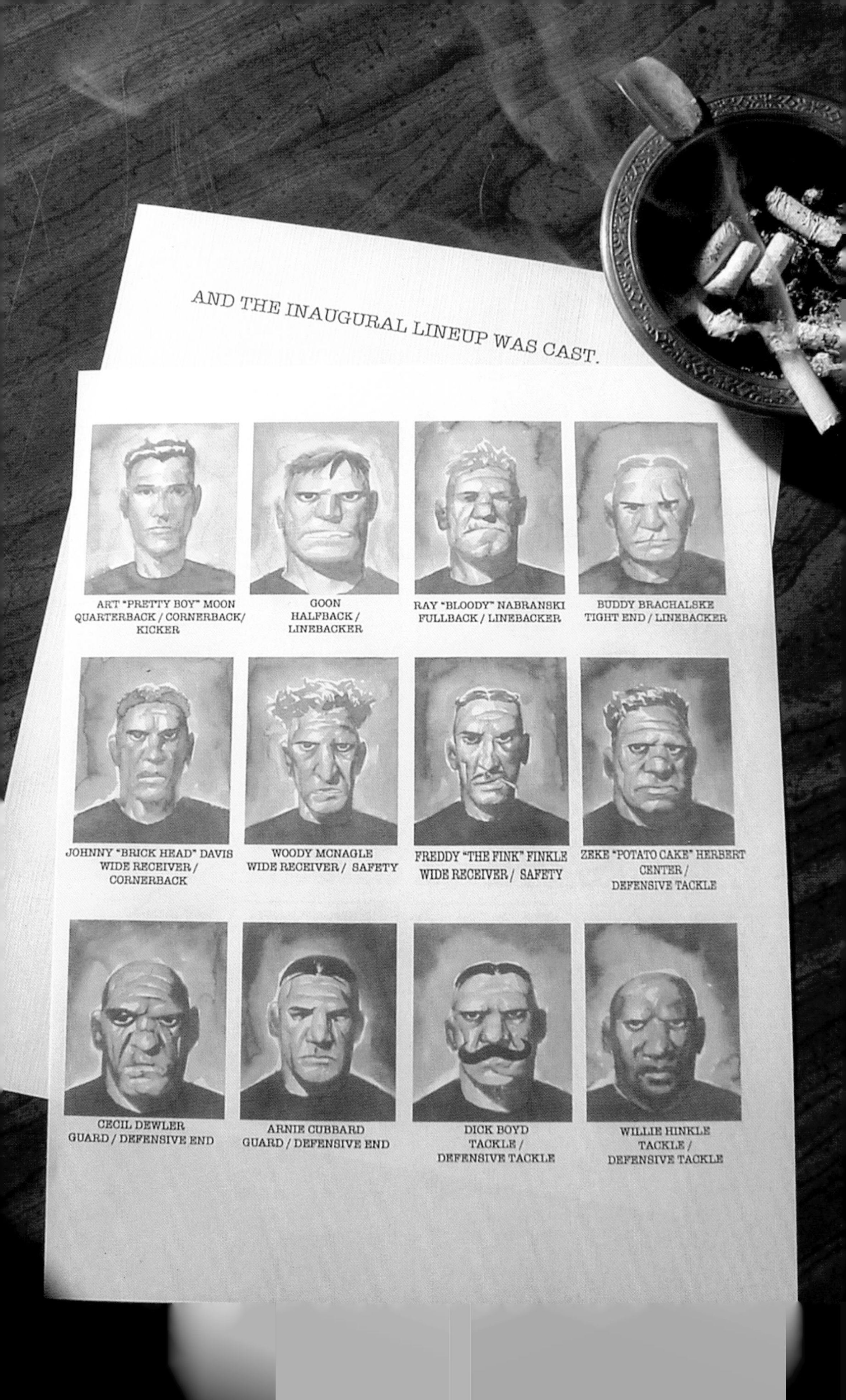
AND THE INAUGURAL LINEUP WAS CAST.
ART "PRETTY BOY" MOON
QUARTERBACK / CORNERBACK/ KICKER
GOON
HALFBACK / LINEBACKER
RAY "BLOODY" NABRANSKI
FULLBACK / LINEBACKER
BUDDY BRACHALSKE
TIGHT END / LINEBACKER
JOHNNY "BRICK HEAD" DAVIS
WIDE RECEIVER / CORNERBACK
WOODY MCNAGLE
WIDE RECEIVER / SAFETY
FREDDY "THE FINK" FINKLE
WIDE RECEIVER / SAFETY
ZEKE "POTATO CAKE" HERBERT
CENTER / DEFENSIVE TACKLE
CECIL DEWLER
GUARD / DEFENSIVE END
ARNIE CUBBARD
GUARD / DEFENSIVE END
DICK BOYD
TACKLE / DEFENSIVE TACKLE
WILLIE HINKLE
TACKLE / DEFENSIVE TACKLE

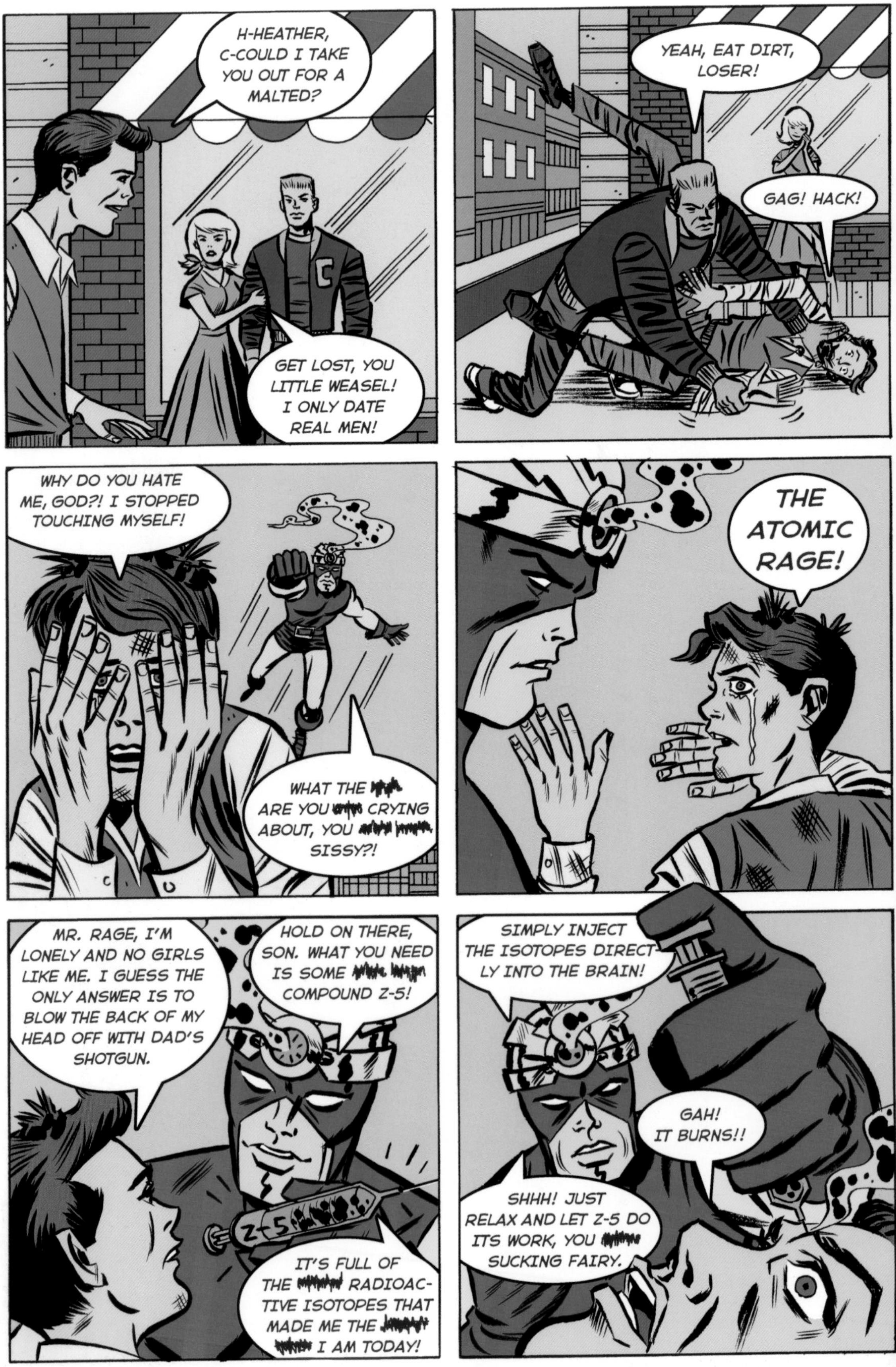
H-HEATHER, C-COULD I TAKE YOU OUT FOR A MALTED?
GET LOST, YOU LITTLE WEASEL! I ONLY DATE REAL MEN!
YEAH, EAT DIRT, LOSER!
GAG! HACK!
WHY DO YOU HATE ME, GOD?! I STOPPED TOUCHING MYSELF!
WHAT THE [redacted] ARE YOU [redacted] CRYING ABOUT, YOU [redacted] SISSY?!
THE ATOMIC RAGE!
MR. RAGE, I'M LONELY AND NO GIRLS LIKE ME. I GUESS THE ONLY ANSWER IS TO BLOW THE BACK OF MY HEAD OFF WITH DAD'S SHOTGUN.
HOLD ON THERE, SON. WHAT YOU NEED IS SOME [redacted] COMPOUND Z-5!
Z-5
IT'S FULL OF THE [redacted] RADIOACTIVE ISOTOPES THAT MADE ME THE [redacted] I AM TODAY!
SIMPLY INJECT THE ISOTOPES DIRECTLY INTO THE BRAIN!
GAH! IT BURNS!!
SHHH! JUST RELAX AND LET Z-5 DO ITS WORK, YOU [redacted] SUCKING FAIRY.

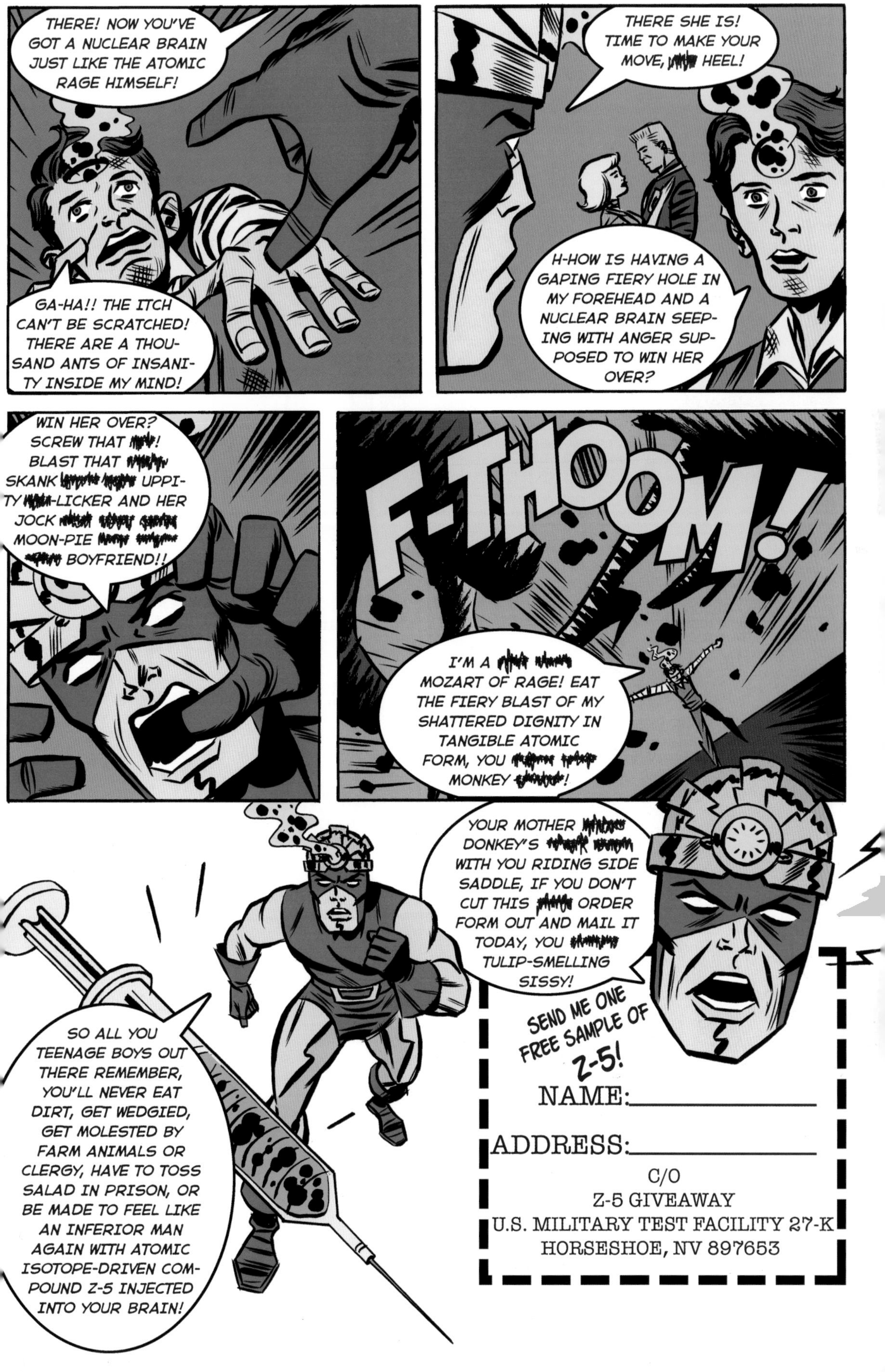
THERE! NOW YOU'VE GOT A NUCLEAR BRAIN JUST LIKE THE ATOMIC RAGE HIMSELF!
GA-HA!! THE ITCH CAN'T BE SCRATCHED! THERE ARE A THOUSAND ANTS OF INSANITY INSIDE MY MIND!
THERE SHE IS! TIME TO MAKE YOUR MOVE, [redacted] HEEL!
H-HOW IS HAVING A GAPING FIERY HOLE IN MY FOREHEAD AND A NUCLEAR BRAIN SEEPING WITH ANGER SUPPOSED TO WIN HER OVER?
WIN HER OVER? SCREW THAT [redacted]! BLAST THAT [redacted] SKANK [redacted] UPPITY [redacted]-LICKER AND HER JOCK [redacted] MOON-PIE [redacted] BOYFRIEND!!
F-THOOM!
I'M A [redacted] MOZART OF RAGE! EAT THE FIERY BLAST OF MY SHATTERED DIGNITY IN TANGIBLE ATOMIC FORM, YOU [redacted] MONKEY [redacted]!
YOUR MOTHER [redacted] DONKEY'S [redacted] WITH YOU RIDING SIDE SADDLE, IF YOU DON'T CUT THIS [redacted] ORDER FORM OUT AND MAIL IT TODAY, YOU [redacted] TULIP-SMELLING SISSY!
SO ALL YOU TEENAGE BOYS OUT THERE REMEMBER, YOU'LL NEVER EAT DIRT, GET WEDGIED, GET MOLESTED BY FARM ANIMALS OR CLERGY, HAVE TO TOSS SALAD IN PRISON, OR BE MADE TO FEEL LIKE AN INFERIOR MAN AGAIN WITH ATOMIC ISOTOPE-DRIVEN COMPOUND Z-5 INJECTED INTO YOUR BRAIN!
SEND ME ONE FREE SAMPLE OF Z-5!
NAME:
ADDRESS:
C/O
Z-5 GIVEAWAY
U.S. MILITARY TEST FACILITY 27-K
HORSESHOE, NV 897653

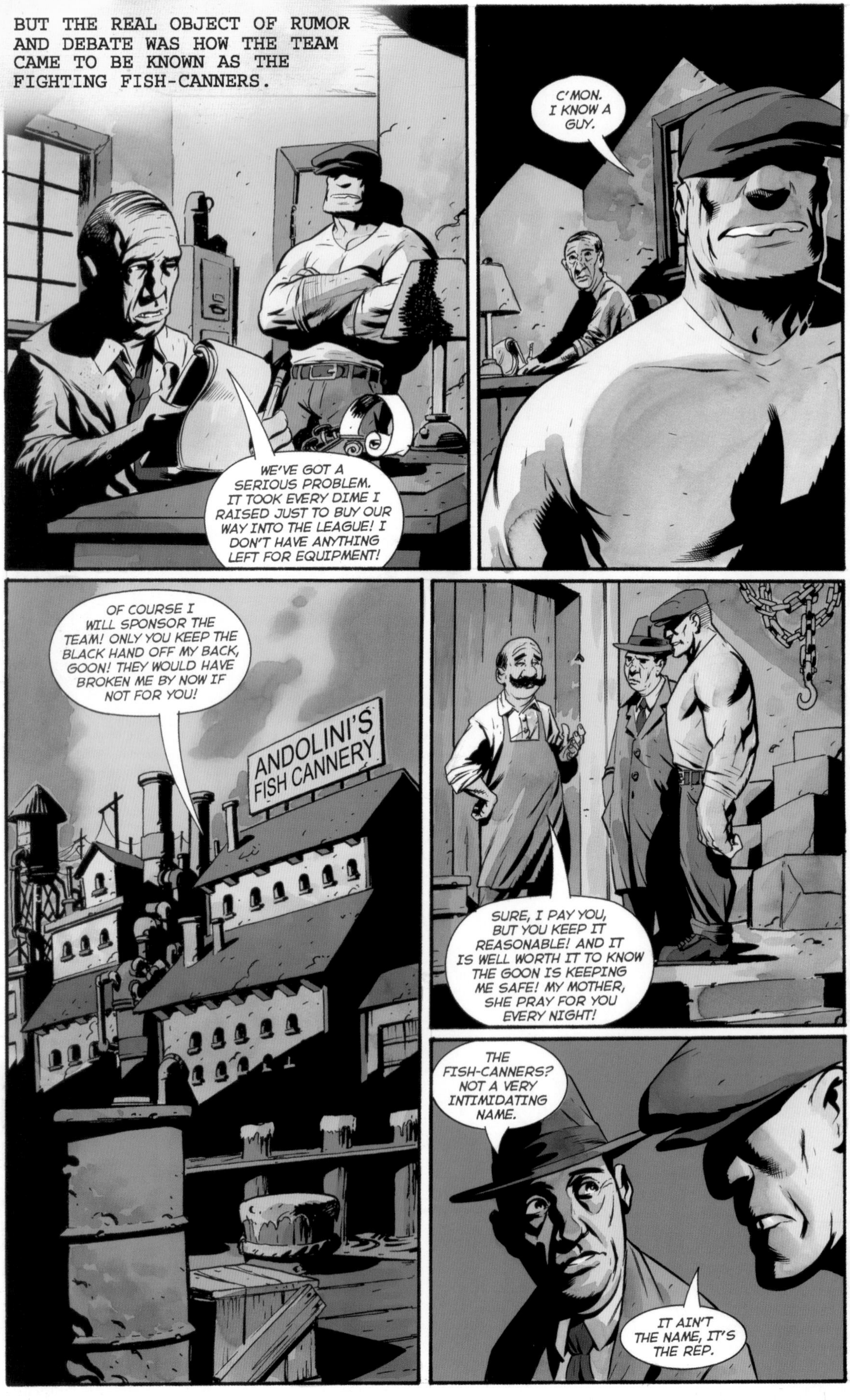
BUT THE REAL OBJECT OF RUMOR AND DEBATE WAS HOW THE TEAM CAME TO BE KNOWN AS THE FIGHTING FISH-CANNERS.
WE'VE GOT A SERIOUS PROBLEM. IT TOOK EVERY DIME I RAISED JUST TO BUY OUR WAY INTO THE LEAGUE! I DON'T HAVE ANYTHING LEFT FOR EQUIPMENT!
C'MON. I KNOW A GUY.
OF COURSE I WILL SPONSOR THE TEAM! ONLY YOU KEEP THE BLACK HAND OFF MY BACK, GOON! THEY WOULD HAVE BROKEN ME BY NOW IF NOT FOR YOU!
ANDOLINI'S FISH CANNERY
SURE, I PAY YOU, BUT YOU KEEP IT REASONABLE! AND IT IS WELL WORTH IT TO KNOW THE GOON IS KEEPING ME SAFE! MY MOTHER, SHE PRAY FOR YOU EVERY NIGHT!
THE FISH-CANNERS? NOT A VERY INTIMIDATING NAME.
IT AIN'T THE NAME, IT'S THE REP.

THE VERY FIRST GAME OF THIS UPSTART LINEUP WAS A STUNNING 42-3 VICTORY OVER THE HEAVILY FAVORED OPPONENT. SEVERAL INJURIES OCCURED DURING THE COURSE OF THE GAME. ALL OF WHICH, ODDLY ENOUGH, HAPPENED TO THE OPPOSING TEAM. NABRANSKI WAS EJECTED FROM THE GAME FOR KIDNEY PUNCHING THE REFEREE, AND GOON SET A FRANCHISE RUSHING RECORD OF 423 YARDS, WHICH STILL HAS NOT BEEN BROKEN TO THIS DAY.

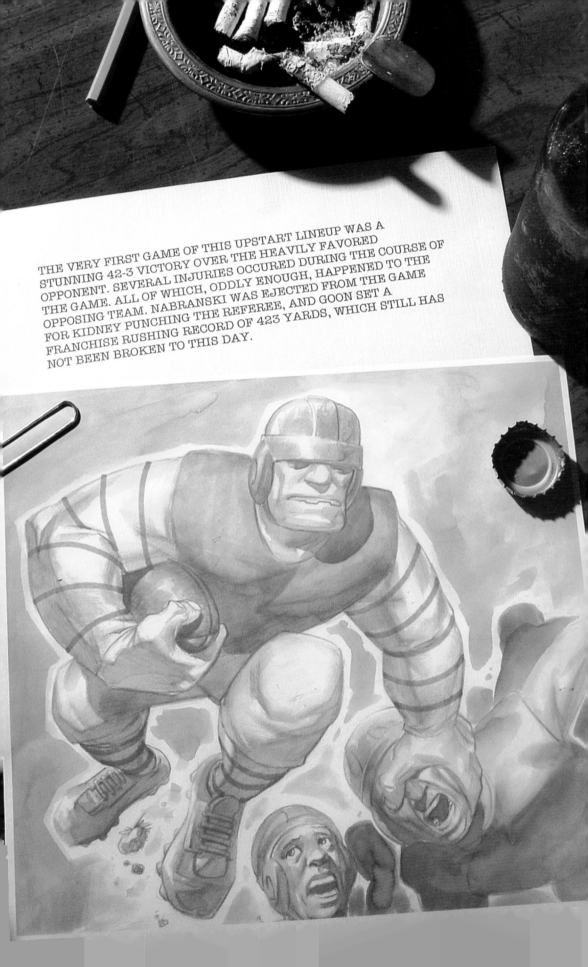

BUT IT WAS THIS EARLY SUCCESS AND GOON'S INVOLVEMENT THAT CAUGHT THE
EYE OF THE LABRAZIO GANG'S RIVAL FAMILIES... THE CALABRESI AND THE FERRARA.

IT'S A RACKET, I TELL YA!

WHY WOULD LABRAZIO HAVE HIS NUMBER-ONE GUY OUT THERE PLAYIN' IN THE MUD?!

IT'S A FIX! AND LABRAZIO IS ABOUT TO CLEAN UP!

BET EVERYTHING WE GOT AGAINST THE FISH-CANNERS IN THEIR NEXT GAME!

WE GOTTA BET ON THAT NEXT GAME, SEE!

SURE THEY WIN BIG THE LAST GAME, BUILD UP THE CONFIDENCE, BUT THEN GOON'S GONNA THROW THE NEXT ONE!

BET EVERYTHING WE GOT AGAINST THE FISH-CANNERS!!

THE CANNERS' NEXT OUTING WAS ALMOST AS IMPRESSIVE AS THEIR FIRST AS THEY POUNDED THEIR WAY TO A 32-7 VICTORY. AGAIN THE TEAM DOMINATED WITH THE GOON'S DOZER-LIKE RUNNING AND BRUTAL DEFENSIVE PLAY.

TO A POPULACE OF THE IMPOVERISHED LIVING IN FEAR, THE FISH-CANNERS BECAME A REASON TO GET UP IN THE MORNING...

DID YOU HEAR THE CANNERS' GAME ON THE RADIO LAST NIGHT?! THEY SLAUGHTERED THOSE KALAMAZOO BOYS!

THEY AIN'T GONNA COME DOWN HERE AND WHIP US! YOU GOTTA BE TOUGH TA LIVE IN THIS TOWN!

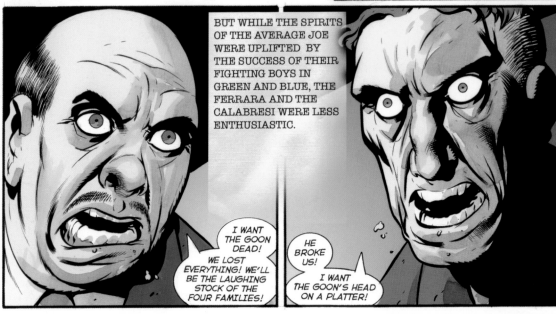

BUT WHILE THE SPIRITS OF THE AVERAGE JOE WERE UPLIFTED BY THE SUCCESS OF THEIR FIGHTING BOYS IN GREEN AND BLUE, THE FERRARA AND THE CALABRESI WERE LESS ENTHUSIASTIC.

I WANT THE GOON DEAD! WE LOST EVERYTHING! WE'LL BE THE LAUGHING STOCK OF THE FOUR FAMILIES!

HE BROKE US!

I WANT THE GOON'S HEAD ON A PLATTER!

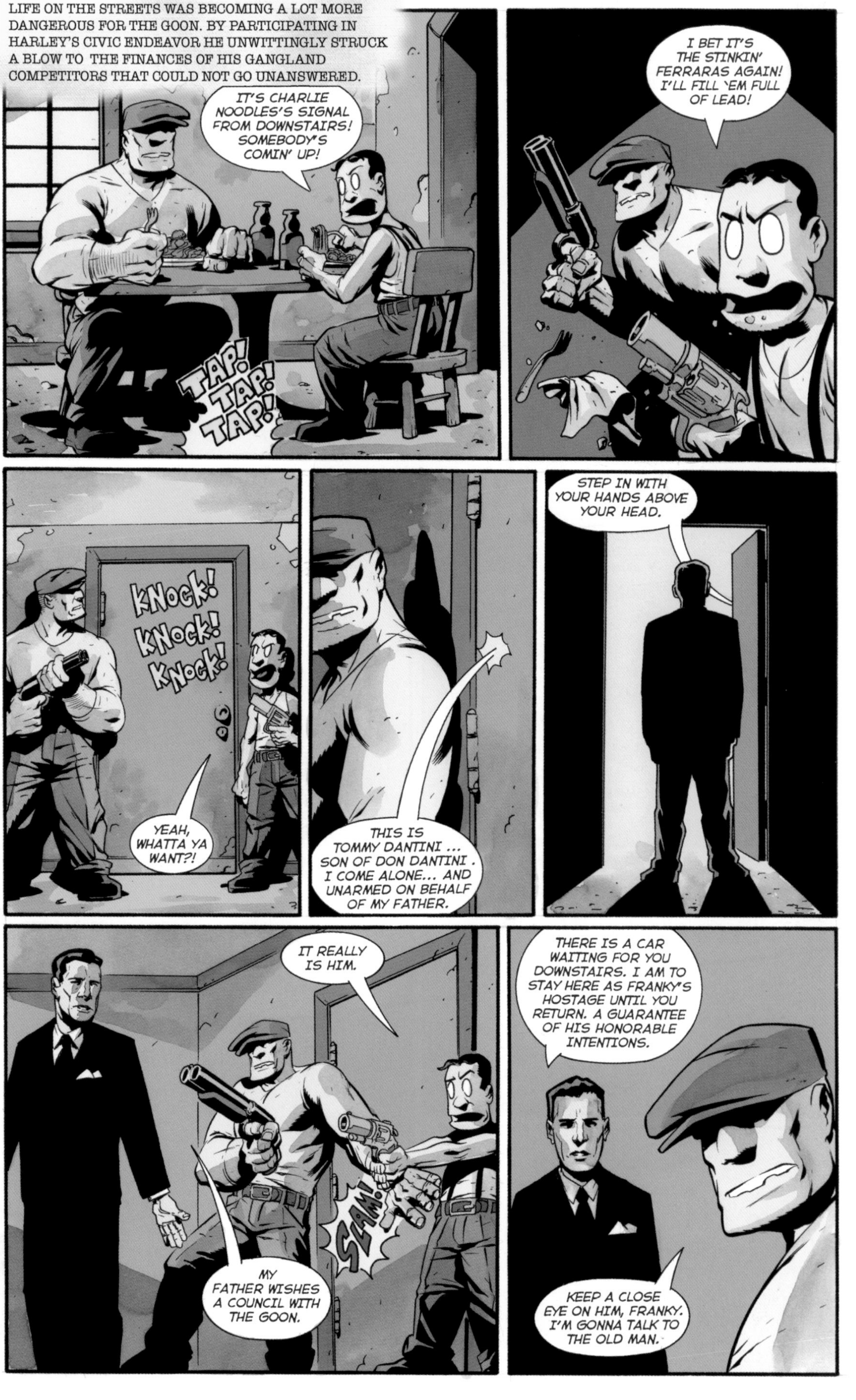
LIFE ON THE STREETS WAS BECOMING A LOT MORE DANGEROUS FOR THE GOON. BY PARTICIPATING IN HARLEY'S CIVIC ENDEAVOR HE UNWITTINGLY STRUCK A BLOW TO THE FINANCES OF HIS GANGLAND COMPETITORS THAT COULD NOT GO UNANSWERED.
IT'S CHARLIE NOODLES'S SIGNAL FROM DOWNSTAIRS! SOMEBODY'S COMIN' UP!
TAP! TAP! TAP!
I BET IT'S THE STINKIN' FERRARAS AGAIN! I'LL FILL 'EM FULL OF LEAD!
KNOCK! KNOCK! KNOCK!
YEAH, WHATTA YA WANT?!
THIS IS TOMMY DANTINI ... SON OF DON DANTINI . I COME ALONE... AND UNARMED ON BEHALF OF MY FATHER.
STEP IN WITH YOUR HANDS ABOVE YOUR HEAD.
IT REALLY IS HIM.
SLAM!
MY FATHER WISHES A COUNCIL WITH THE GOON.
THERE IS A CAR WAITING FOR YOU DOWNSTAIRS. I AM TO STAY HERE AS FRANKY'S HOSTAGE UNTIL YOU RETURN. A GUARANTEE OF HIS HONORABLE INTENTIONS.
KEEP A CLOSE EYE ON HIM, FRANKY. I'M GONNA TALK TO THE OLD MAN.

DON, THE GOON IS HERE.

AH, HELLO, GOON. IT IS A PLEASURE TO FINALLY BE ABLE TO MEET YOU IN PERSON. THE YOUNG MAN WITH SUCH A REPUTATION. HAVE A SEAT.

I'LL STAND.

IF YOU WISH.

I HEAR ODD STORIES THESE DAYS.

ABOUT SOME RACKET WITH YOU PLAYING IN BALL GAMES. I HEAR THE CALABRESIS AND FERRARAS HAVE LOST QUITE A BIT OF MONEY.

THEY SHOULDN'T HAVE BET AGAINST ME. AND IT AIN'T AN ANGLE.

YES, I CAN SEE THAT YOU ARE NOT THE MAN TO BE TAKEN LIGHTLY. BUT YOU KNOW THEY WILL KILL YOU FOR THIS.

ALL OF YOU HAVE BEEN TRYING TO DO THAT FOR A LONG TIME. I AIN'T DEAD YET.

≶SIGH≷ THE ARROGANCE OF YOUTH.

I WON'T BEAT AROUND THE BUSH ANY LONGER. I HAVE BROUGHT YOU HERE FOR TWO REASONS. ONE...

WHY DID YOU KILL LABRAZIO?

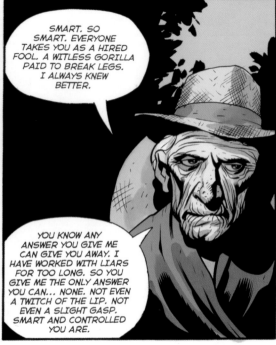

SMART. SO SMART. EVERYONE TAKES YOU AS A HIRED FOOL. A WITLESS GORILLA PAID TO BREAK LEGS. I ALWAYS KNEW BETTER.

YOU KNOW ANY ANSWER YOU GIVE ME CAN GIVE YOU AWAY. I HAVE WORKED WITH LIARS FOR TOO LONG. SO YOU GIVE ME THE ONLY ANSWER YOU CAN... NONE. NOT EVEN A TWITCH OF THE LIP. NOT EVEN A SLIGHT GASP. SMART AND CONTROLLED YOU ARE.

YOU WAIT FOR ME TO RESPOND FIRST. TO GAUGE. TO FIND OUT HOW MUCH I KNOW. EVEN NOW YOU ARE A BLANK WALL.

YOU HAVE NOTHING TO FEAR FROM ME. I HAVE ALWAYS KNOWN THAT LABRAZIO WAS DEAD AND THAT YOU HAD SOMETHING TO DO WITH IT.

I KNEW LABRAZIO WELL. WELL ENOUGH TO KNOW THAT GOING INTO HIDING AND LEAVING A CHILD, NO MATTER HOW FORMIDABLE, TO DO HIS COLLECTING WAS INCONCEIVABLE.

I COULD HAVE HAD YOU KILLED FOR THIS. LABRAZIO WAS A MADE MAN, AND ACCORDING TO THE CODE OF THE BLACK HAND, YOU DESERVED DEATH.

BUT I PREFERRED TO WATCH YOU. I WAS AMAZED THAT ANY BOY COULD PULL OFF SUCH A RUSE.

BUT AS I SAID, YOU HAVE NOTHING TO FEAR FROM ME. YOU HAVE NOTHING TO FEAR BECAUSE OF THE SECOND REASON I ASKED YOU HERE. I AM STEPPING DOWN AS DON OF THE DANTINI FAMILY.

MY FAMILY WILL BE GOING LEGITIMATE AS SOON AS I HAND OVER MY OPERATIONS TO MY SON, TOMMY. I DO NOT WANT MY SINS TO BECOME HIS. AS PER THE CODE, MY TERRITORIES WILL BE DIVIDED BETWEEN YOU, THE CALABRESI, AND THE FERRARA.

YOU MAY NOT KNOW IT, BUT IN SOME SMALL DEGREE, I HAVE KEPT THE OTHER FAMILIES OFF OF YOU. I HAVE DISTRACTED THEM AT TIMES. TRIED TO REDIRECT THEIR HOSTILITIES.

NOW THAT I WILL BE THERE NO MORE, IT WILL BE A RACE FOR YOUR HEAD. I WANTED TO WARN YOU.

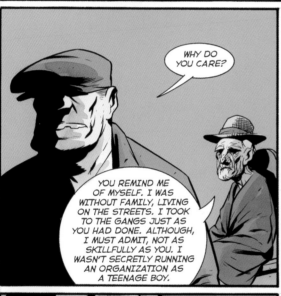

WHY DO YOU CARE?

YOU REMIND ME OF MYSELF. I WAS WITHOUT FAMILY, LIVING ON THE STREETS. I TOOK TO THE GANGS JUST AS YOU HAD DONE. ALTHOUGH, I MUST ADMIT, NOT AS SKILLFULLY AS YOU. I WASN'T SECRETLY RUNNING AN ORGANIZATION AS A TEENAGE BOY.

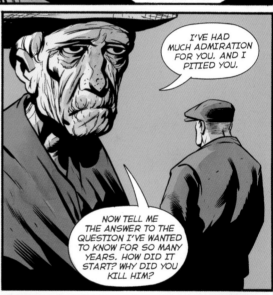

I'VE HAD MUCH ADMIRATION FOR YOU. AND I PITIED YOU.

NOW TELL ME THE ANSWER TO THE QUESTION I'VE WANTED TO KNOW FOR SO MANY YEARS. HOW DID IT START? WHY DID YOU KILL HIM?

HE KILLED THE ONLY PERSON IN THIS MISERABLE WORLD THAT EVER GAVE A DAMN ABOUT ME.

THEN HE DESERVED TO DIE. I AM SORRY FOR YOUR LOSS.

PLEASE SEE THAT MY SON IS RETURNED SAFELY. FROM THIS DAY ON MY FAMILY IS BLACK HAND NO MORE.

IN THE FOLLOWING MONTHS, THE ESCALATED VIOLENCE BETWEEN THE LABRAZIO, CALABRESI, AND FERRARA FAMILIES DID LITTLE TO HURT THE PERFORMANCE OF THE CANNERS. THEY POUNDED THEIR WAY TO THE FRANCHISE'S FIRST AND ONLY UNDEFEATED REGULAR SEASON. BUT THE BITTER EVENTS SURROUNDING THE CHAMPIONSHIP GAME WILL ALWAYS LEAVE US WONDERING WHAT MIGHT HAVE BEEN.

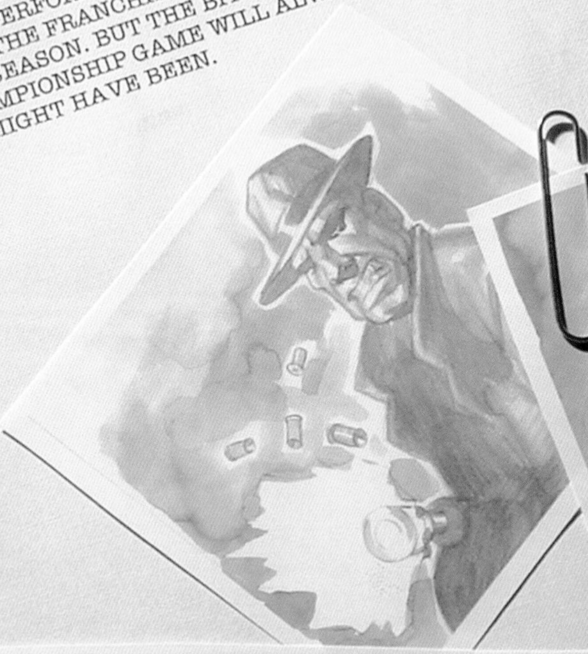

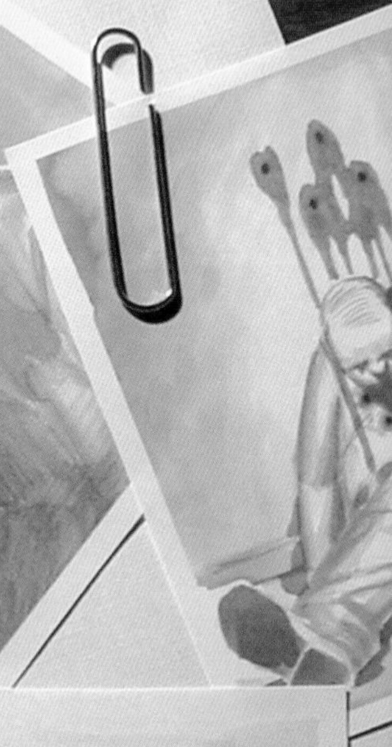

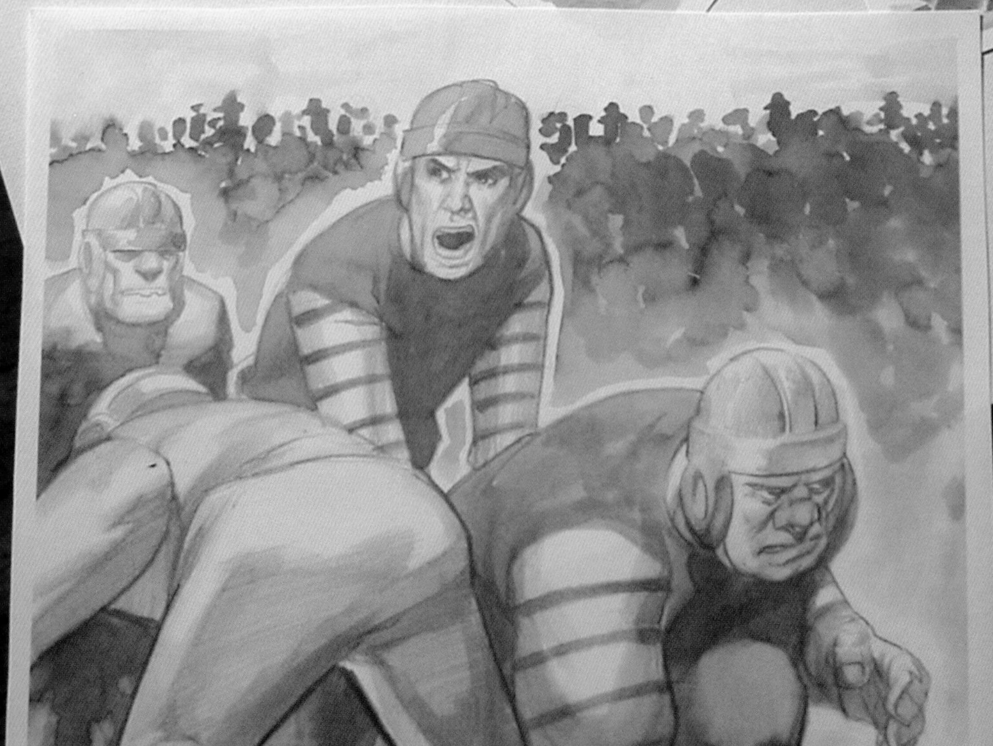

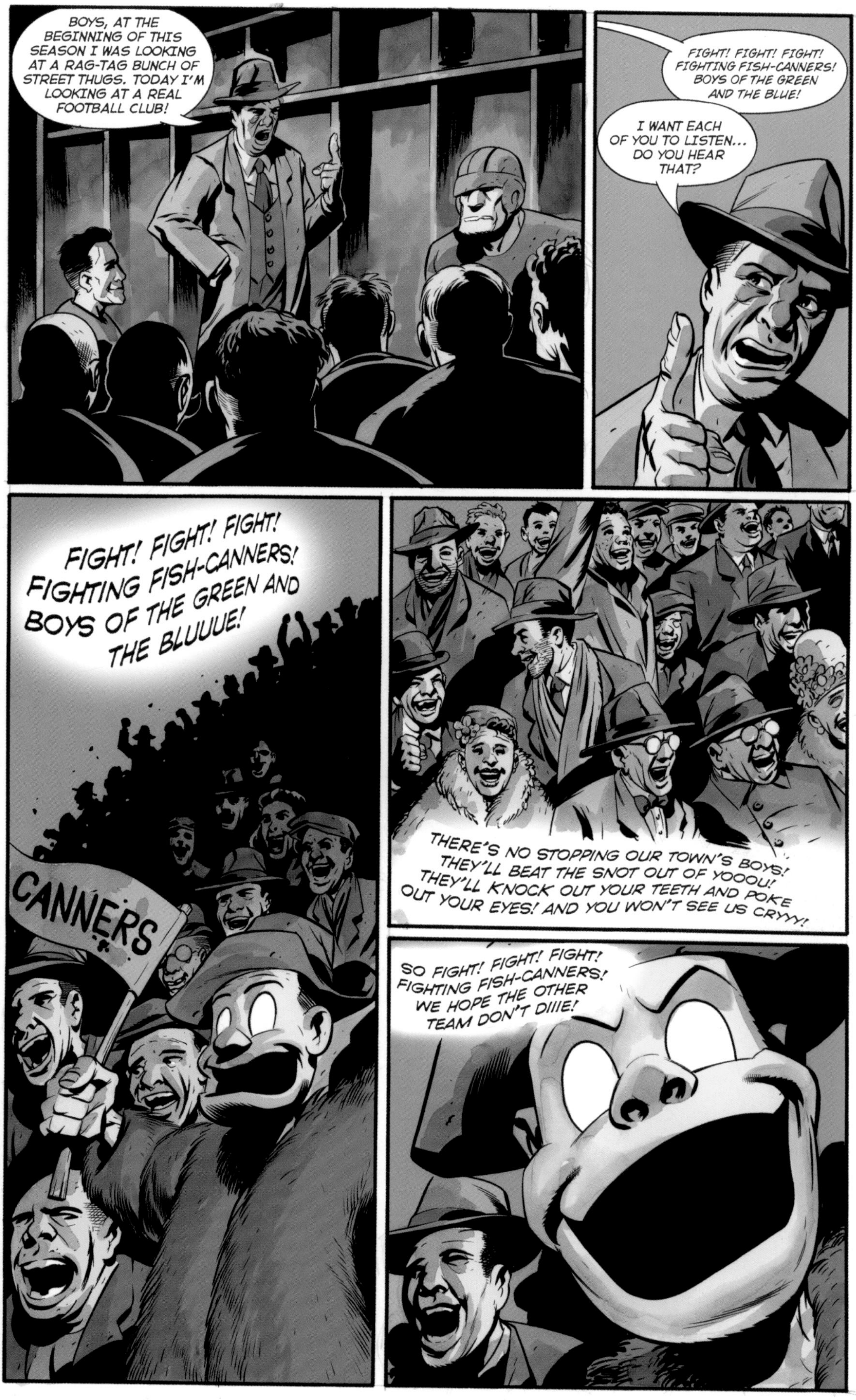
BOYS, AT THE BEGINNING OF THIS SEASON I WAS LOOKING AT A RAG-TAG BUNCH OF STREET THUGS. TODAY I'M LOOKING AT A REAL FOOTBALL CLUB!
FIGHT! FIGHT! FIGHT! FIGHTING FISH-CANNERS! BOYS OF THE GREEN AND THE BLUE!
I WANT EACH OF YOU TO LISTEN... DO YOU HEAR THAT?
FIGHT! FIGHT! FIGHT! FIGHTING FISH-CANNERS! FIGHTING FISH-CANNERS! BOYS OF THE GREEN AND THE BLUUUE!
CANNERS
THERE'S NO STOPPING OUR TOWN'S BOYS! THEY'LL BEAT THE SNOT OUT OF YOOOU! THEY'LL KNOCK OUT YOUR TEETH AND POKE OUT YOUR EYES! AND YOU WON'T SEE US CRYYY!
SO FIGHT! FIGHT! FIGHT! FIGHTING FISH-CANNERS! WE HOPE THE OTHER TEAM DON'T DIIIE!

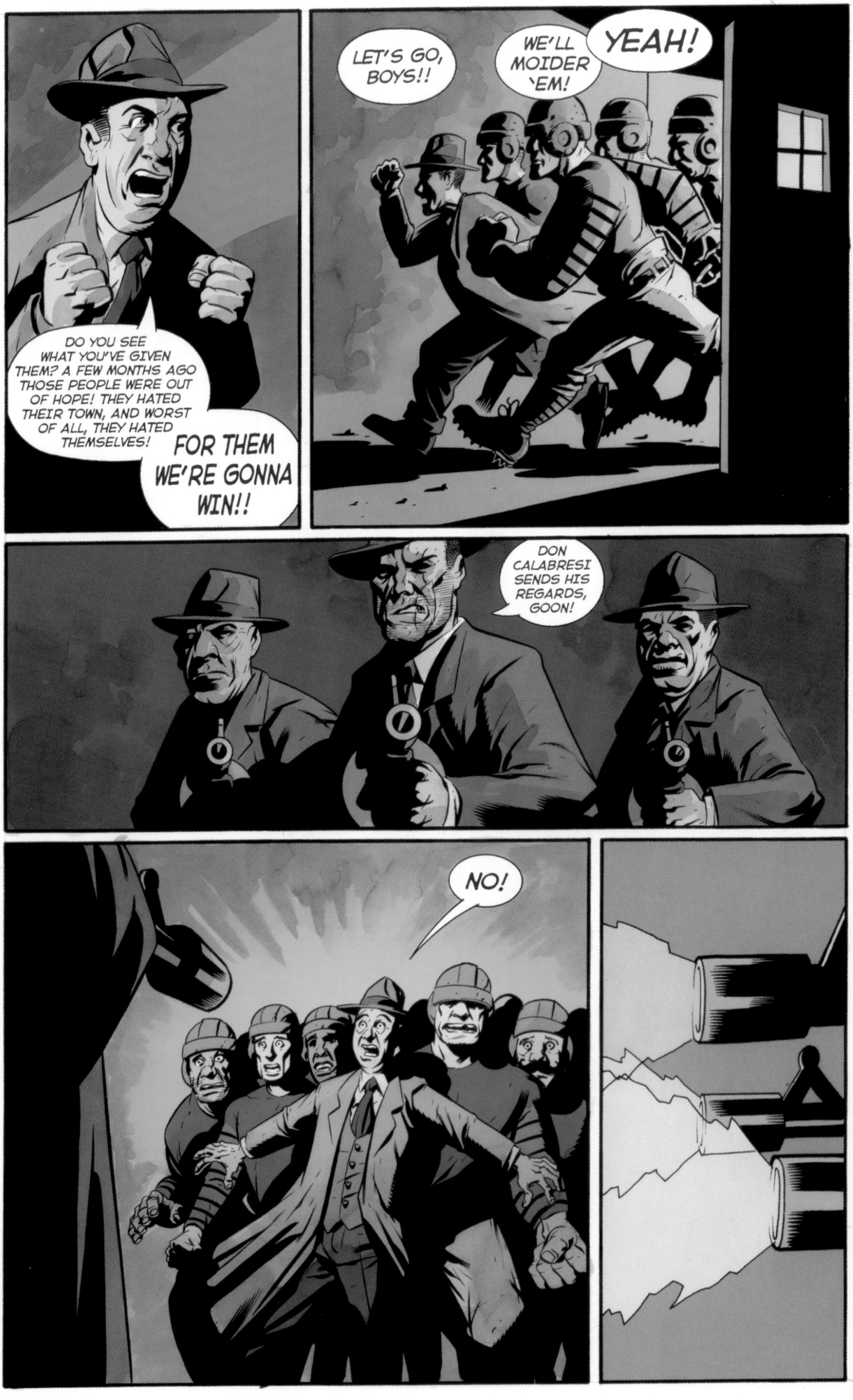
DO YOU SEE WHAT YOU'VE GIVEN THEM? A FEW MONTHS AGO THOSE PEOPLE WERE OUT OF HOPE! THEY HATED THEIR TOWN, AND WORST OF ALL, THEY HATED THEMSELVES!
FOR THEM WE'RE GONNA WIN!!
LET'S GO, BOYS!!
WE'LL MOIDER 'EM!
YEAH!
DON CALABRESI SENDS HIS REGARDS, GOON!
NO!

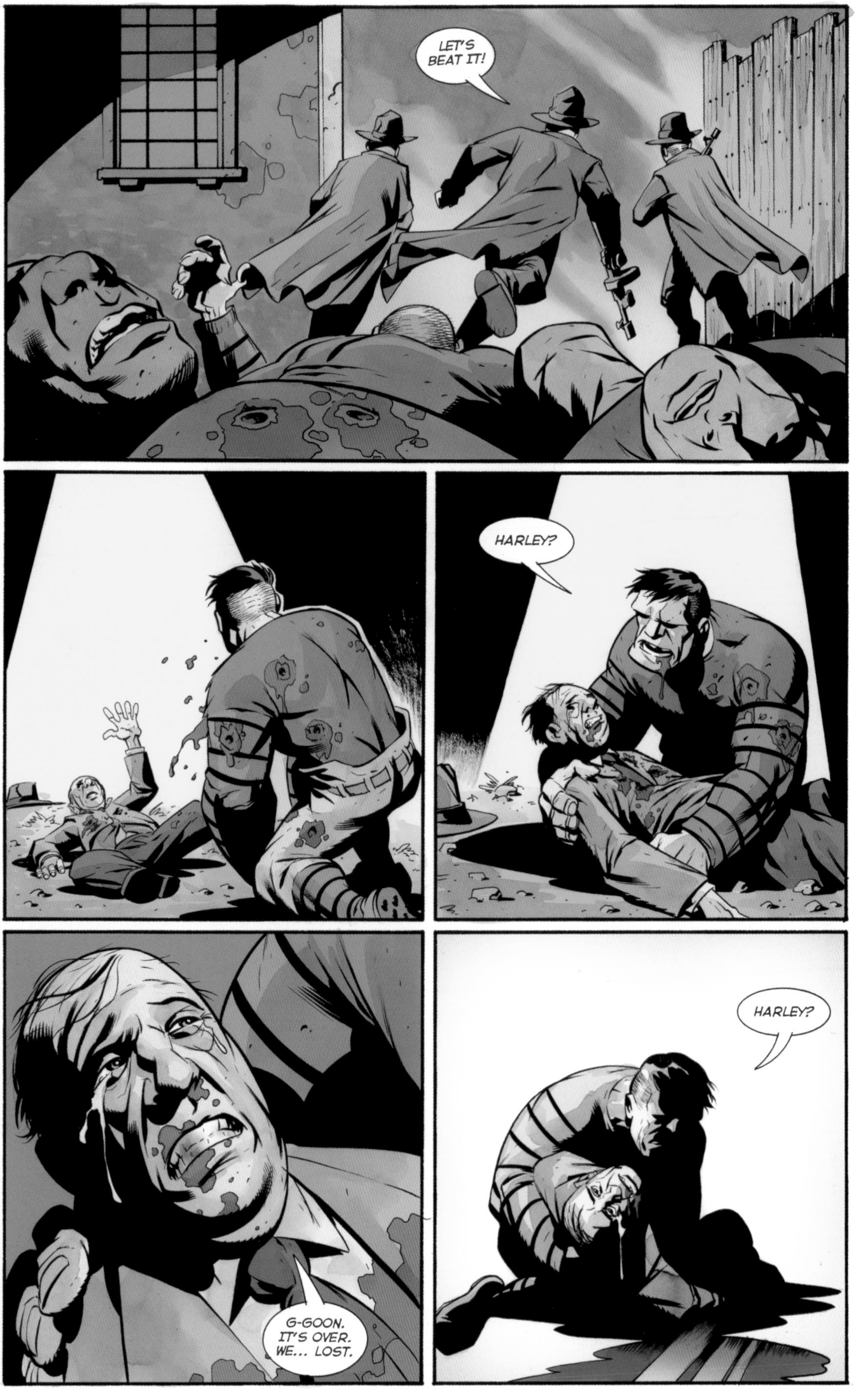
LET'S BEAT IT!
HARLEY?
G-GOON. IT'S OVER. WE... LOST.
HARLEY?

THE STORYBOOK SEASON OF THE CANNERS CAME TO A TRAGIC CLOSE WITH THE ASSASSINATIONS OF HARLEY LABEAU, ART MOON, CECIL DEWLER, ARNIE CUBBARD, WILLIE HINKLE, ZEKE HERBERT, AND DICK BOYD. THE REMAINING MEMBERS OF THE TEAM WERE ALL HOSPITALIZED FROM GUNSHOT WOUNDS BUT RECOVERED IN TIME. THE CANNERS HAD TO FORFEIT THE CHAMPIONSHIP GAME AND HAVE YET TO HAVE ANOTHER WINNING SEASON, LET ALONE RETURN TO THE CHAMPIONSHIP. THE GOON NEVER PLAYED AGAIN AFTER THAT NIGHT.

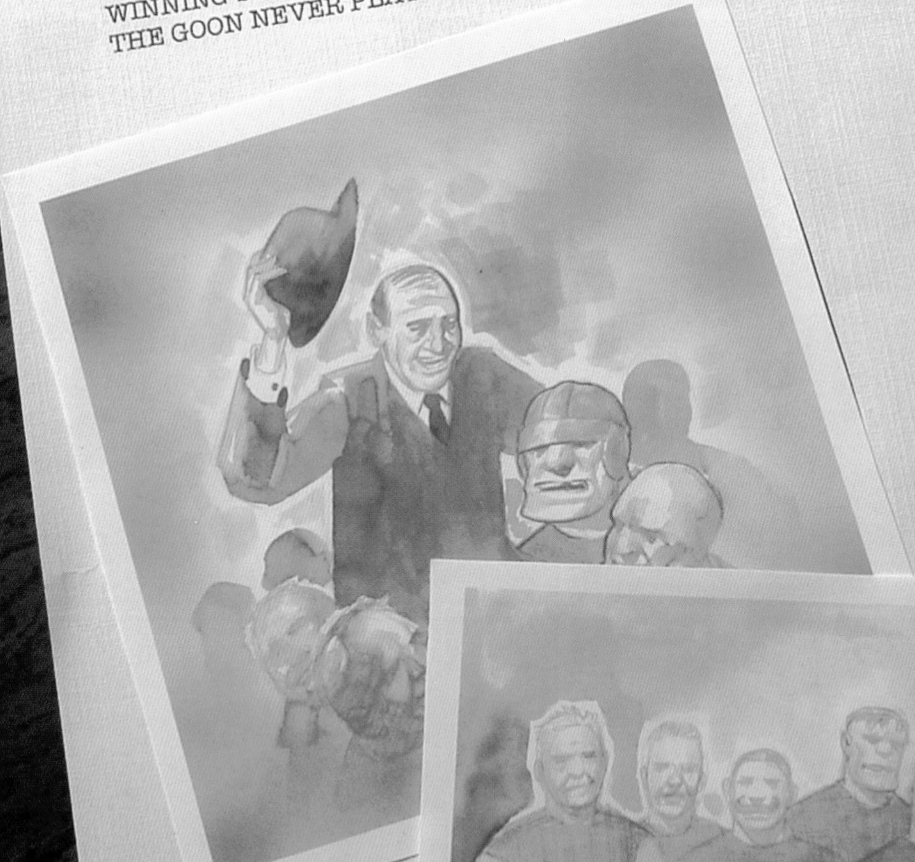

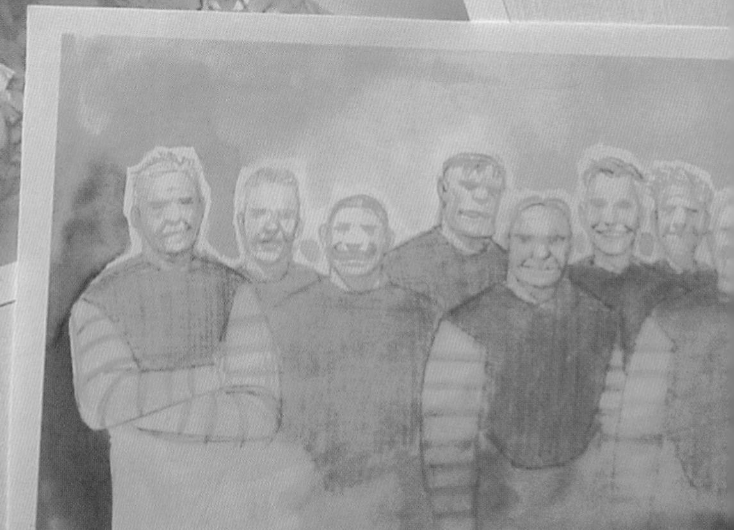

THE MALICIOUSNESS OF THE BLACK HAND WAS, IN THE END, THEIR OWN UNDOING. THEY HAD KEPT THEM UNDER NEAR UNLIVABLE CONDITIONS FOR TOO LONG TO SPEAK OF, BUT WHEN THEY STRUCK OUT AT THE ONE THING THAT GAVE THE PEOPLE A LITTLE JOY, A TORRENT OF EMOTION WAS UNLEASHED. THE ENSUING RIOTS ENDED IN THE CORNERING OF THE CALABRESI AND FERRARA GANGS ON LONELY STREET.

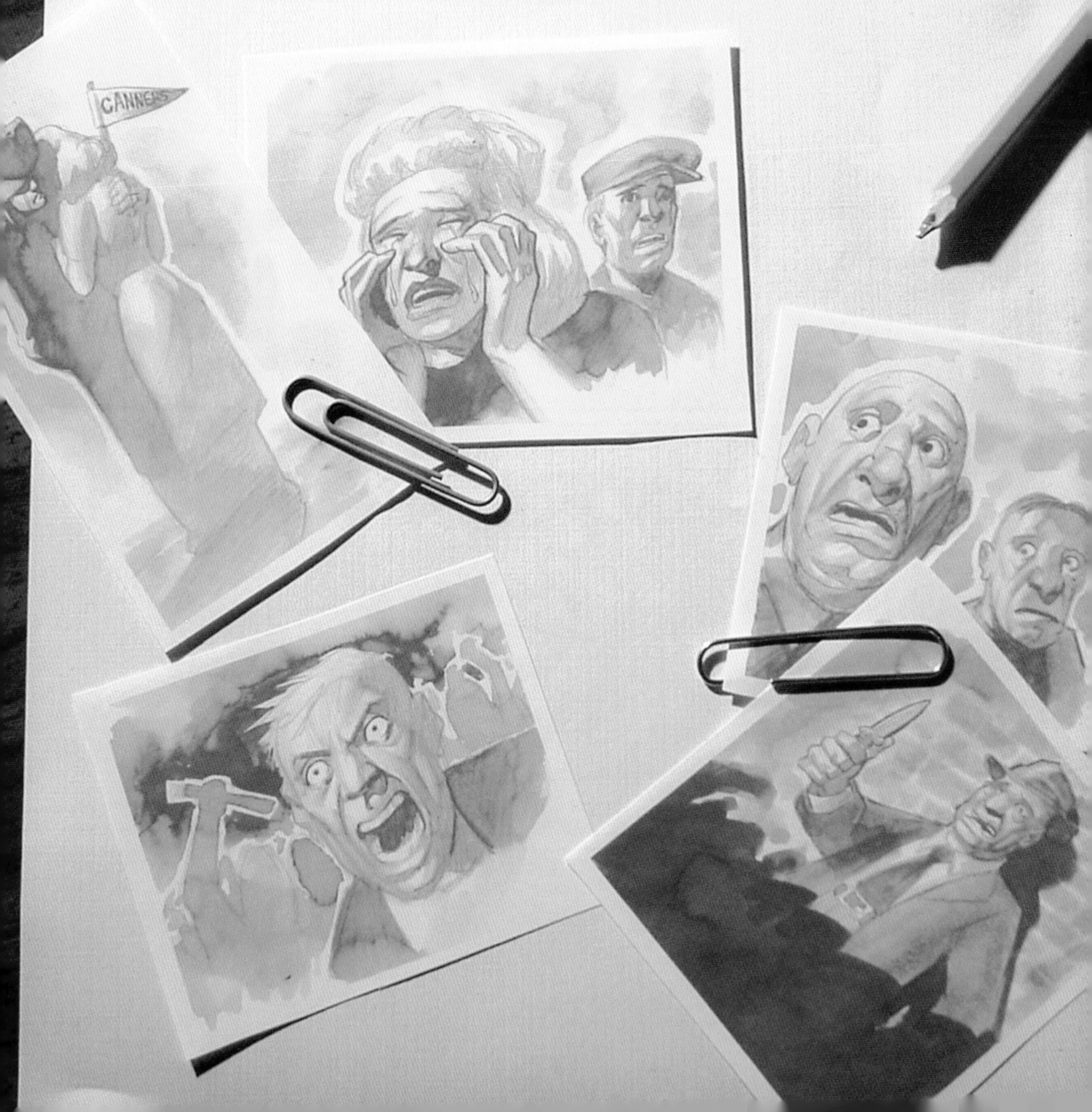
CANNERS

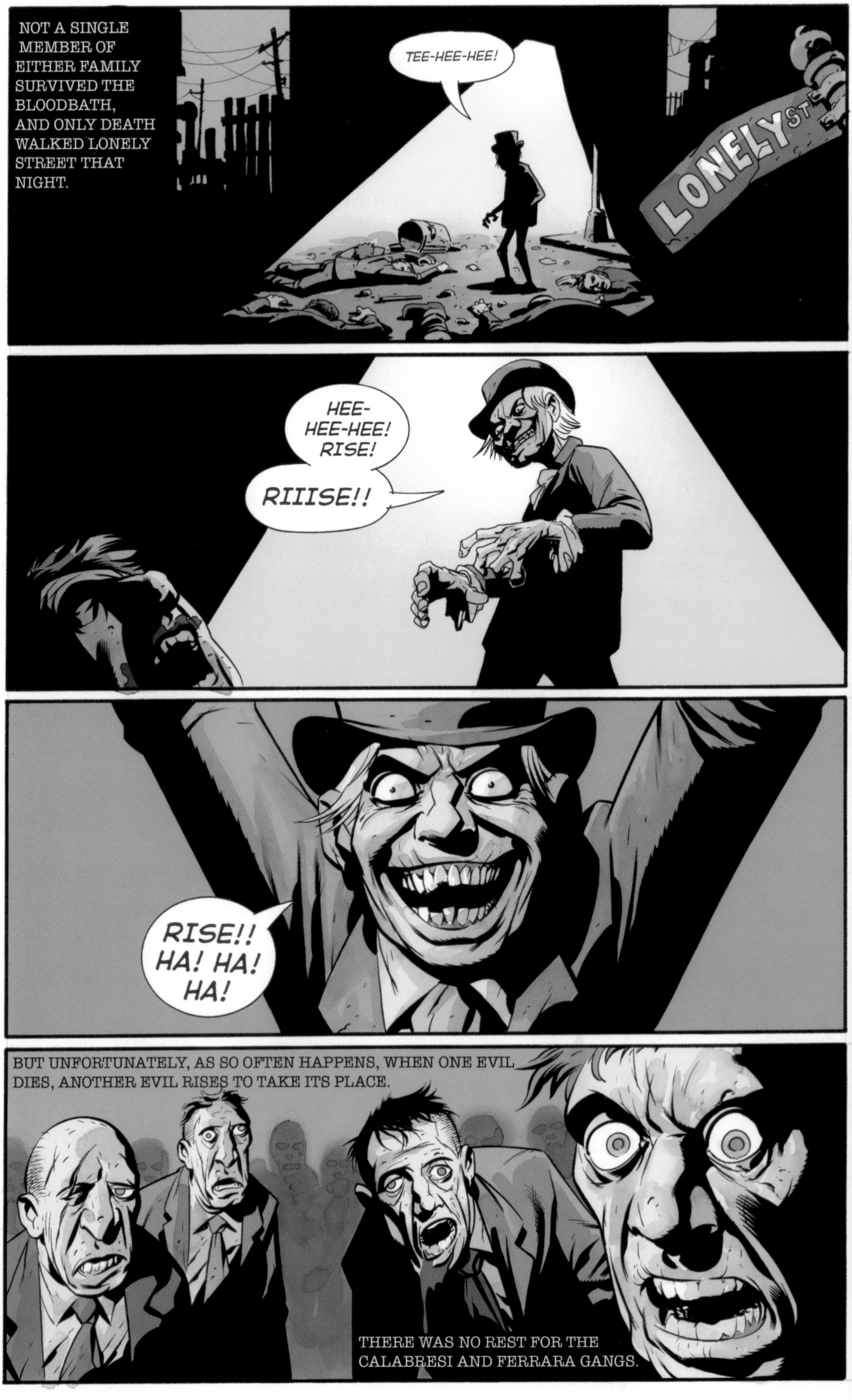
NOT A SINGLE MEMBER OF EITHER FAMILY SURVIVED THE BLOODBATH, AND ONLY DEATH WALKED LONELY STREET THAT NIGHT.
TEE-HEE-HEE!
LONELY ST
HEE-HEE-HEE! RISE!
RIIISE!!
RISE!! HA! HA! HA!
BUT UNFORTUNATELY, AS SO OFTEN HAPPENS, WHEN ONE EVIL DIES, ANOTHER EVIL RISES TO TAKE ITS PLACE.
THERE WAS NO REST FOR THE CALABRESI AND FERRARA GANGS.

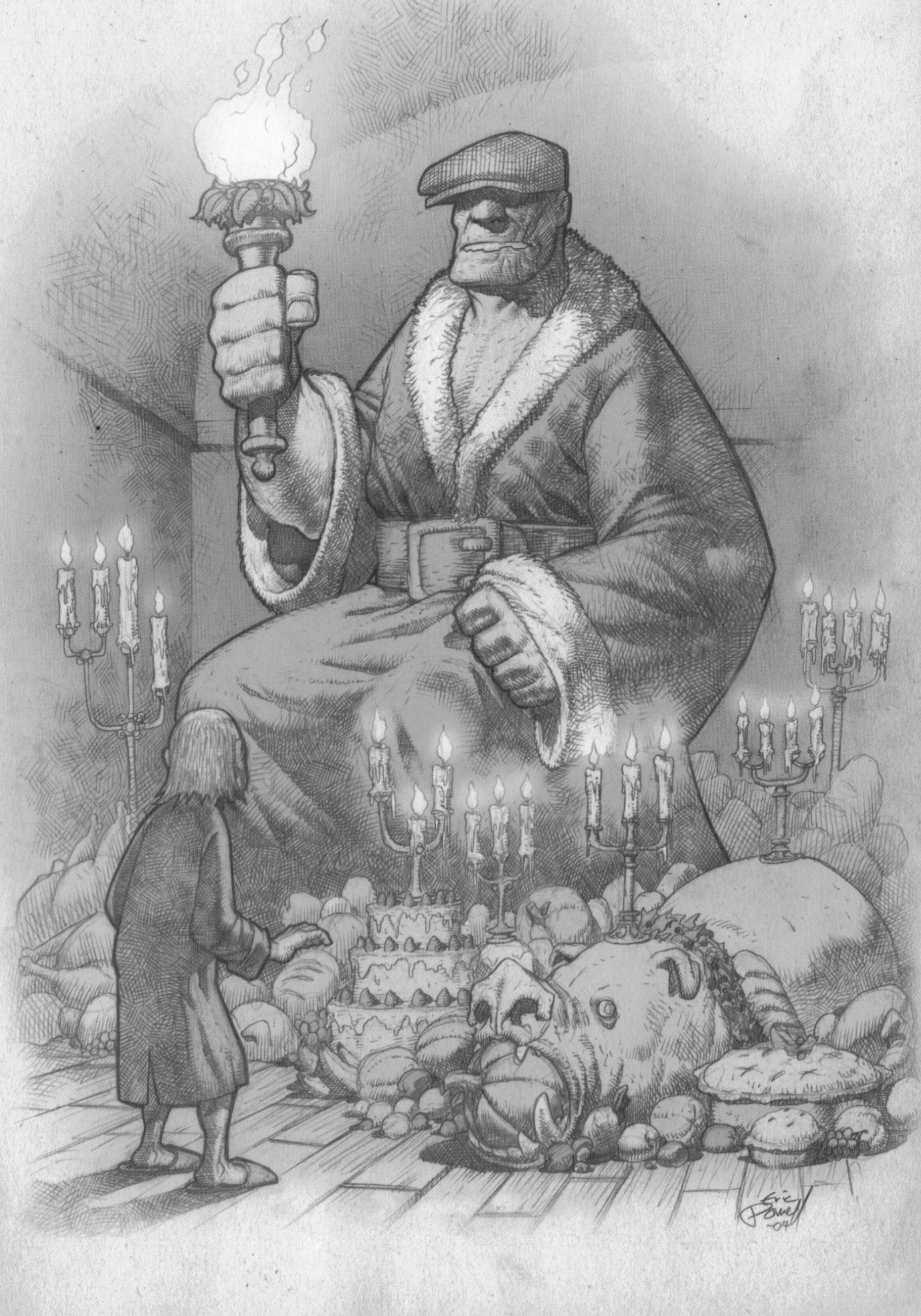

THE CAST OF THE GOON WOULD LIKE TO PRESENT...
CHARLES DICKENS'
A CHRISTMAS CAROL
A COMPLETE BASTARDIZATION OF A PIECE OF CLASSIC HOLIDAY LITERATURE

MERLE
AS
BOB CRATCHIT

THE NAMELESS MAN
AS
EBENEZER SCROOGE

THE MUD BROTHERS
AS
THE COLLECTORS FOR THE POOR

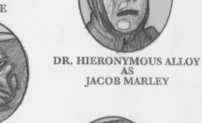

DR. HIERONYMOUS ALLOY
AS
JACOB MARLEY

FRANKY
AS
THE GHOST OF
CHRISTMAS PAST

PEACHES VALENTINE
AS
TINY TIM

GOON
AS
THE GHOST OF
CHRISTMAS PRESENT

AS
THE GHOST OF
CHRISTMAS FUTURE

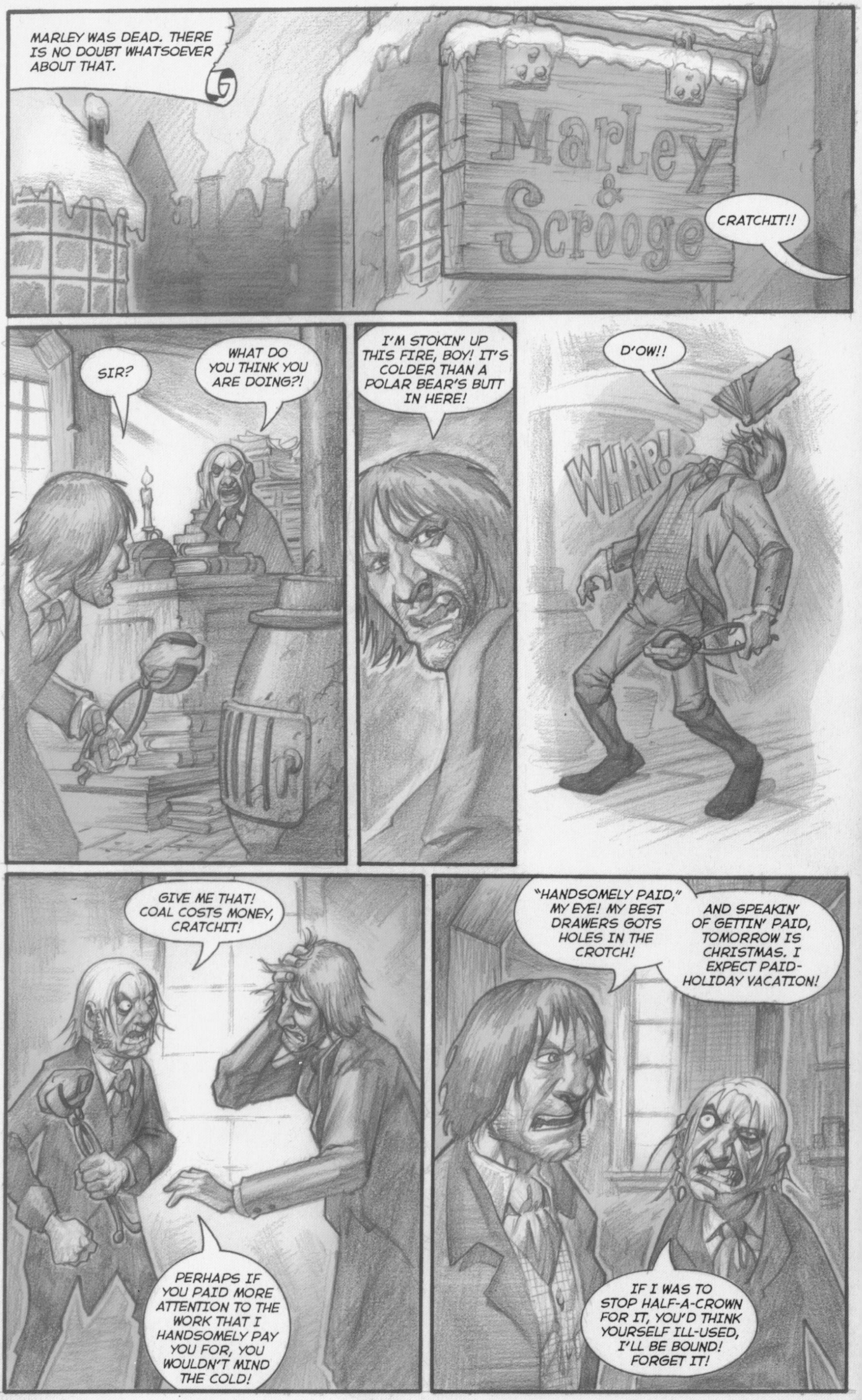
MARLEY WAS DEAD. THERE IS NO DOUBT WHATSOEVER ABOUT THAT.
Marley & Scrooge
CRATCHIT!!
SIR?
WHAT DO YOU THINK YOU ARE DOING?!
I'M STOKIN' UP THIS FIRE, BOY! IT'S COLDER THAN A POLAR BEAR'S BUTT IN HERE!
D'OW!!
WHAP!
GIVE ME THAT! COAL COSTS MONEY, CRATCHIT!
PERHAPS IF YOU PAID MORE ATTENTION TO THE WORK THAT I HANDSOMELY PAY YOU FOR, YOU WOULDN'T MIND THE COLD!
"HANDSOMELY PAID," MY EYE! MY BEST DRAWERS GOTS HOLES IN THE CROTCH!
AND SPEAKIN' OF GETTIN' PAID, TOMORROW IS CHRISTMAS. I EXPECT PAID-HOLIDAY VACATION!
IF I WAS TO STOP HALF-A-CROWN FOR IT, YOU'D THINK YOURSELF ILL-USED, I'LL BE BOUND! FORGET IT!

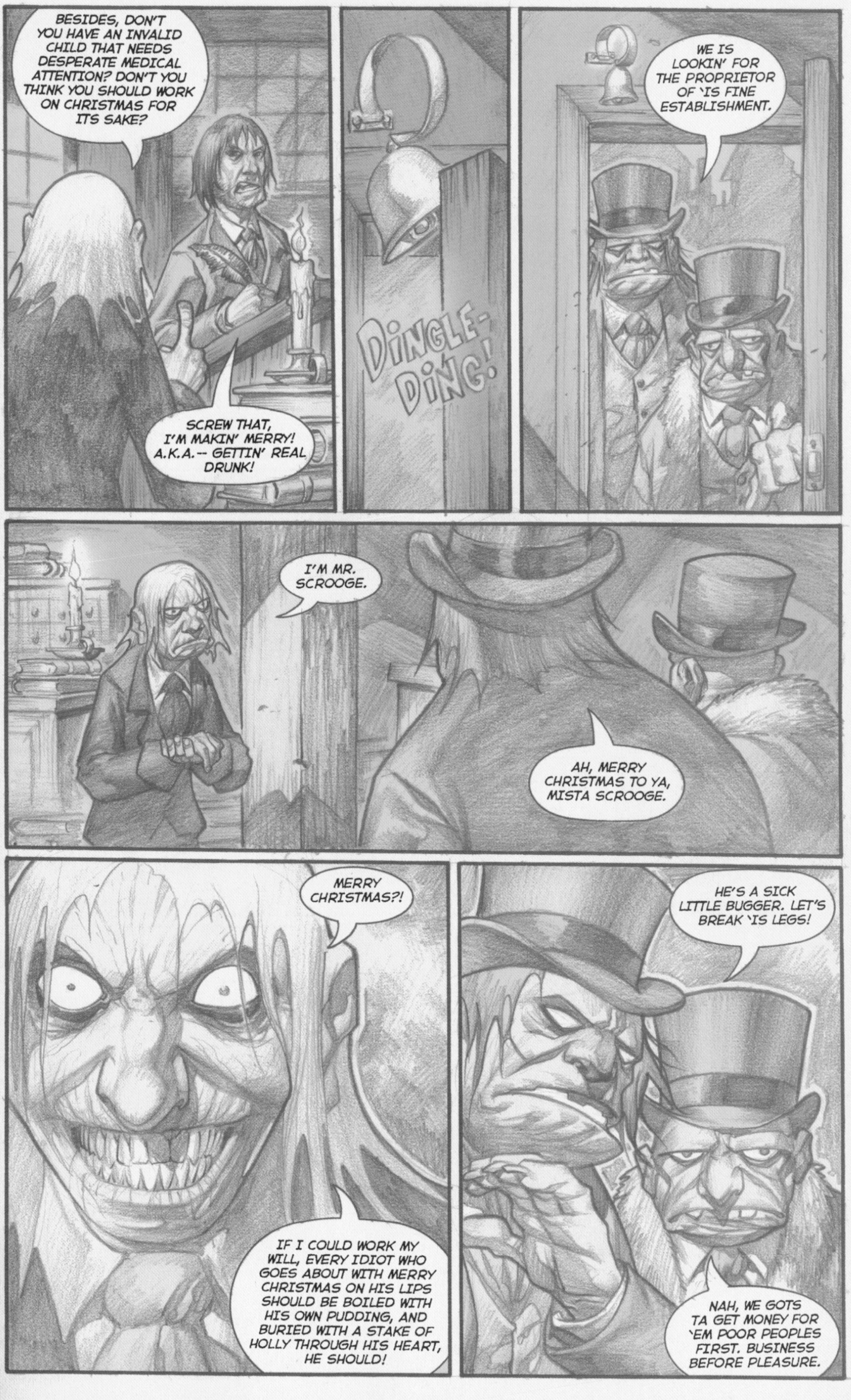

BESIDES, DON'T YOU HAVE AN INVALID CHILD THAT NEEDS DESPERATE MEDICAL ATTENTION? DON'T YOU THINK YOU SHOULD WORK ON CHRISTMAS FOR ITS SAKE?
SCREW THAT, I'M MAKIN' MERRY! A.K.A.-- GETTIN' REAL DRUNK!
DINGLE-DING!
WE IS LOOKIN' FOR THE PROPRIETOR OF 'IS FINE ESTABLISHMENT.
I'M MR. SCROOGE.
AH, MERRY CHRISTMAS TO YA, MISTA SCROOGE.
MERRY CHRISTMAS?!
IF I COULD WORK MY WILL, EVERY IDIOT WHO GOES ABOUT WITH MERRY CHRISTMAS ON HIS LIPS SHOULD BE BOILED WITH HIS OWN PUDDING, AND BURIED WITH A STAKE OF HOLLY THROUGH HIS HEART, HE SHOULD!
HE'S A SICK LITTLE BUGGER. LET'S BREAK 'IS LEGS!
NAH, WE GOTS TA GET MONEY FOR 'EM POOR PEOPLES FIRST. BUSINESS BEFORE PLEASURE.

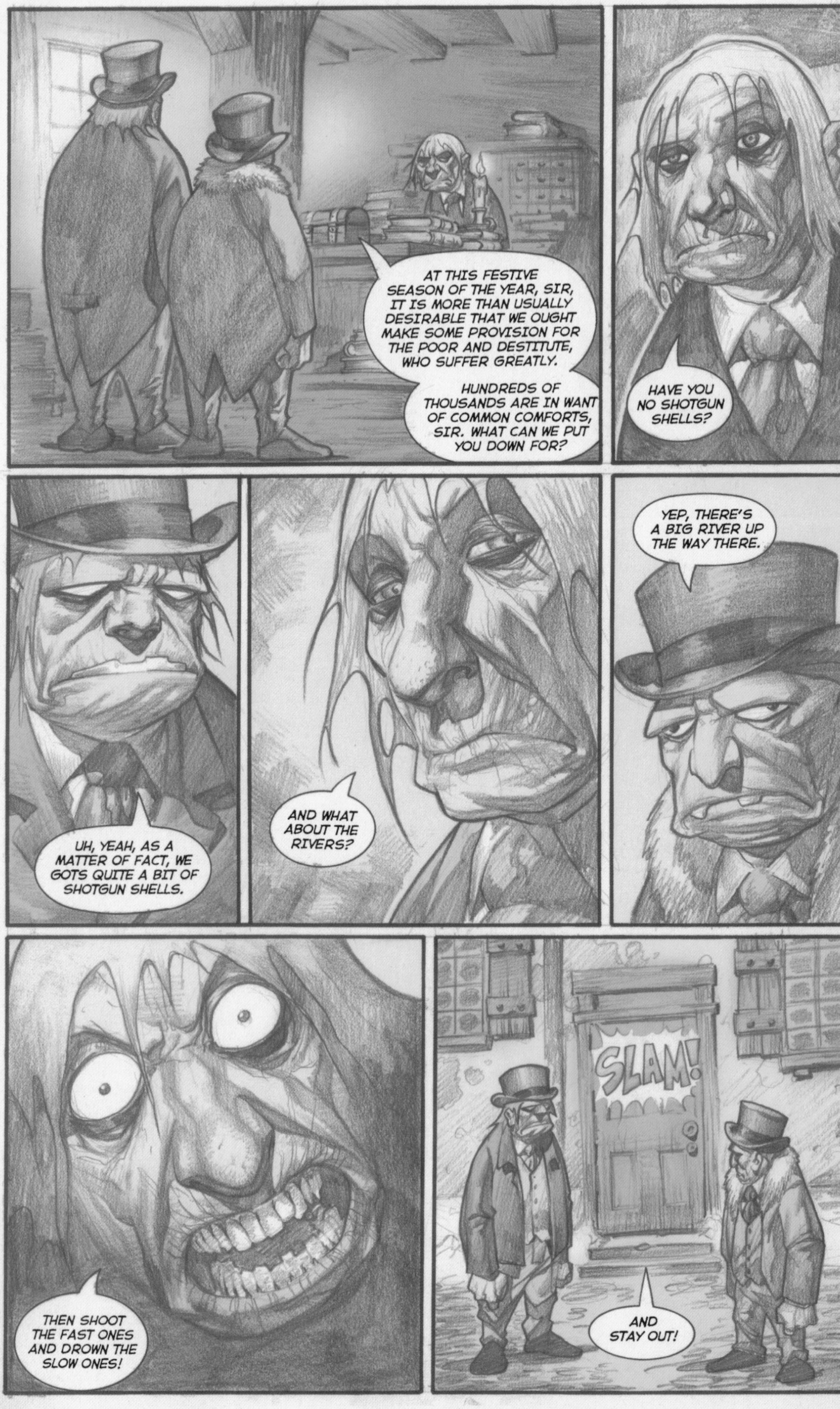
AT THIS FESTIVE SEASON OF THE YEAR, SIR, IT IS MORE THAN USUALLY DESIRABLE THAT WE OUGHT MAKE SOME PROVISION FOR THE POOR AND DESTITUTE, WHO SUFFER GREATLY.
HUNDREDS OF THOUSANDS ARE IN WANT OF COMMON COMFORTS, SIR. WHAT CAN WE PUT YOU DOWN FOR?
HAVE YOU NO SHOTGUN SHELLS?
UH, YEAH, AS A MATTER OF FACT, WE GOTS QUITE A BIT OF SHOTGUN SHELLS.
AND WHAT ABOUT THE RIVERS?
YEP, THERE'S A BIG RIVER UP THE WAY THERE.
THEN SHOOT THE FAST ONES AND DROWN THE SLOW ONES!
SLAM!
AND STAY OUT!

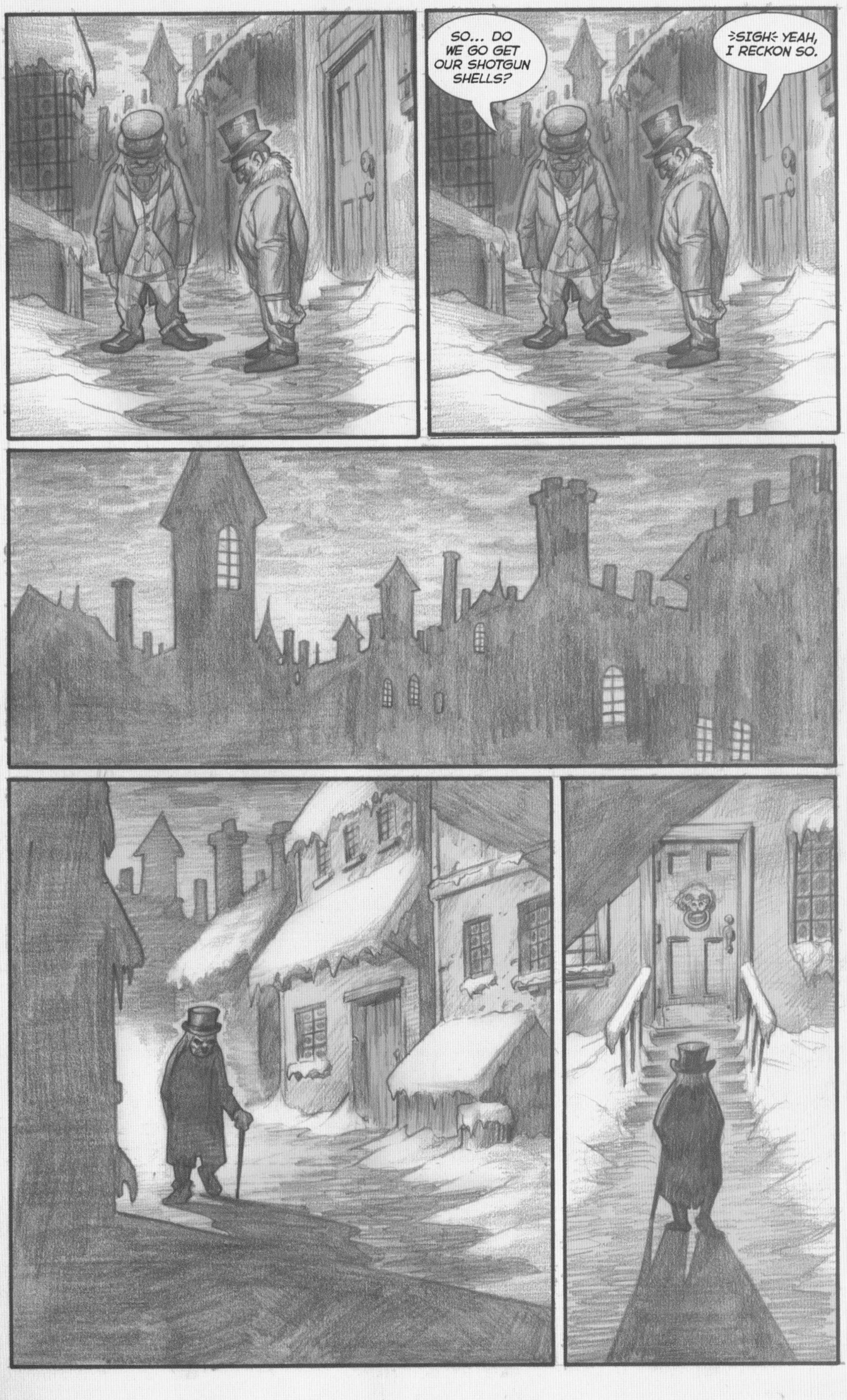
SO... DO WE GO GET OUR SHOTGUN SHELLS?
⪢SIGH⪡ YEAH, I RECKON SO.

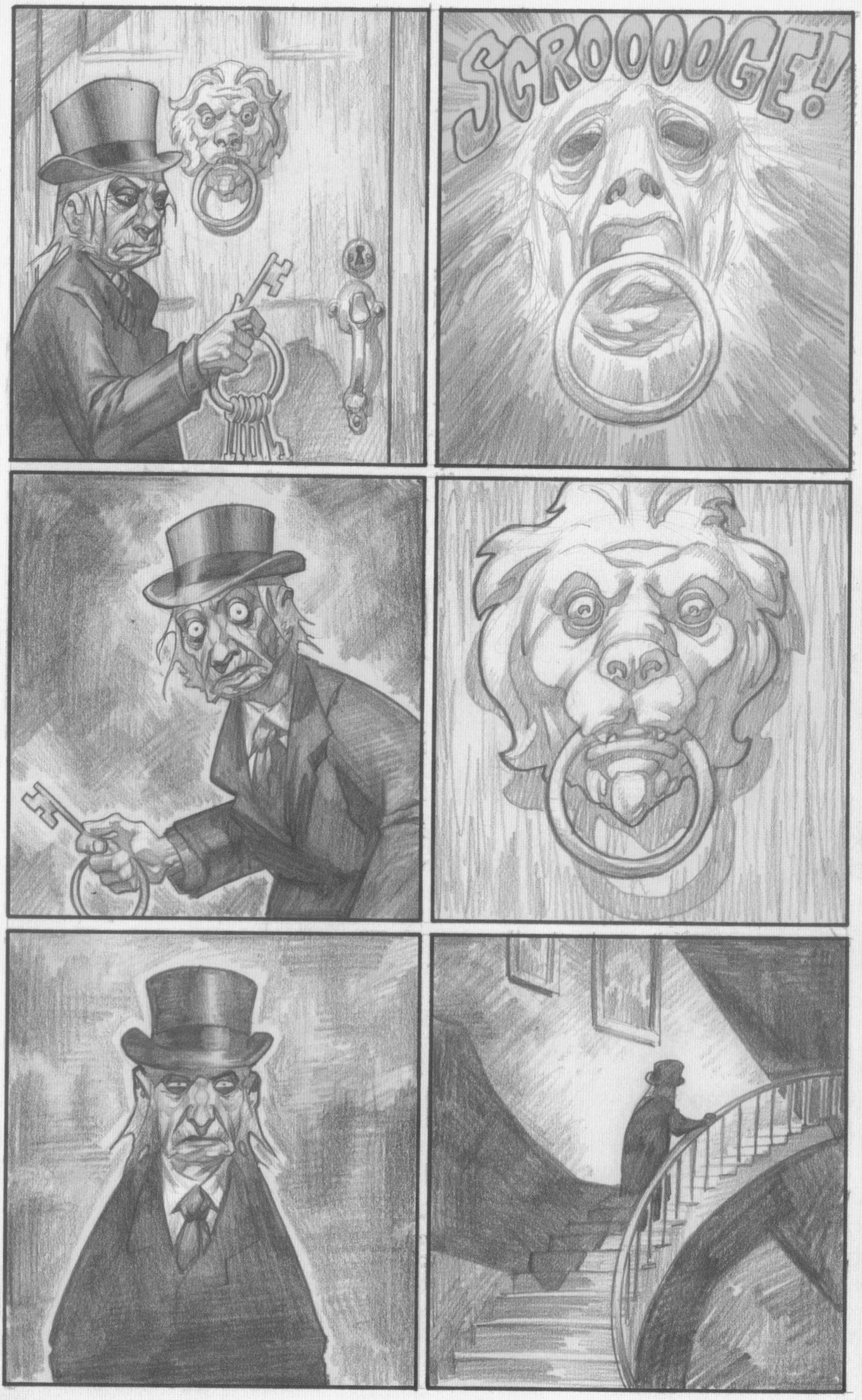
SCROOOOGE!

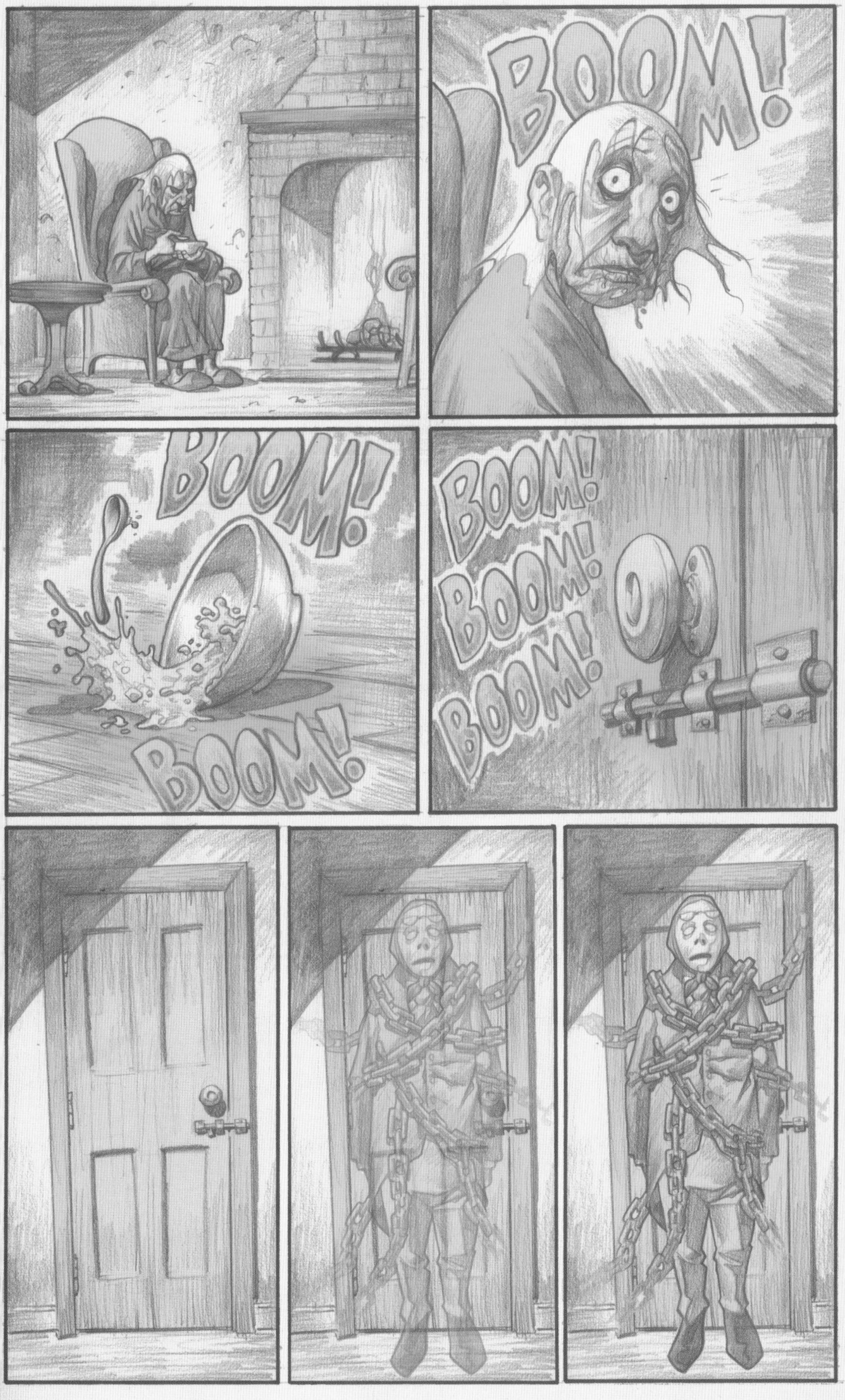
BOOM!
BOOM!
BOOM!
BOOM!
BOOM!
BOOM!

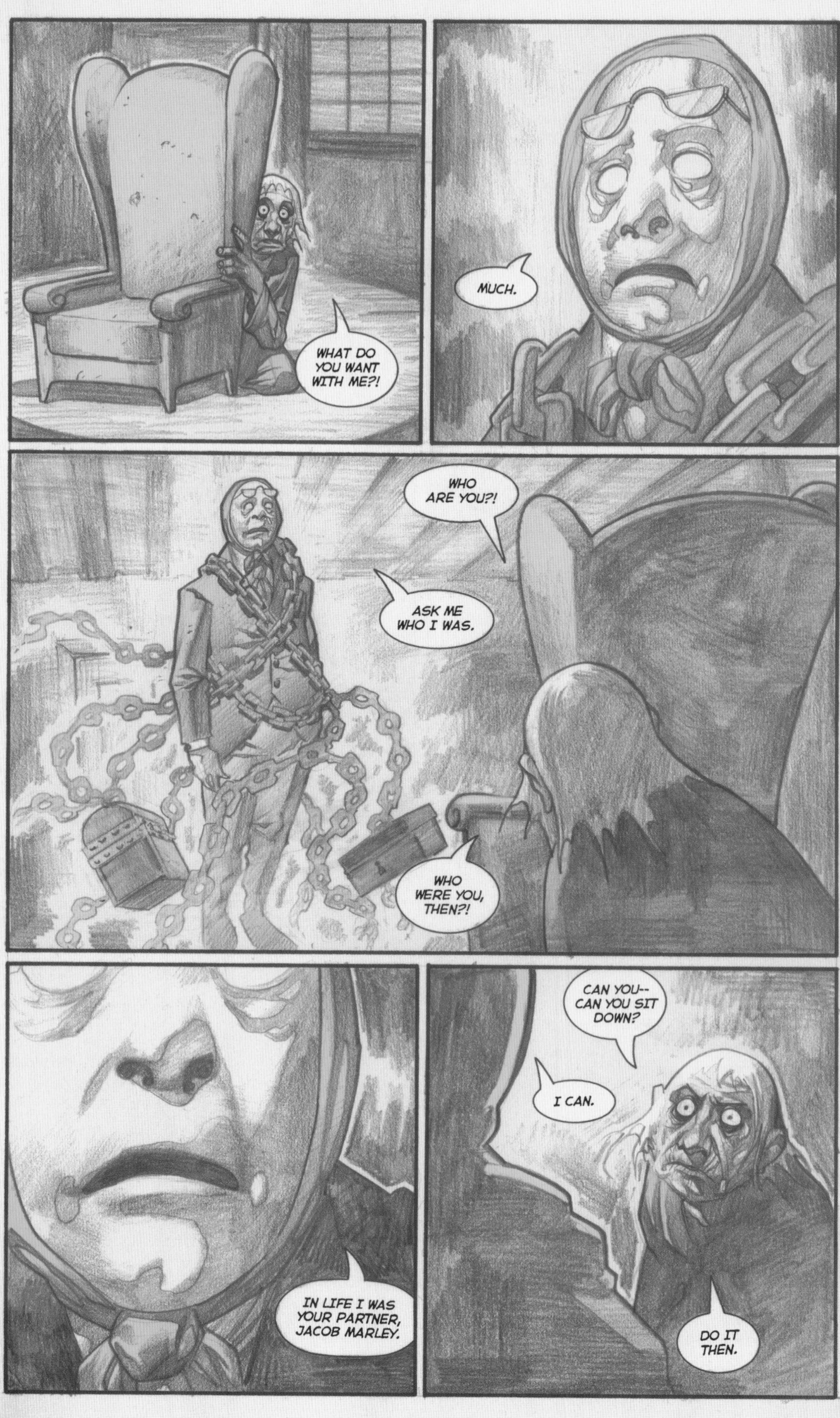
WHAT DO YOU WANT WITH ME?!
MUCH.
WHO ARE YOU?!
ASK ME WHO I WAS.
WHO WERE YOU, THEN?!
IN LIFE I WAS YOUR PARTNER, JACOB MARLEY.
CAN YOU-- CAN YOU SIT DOWN?
I CAN.
DO IT THEN.

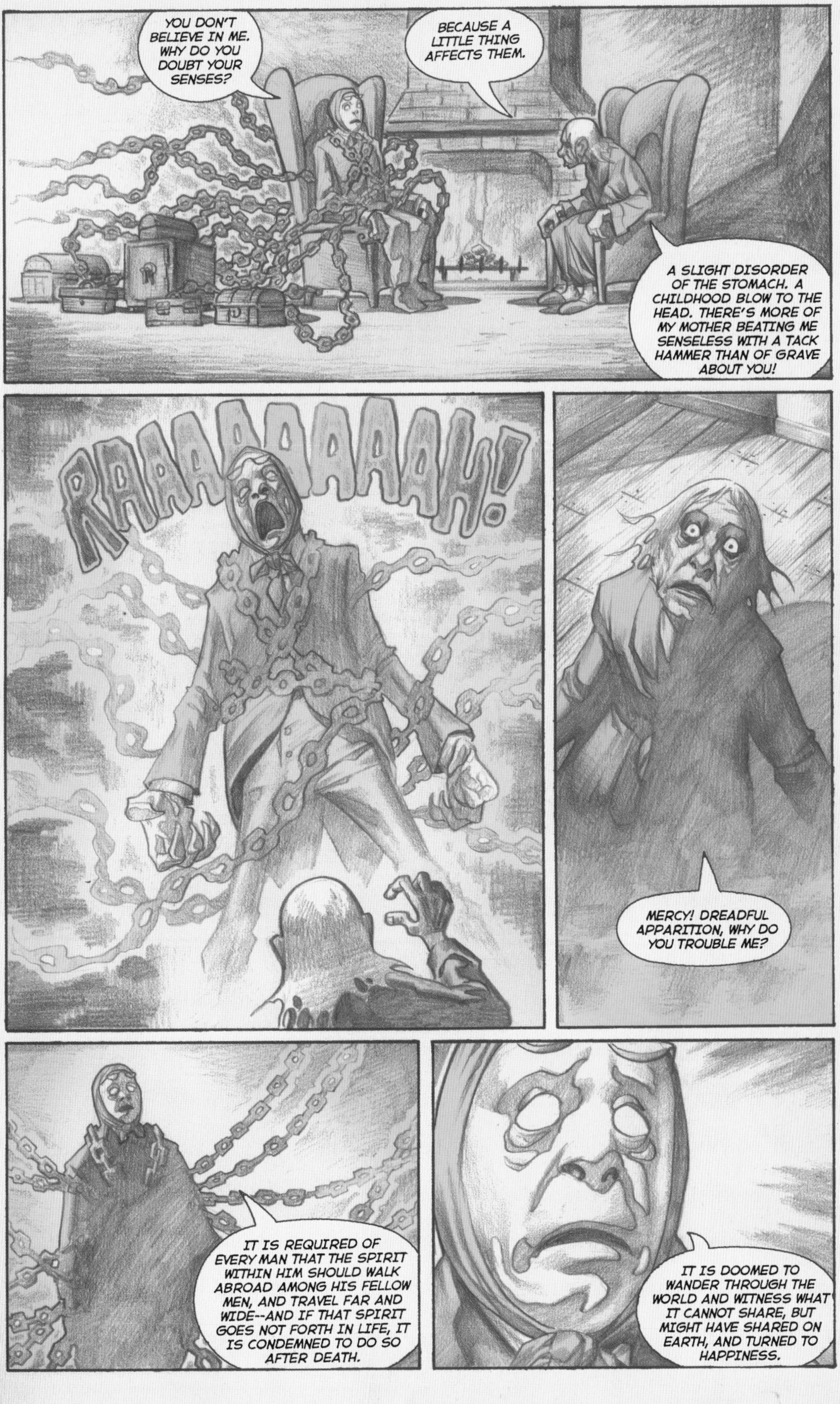
YOU DON'T BELIEVE IN ME. WHY DO YOU DOUBT YOUR SENSES?
BECAUSE A LITTLE THING AFFECTS THEM.
A SLIGHT DISORDER OF THE STOMACH. A CHILDHOOD BLOW TO THE HEAD. THERE'S MORE OF MY MOTHER BEATING ME SENSELESS WITH A TACK HAMMER THAN OF GRAVE ABOUT YOU!
RAAAAAAAAH!
MERCY! DREADFUL APPARITION, WHY DO YOU TROUBLE ME?
IT IS REQUIRED OF EVERY MAN THAT THE SPIRIT WITHIN HIM SHOULD WALK ABROAD AMONG HIS FELLOW MEN, AND TRAVEL FAR AND WIDE--AND IF THAT SPIRIT GOES NOT FORTH IN LIFE, IT IS CONDEMNED TO DO SO AFTER DEATH.
IT IS DOOMED TO WANDER THROUGH THE WORLD AND WITNESS WHAT IT CANNOT SHARE, BUT MIGHT HAVE SHARED ON EARTH, AND TURNED TO HAPPINESS.

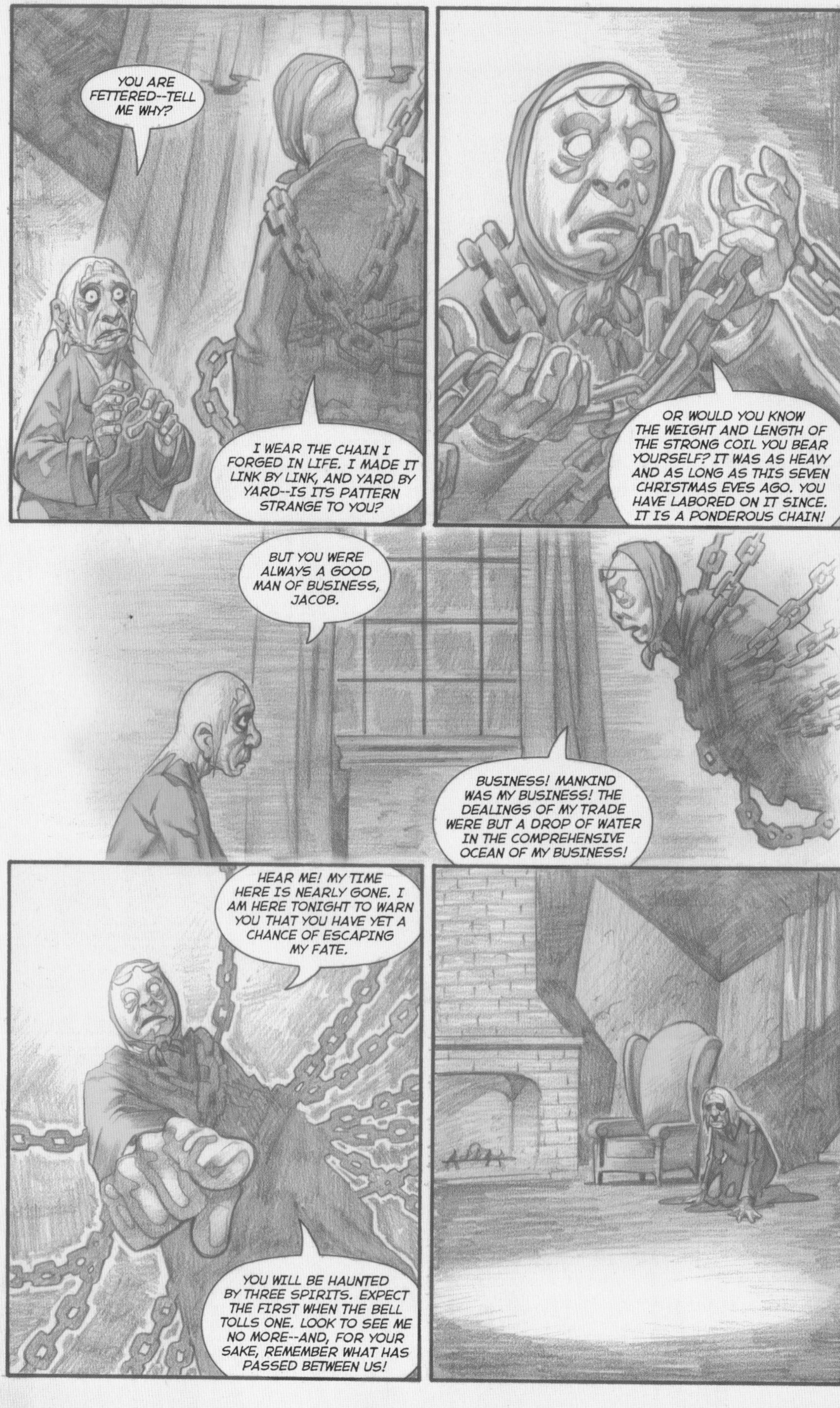
YOU ARE FETTERED--TELL ME WHY?
I WEAR THE CHAIN I FORGED IN LIFE. I MADE IT LINK BY LINK, AND YARD BY YARD--IS ITS PATTERN STRANGE TO YOU?
OR WOULD YOU KNOW THE WEIGHT AND LENGTH OF THE STRONG COIL YOU BEAR YOURSELF? IT WAS AS HEAVY AND AS LONG AS THIS SEVEN CHRISTMAS EVES AGO. YOU HAVE LABORED ON IT SINCE. IT IS A PONDEROUS CHAIN!
BUT YOU WERE ALWAYS A GOOD MAN OF BUSINESS, JACOB.
BUSINESS! MANKIND WAS MY BUSINESS! THE DEALINGS OF MY TRADE WERE BUT A DROP OF WATER IN THE COMPREHENSIVE OCEAN OF MY BUSINESS!
HEAR ME! MY TIME HERE IS NEARLY GONE. I AM HERE TONIGHT TO WARN YOU THAT YOU HAVE YET A CHANCE OF ESCAPING MY FATE.
YOU WILL BE HAUNTED BY THREE SPIRITS. EXPECT THE FIRST WHEN THE BELL TOLLS ONE. LOOK TO SEE ME NO MORE--AND, FOR YOUR SAKE, REMEMBER WHAT HAS PASSED BETWEEN US!

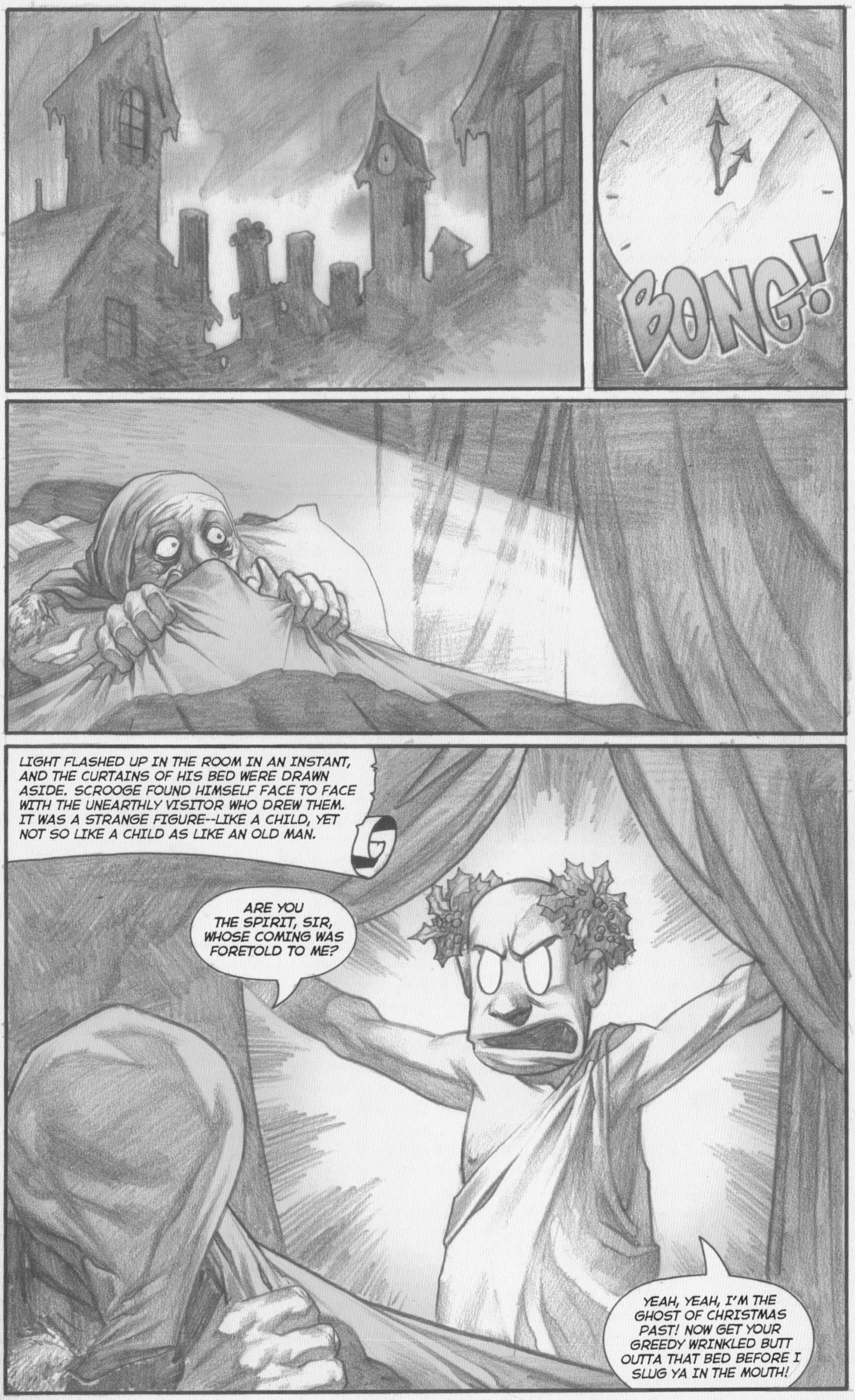
BONG!
LIGHT FLASHED UP IN THE ROOM IN AN INSTANT, AND THE CURTAINS OF HIS BED WERE DRAWN ASIDE. SCROOGE FOUND HIMSELF FACE TO FACE WITH THE UNEARTHLY VISITOR WHO DREW THEM. IT WAS A STRANGE FIGURE--LIKE A CHILD, YET NOT SO LIKE A CHILD AS LIKE AN OLD MAN.
ARE YOU THE SPIRIT, SIR, WHOSE COMING WAS FORETOLD TO ME?
YEAH, YEAH, I'M THE GHOST OF CHRISTMAS PAST! NOW GET YOUR GREEDY WRINKLED BUTT OUTTA THAT BED BEFORE I SLUG YA IN THE MOUTH!

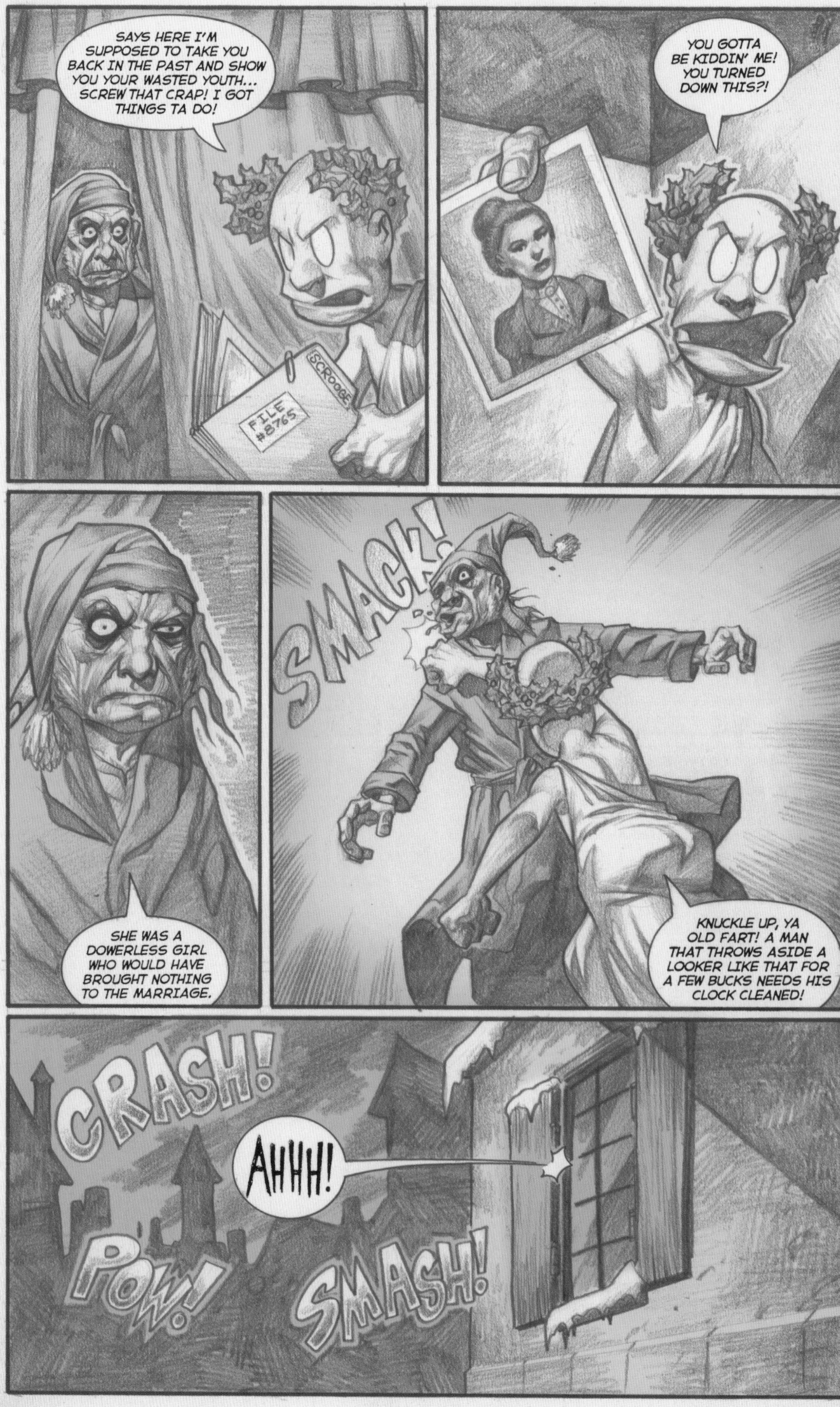
SAYS HERE I'M SUPPOSED TO TAKE YOU BACK IN THE PAST AND SHOW YOU YOUR WASTED YOUTH... SCREW THAT CRAP! I GOT THINGS TA DO!
SCROOGE
FILE #8765
YOU GOTTA BE KIDDIN' ME! YOU TURNED DOWN THIS?!
SHE WAS A DOWERLESS GIRL WHO WOULD HAVE BROUGHT NOTHING TO THE MARRIAGE.
SMACK!
KNUCKLE UP, YA OLD FART! A MAN THAT THROWS ASIDE A LOOKER LIKE THAT FOR A FEW BUCKS NEEDS HIS CLOCK CLEANED!
CRASH!
AHHH!
POW!
SMASH!

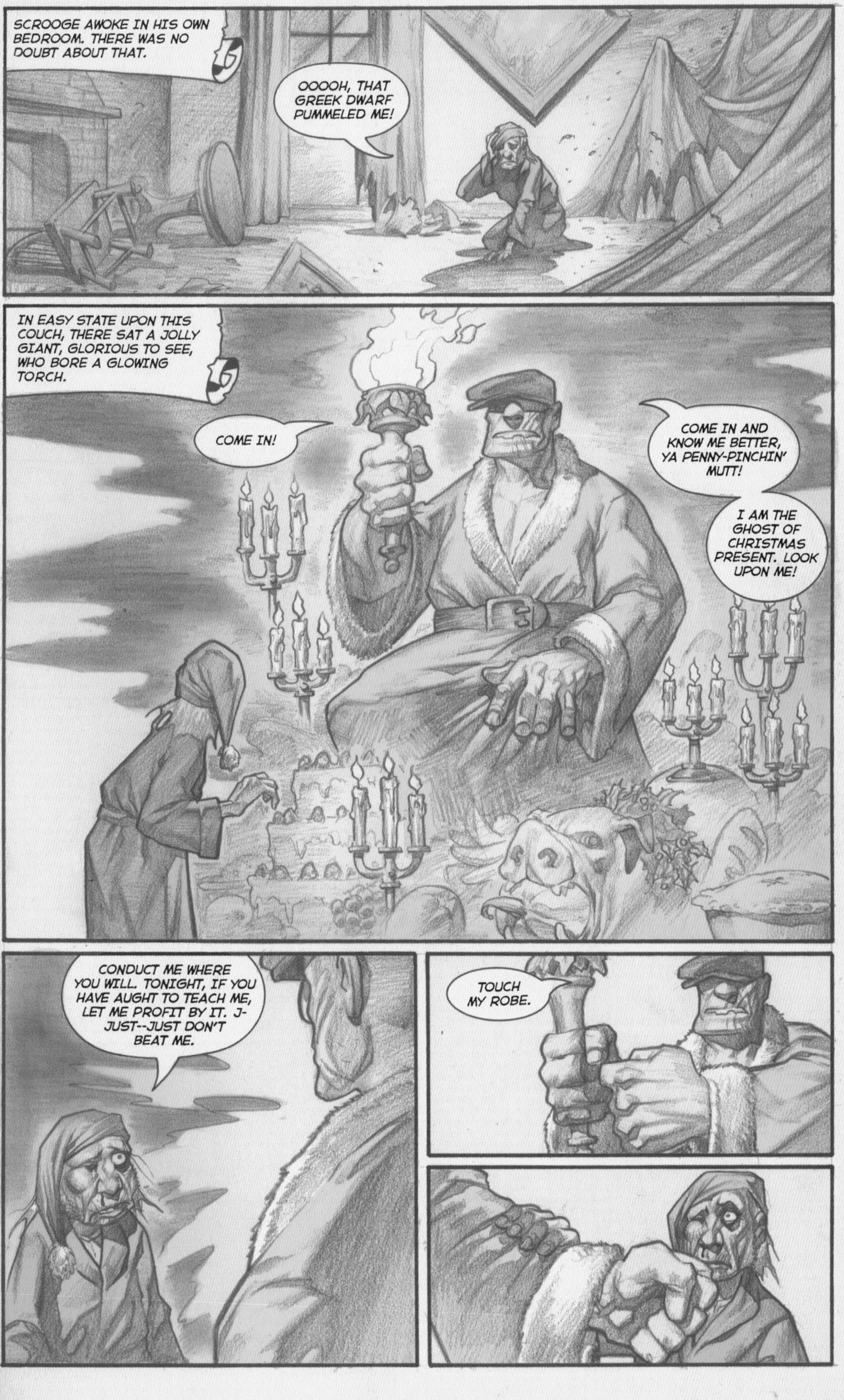
SCROOGE AWOKE IN HIS OWN BEDROOM. THERE WAS NO DOUBT ABOUT THAT.
OOOOH, THAT GREEK DWARF PUMMELED ME!
IN EASY STATE UPON THIS COUCH, THERE SAT A JOLLY GIANT, GLORIOUS TO SEE, WHO BORE A GLOWING TORCH.
COME IN!
COME IN AND KNOW ME BETTER, YA PENNY-PINCHIN' MUTT!
I AM THE GHOST OF CHRISTMAS PRESENT. LOOK UPON ME!
CONDUCT ME WHERE YOU WILL. TONIGHT, IF YOU HAVE AUGHT TO TEACH ME, LET ME PROFIT BY IT. J-JUST--JUST DON'T BEAT ME.
TOUCH MY ROBE.

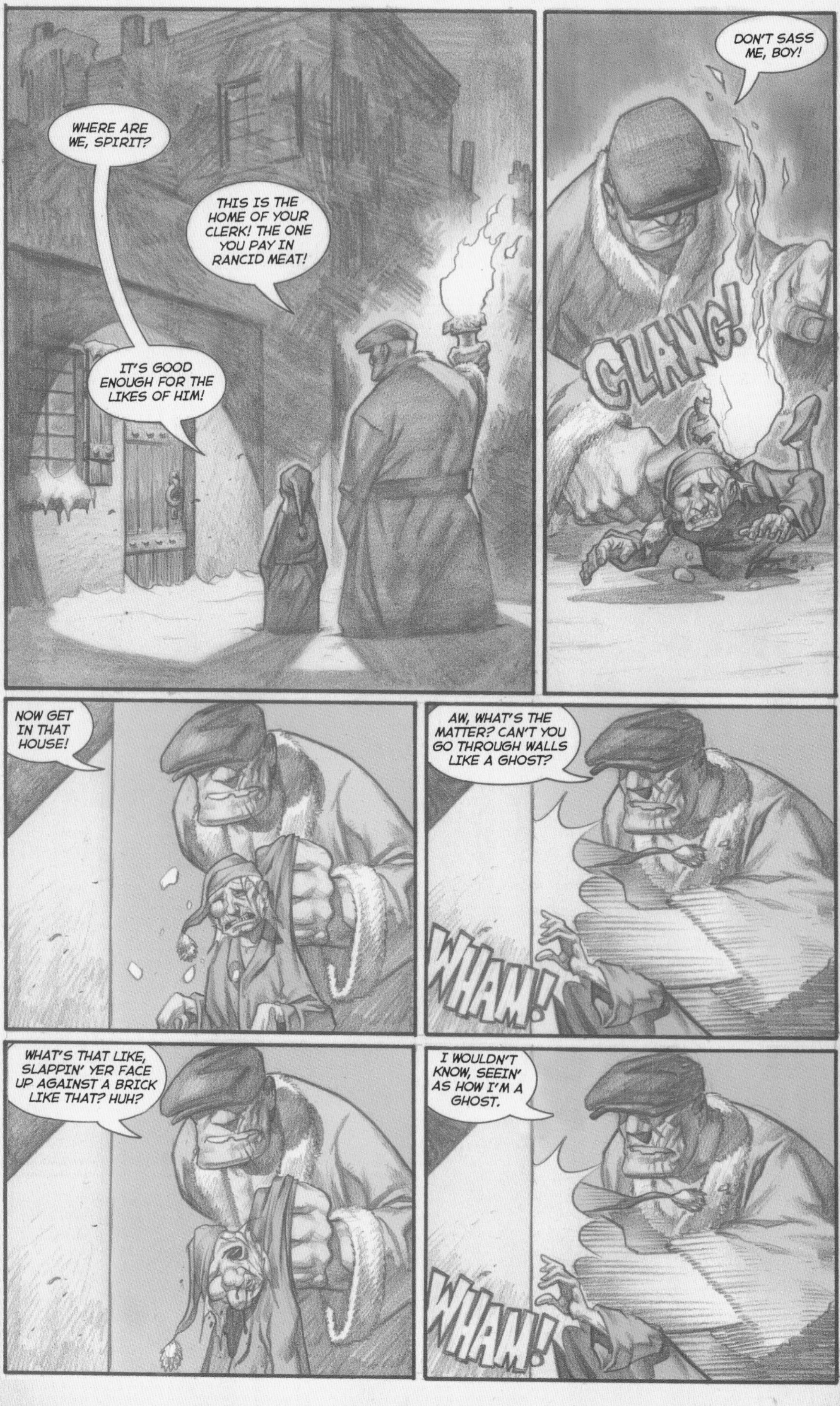
WHERE ARE WE, SPIRIT?
THIS IS THE HOME OF YOUR CLERK! THE ONE YOU PAY IN RANCID MEAT!
IT'S GOOD ENOUGH FOR THE LIKES OF HIM!
DON'T SASS ME, BOY!
CLANG!
NOW GET IN THAT HOUSE!
AW, WHAT'S THE MATTER? CAN'T YOU GO THROUGH WALLS LIKE A GHOST?
WHAM!
WHAT'S THAT LIKE, SLAPPIN' YER FACE UP AGAINST A BRICK LIKE THAT? HUH?
I WOULDN'T KNOW, SEEIN' AS HOW I'M A GHOST.
WHAM!

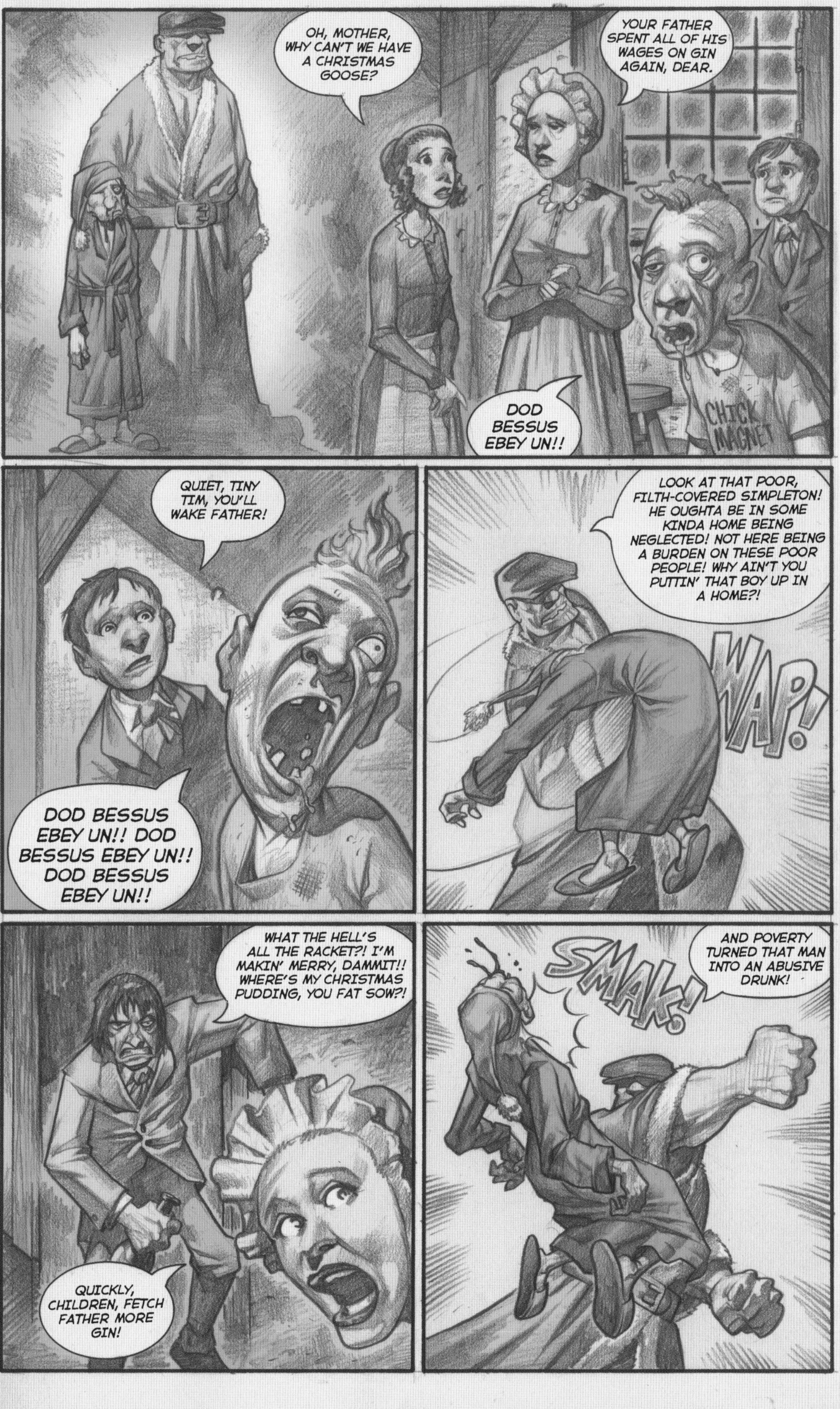
OH, MOTHER, WHY CAN'T WE HAVE A CHRISTMAS GOOSE?
YOUR FATHER SPENT ALL OF HIS WAGES ON GIN AGAIN, DEAR.
DOD BESSUS EBEY UN!!
CHICK MAGNET
QUIET, TINY TIM, YOU'LL WAKE FATHER!
DOD BESSUS EBEY UN!! DOD BESSUS EBEY UN!! DOD BESSUS EBEY UN!!
LOOK AT THAT POOR, FILTH-COVERED SIMPLETON! HE OUGHTA BE IN SOME KINDA HOME BEING NEGLECTED! NOT HERE BEING A BURDEN ON THESE POOR PEOPLE! WHY AIN'T YOU PUTTIN' THAT BOY UP IN A HOME?!
WAP!
WHAT THE HELL'S ALL THE RACKET?! I'M MAKIN' MERRY, DAMMIT!! WHERE'S MY CHRISTMAS PUDDING, YOU FAT SOW?!
QUICKLY, CHILDREN, FETCH FATHER MORE GIN!
SMAK!
AND POVERTY TURNED THAT MAN INTO AN ABUSIVE DRUNK!

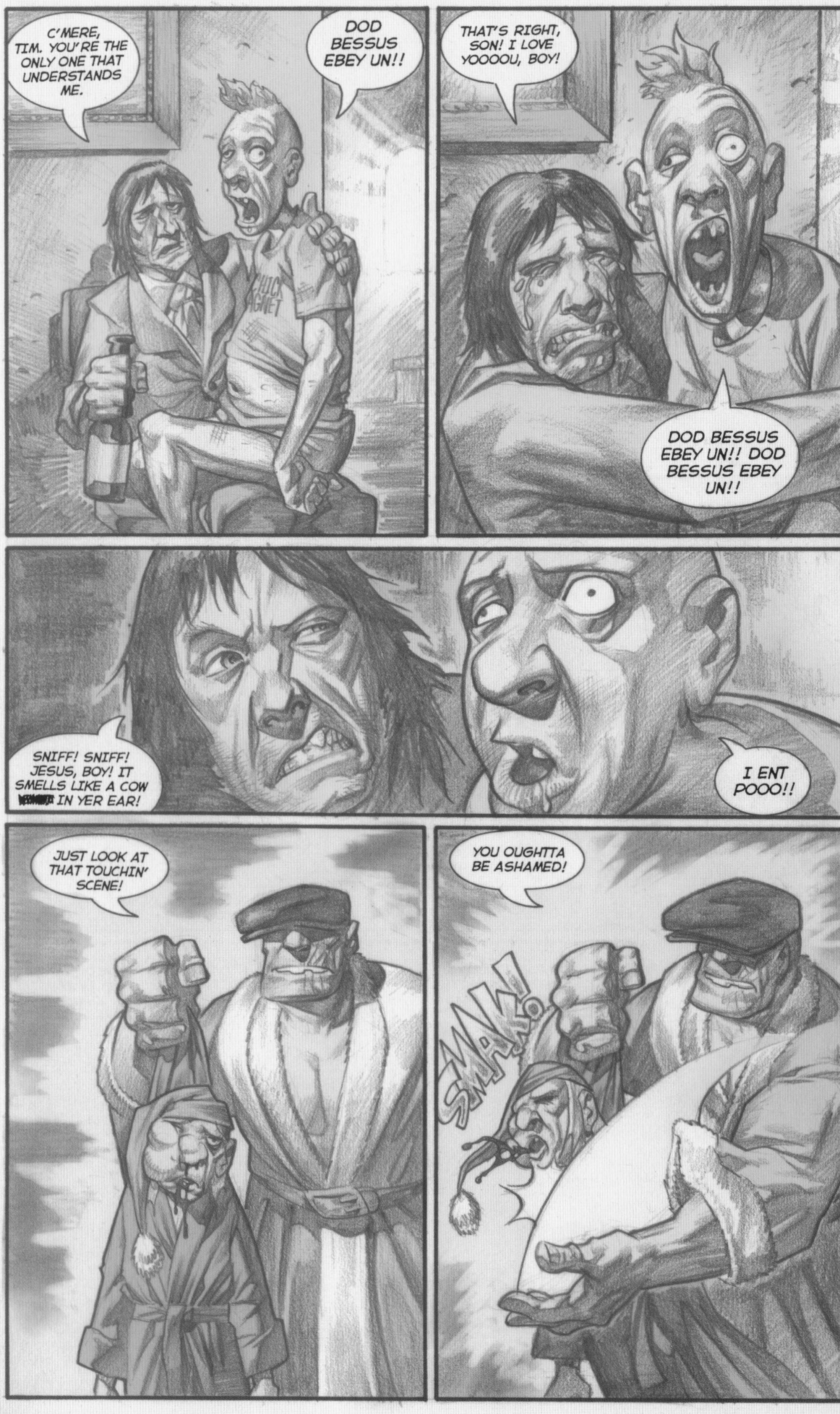
C'MERE, TIM. YOU'RE THE ONLY ONE THAT UNDERSTANDS ME.
DOD BESSUS EBEY UN!!
THAT'S RIGHT, SON! I LOVE YOOOOU, BOY!
DOD BESSUS EBEY UN!! DOD BESSUS EBEY UN!!
SNIFF! SNIFF! JESUS, BOY! IT SMELLS LIKE A COW [redacted] IN YER EAR!
I ENT POOO!!
JUST LOOK AT THAT TOUCHIN' SCENE!
YOU OUGHTTA BE ASHAMED!
SMAK!

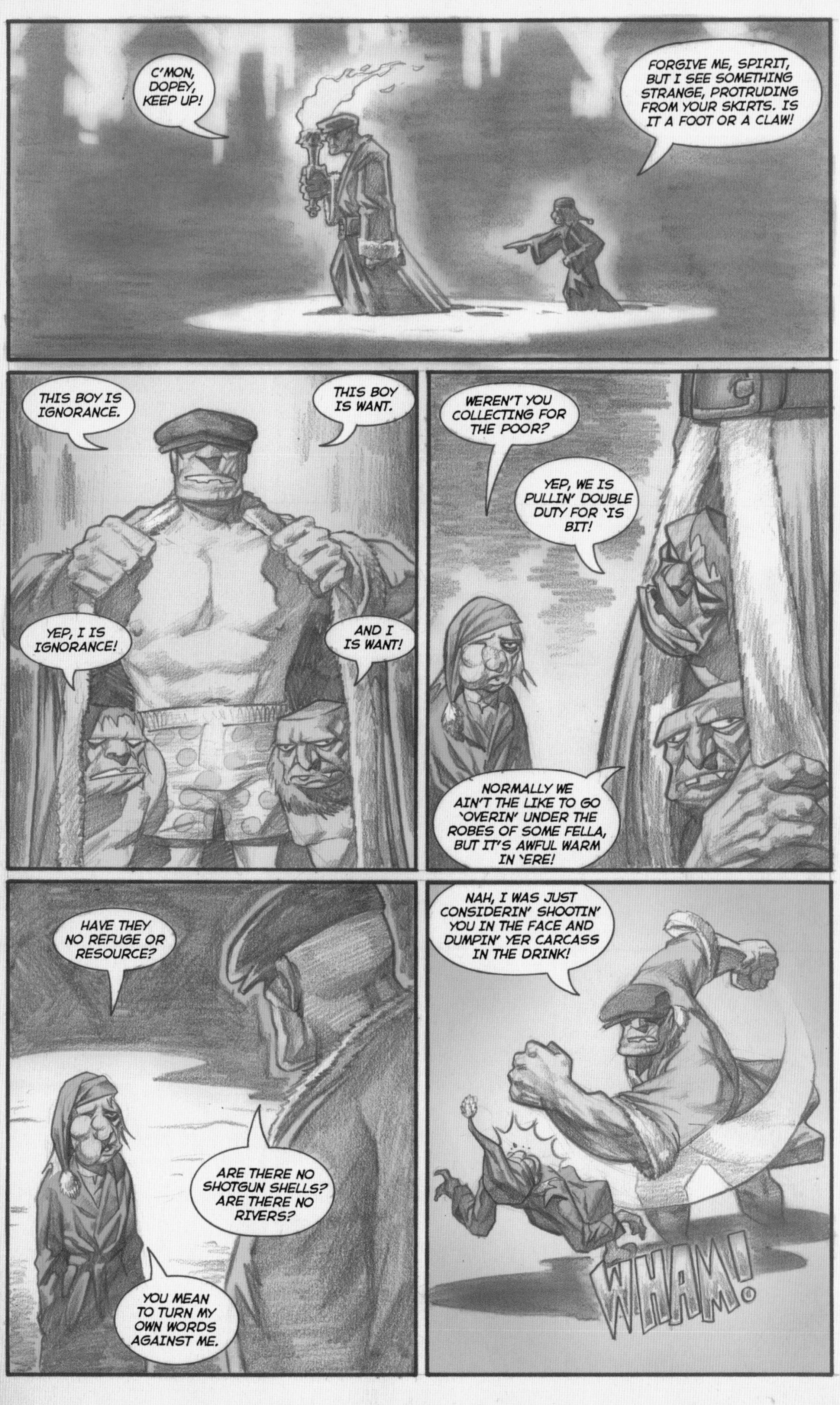

C'MON, DOPEY, KEEP UP!
FORGIVE ME, SPIRIT, BUT I SEE SOMETHING STRANGE, PROTRUDING FROM YOUR SKIRTS. IS IT A FOOT OR A CLAW!
THIS BOY IS IGNORANCE.
THIS BOY IS WANT.
YEP, I IS IGNORANCE!
AND I IS WANT!
WEREN'T YOU COLLECTING FOR THE POOR?
YEP, WE IS PULLIN' DOUBLE DUTY FOR 'IS BIT!
NORMALLY WE AIN'T THE LIKE TO GO 'OVERIN' UNDER THE ROBES OF SOME FELLA, BUT IT'S AWFUL WARM IN 'ERE!
HAVE THEY NO REFUGE OR RESOURCE?
ARE THERE NO SHOTGUN SHELLS? ARE THERE NO RIVERS?
YOU MEAN TO TURN MY OWN WORDS AGAINST ME.
NAH, I WAS JUST CONSIDERIN' SHOOTIN' YOU IN THE FACE AND DUMPIN' YER CARCASS IN THE DRINK!
WHAM!

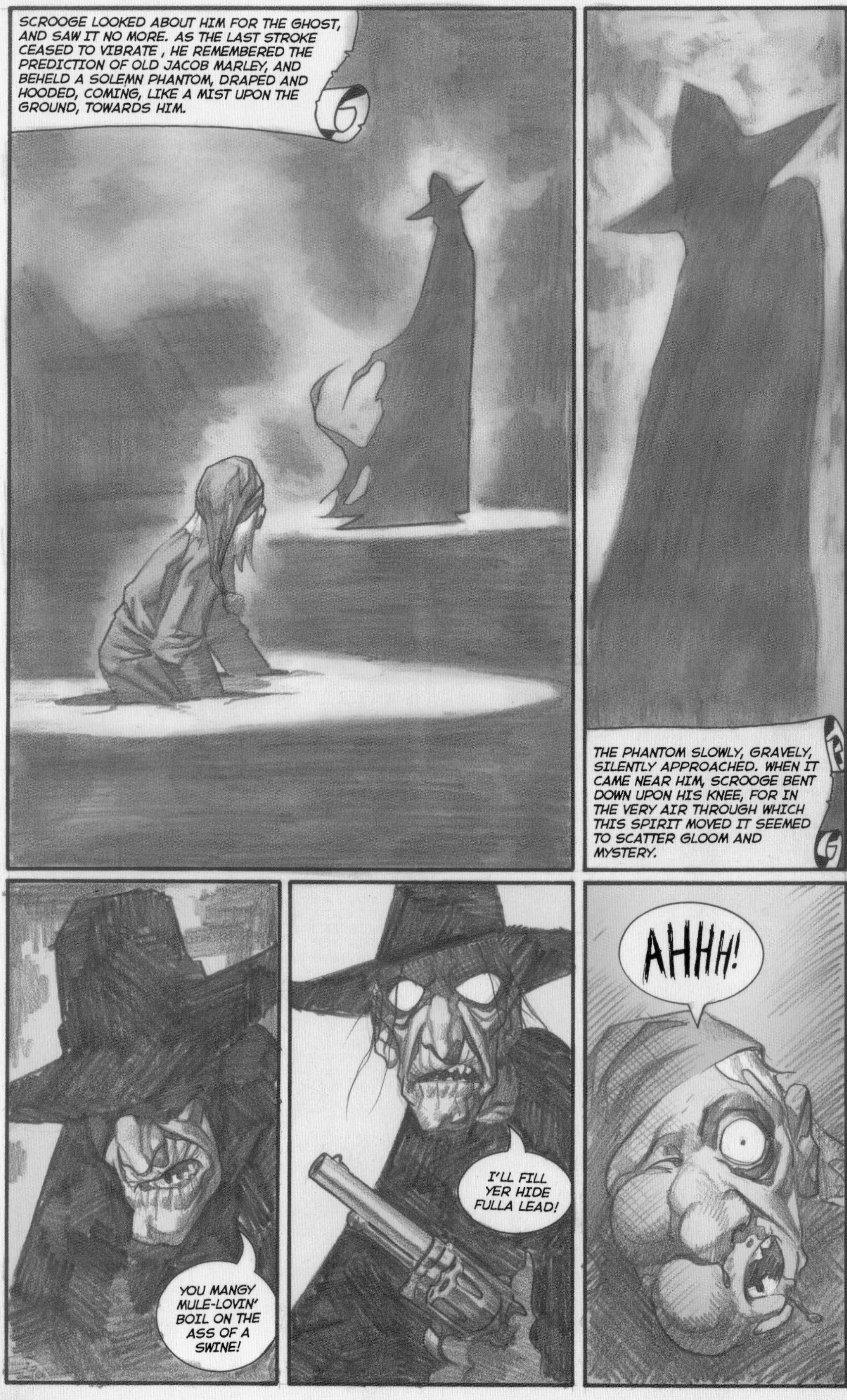
SCROOGE LOOKED ABOUT HIM FOR THE GHOST, AND SAW IT NO MORE. AS THE LAST STROKE CEASED TO VIBRATE , HE REMEMBERED THE PREDICTION OF OLD JACOB MARLEY, AND BEHELD A SOLEMN PHANTOM, DRAPED AND HOODED, COMING, LIKE A MIST UPON THE GROUND, TOWARDS HIM.
THE PHANTOM SLOWLY, GRAVELY, SILENTLY APPROACHED. WHEN IT CAME NEAR HIM, SCROOGE BENT DOWN UPON HIS KNEE, FOR IN THE VERY AIR THROUGH WHICH THIS SPIRIT MOVED IT SEEMED TO SCATTER GLOOM AND MYSTERY.
YOU MANGY MULE-LOVIN' BOIL ON THE ASS OF A SWINE!
I'LL FILL YER HIDE FULLA LEAD!
AHHH!

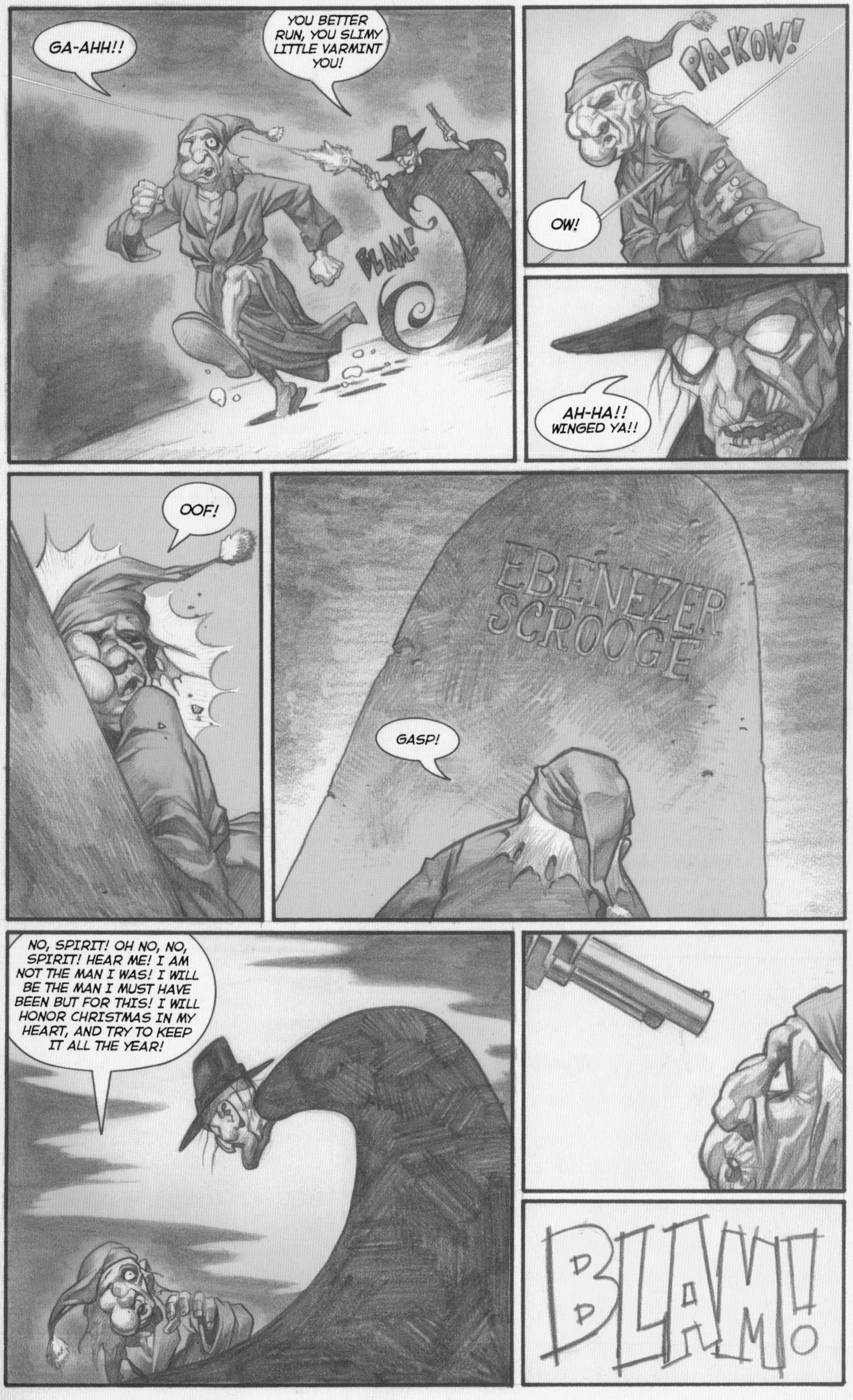
GA-AHH!!
YOU BETTER RUN, YOU SLIMY LITTLE VARMINT YOU!
BLAM!
PA-KOW!
OW!
AH-HA!! WINGED YA!!
OOF!
EBENEZER SCROOGE
GASP!
NO, SPIRIT! OH NO, NO, SPIRIT! HEAR ME! I AM NOT THE MAN I WAS! I WILL BE THE MAN I MUST HAVE BEEN BUT FOR THIS! I WILL HONOR CHRISTMAS IN MY HEART, AND TRY TO KEEP IT ALL THE YEAR!
BLAM!

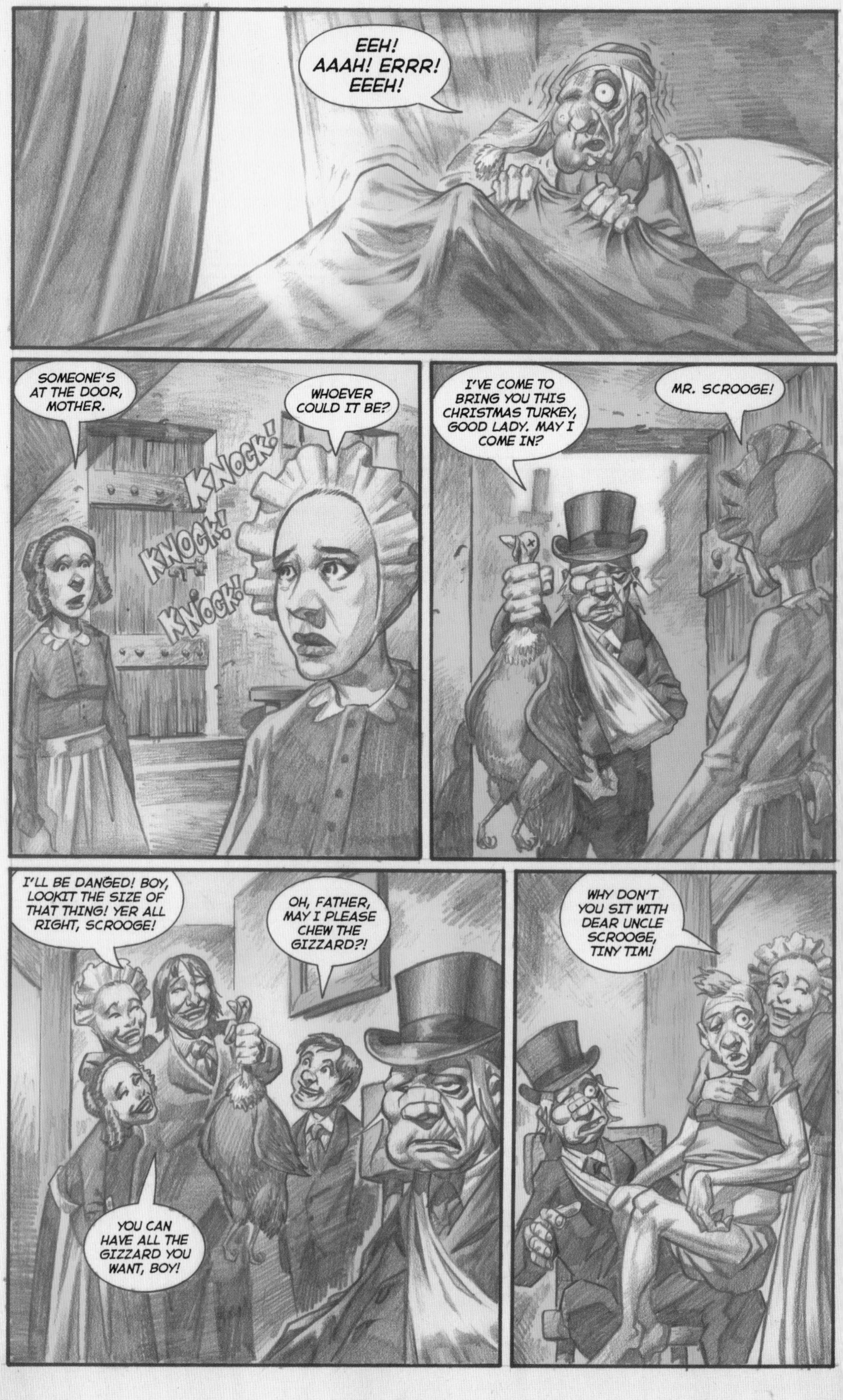
EEH! AAAH! ERRR! EEEH!
SOMEONE'S AT THE DOOR, MOTHER.
WHOEVER COULD IT BE?
KNOCK! KNOCK! KNOCK!
I'VE COME TO BRING YOU THIS CHRISTMAS TURKEY, GOOD LADY. MAY I COME IN?
MR. SCROOGE!
I'LL BE DANGED! BOY, LOOKIT THE SIZE OF THAT THING! YER ALL RIGHT, SCROOGE!
OH, FATHER, MAY I PLEASE CHEW THE GIZZARD?!
YOU CAN HAVE ALL THE GIZZARD YOU WANT, BOY!
WHY DON'T YOU SIT WITH DEAR UNCLE SCROOGE, TINY TIM!

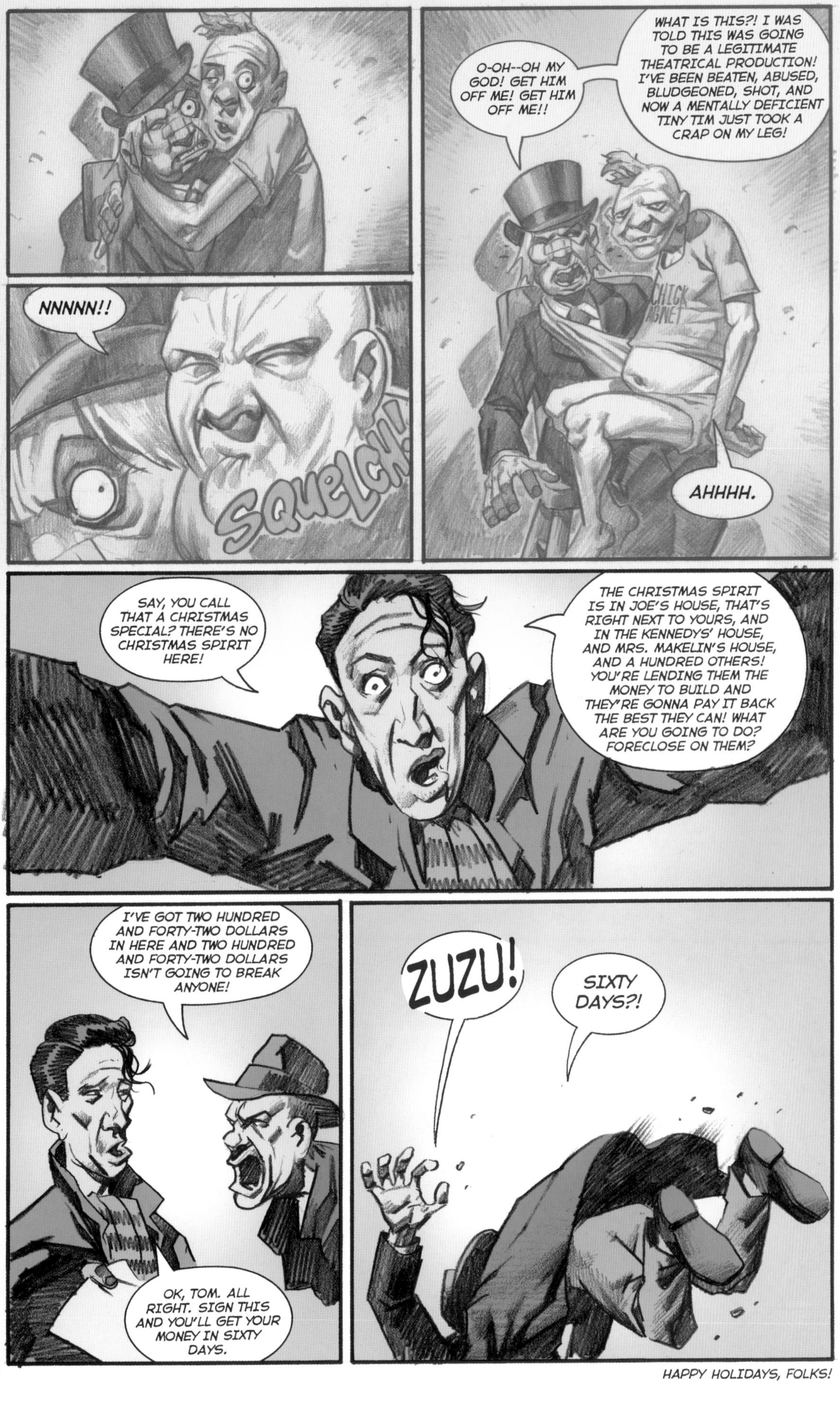
NNNNN!!
SQUELCH!
O-OH--OH MY GOD! GET HIM OFF ME! GET HIM OFF ME!!
WHAT IS THIS?! I WAS TOLD THIS WAS GOING TO BE A LEGITIMATE THEATRICAL PRODUCTION! I'VE BEEN BEATEN, ABUSED, BLUDGEONED, SHOT, AND NOW A MENTALLY DEFICIENT TINY TIM JUST TOOK A CRAP ON MY LEG!
AHHHH.
SAY, YOU CALL THAT A CHRISTMAS SPECIAL? THERE'S NO CHRISTMAS SPIRIT HERE!
THE CHRISTMAS SPIRIT IS IN JOE'S HOUSE, THAT'S RIGHT NEXT TO YOURS, AND IN THE KENNEDYS' HOUSE, AND MRS. MAKELIN'S HOUSE, AND A HUNDRED OTHERS! YOU'RE LENDING THEM THE MONEY TO BUILD AND THEY'RE GONNA PAY IT BACK THE BEST THEY CAN! WHAT ARE YOU GOING TO DO? FORECLOSE ON THEM?
I'VE GOT TWO HUNDRED AND FORTY-TWO DOLLARS IN HERE AND TWO HUNDRED AND FORTY-TWO DOLLARS ISN'T GOING TO BREAK ANYONE!
OK, TOM. ALL RIGHT. SIGN THIS AND YOU'LL GET YOUR MONEY IN SIXTY DAYS.
ZUZU!
SIXTY DAYS?!

HAPPY HOLIDAYS, FOLKS!

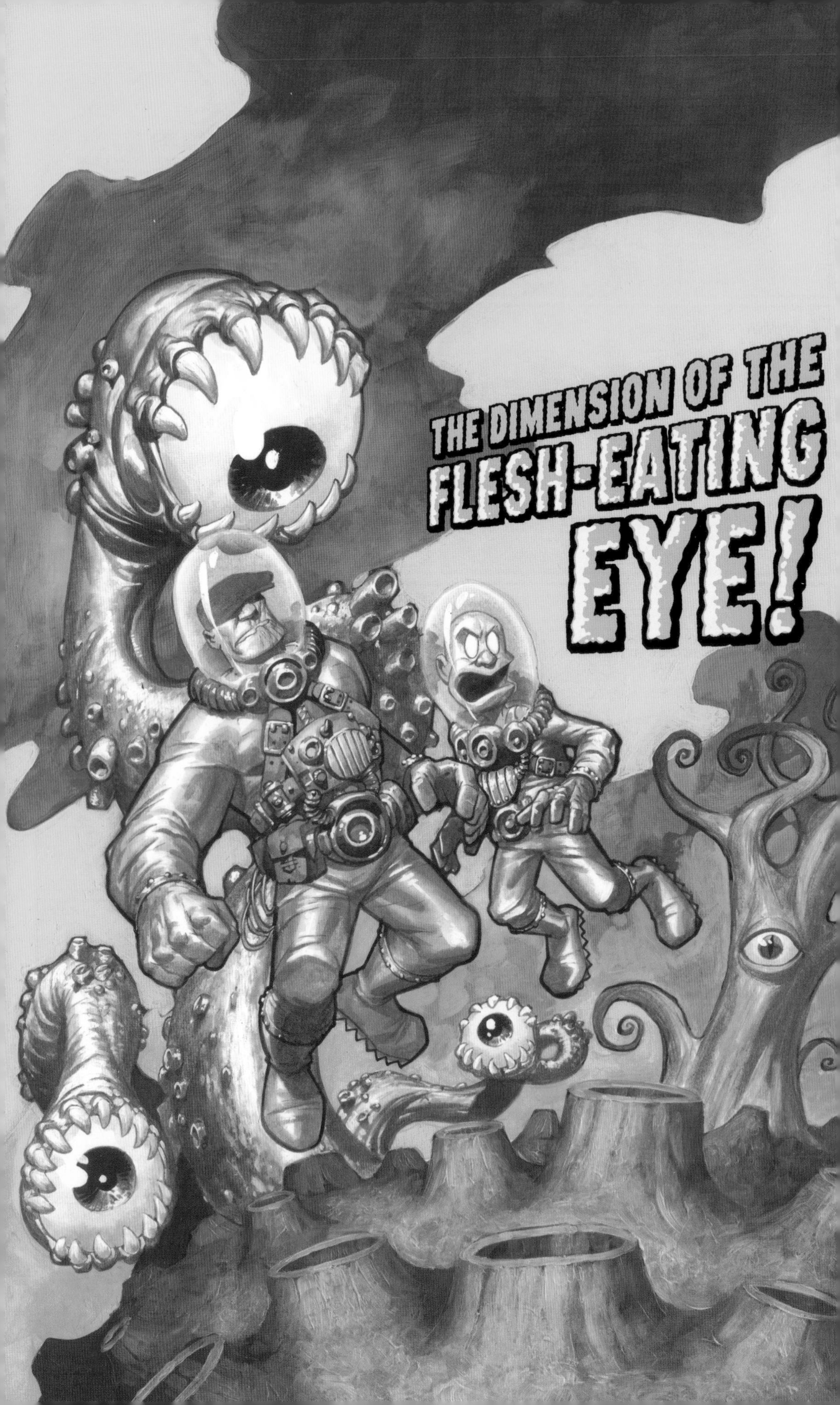
THE DIMENSION OF THE
FLESH-EATING
EYE!

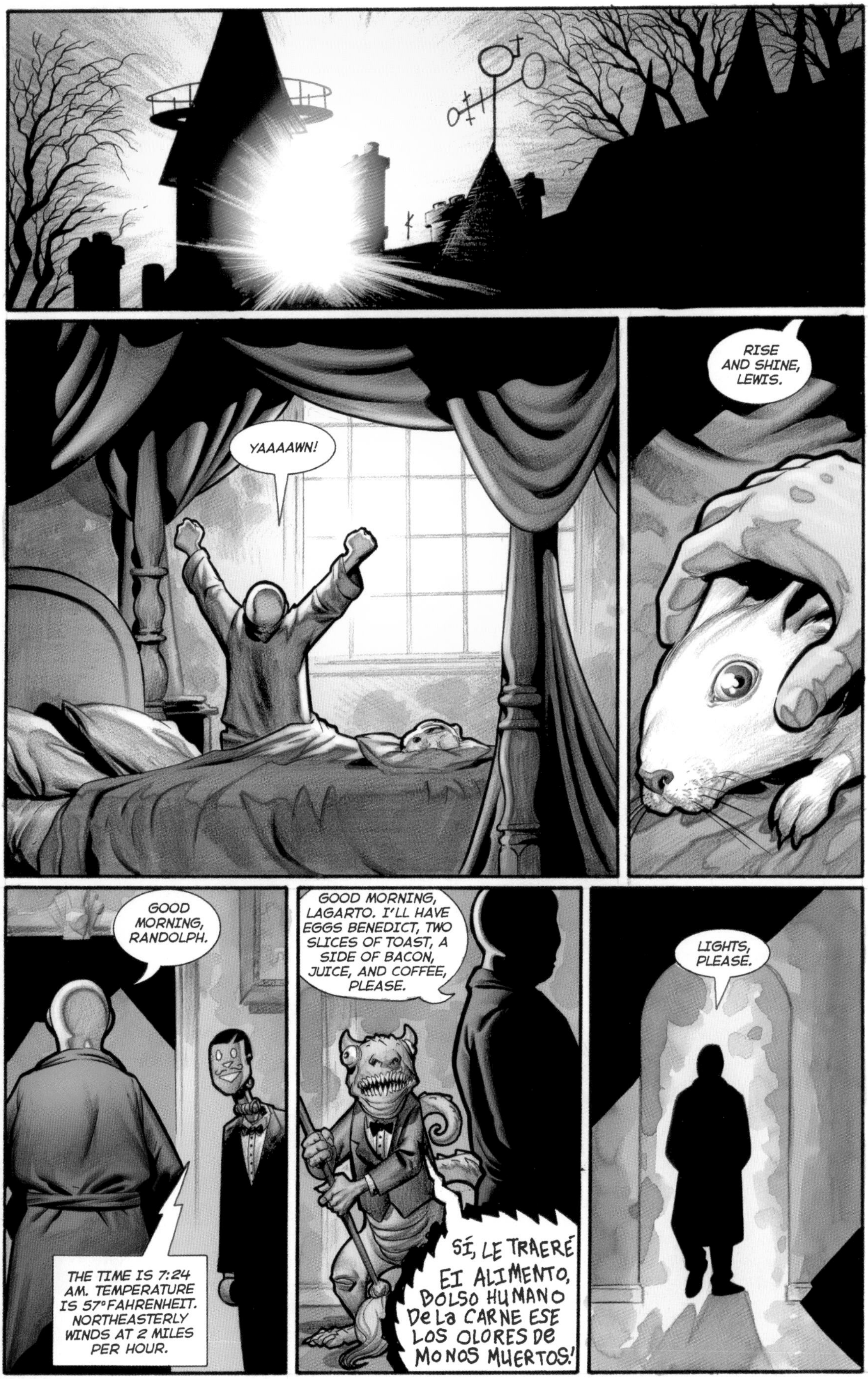

YAAAAWN!
RISE AND SHINE, LEWIS.
GOOD MORNING, RANDOLPH.
THE TIME IS 7:24 AM. TEMPERATURE IS 57° FAHRENHEIT. NORTHEASTERLY WINDS AT 2 MILES PER HOUR.
GOOD MORNING, LAGARTO. I'LL HAVE EGGS BENEDICT, TWO SLICES OF TOAST, A SIDE OF BACON, JUICE, AND COFFEE, PLEASE.
SÍ, LE TRAERÉ EI ALIMENTO, BOLSO HUMANO DE LA CARNE ESE LOS OLORES DE MONOS MUERTOS!
LIGHTS, PLEASE.

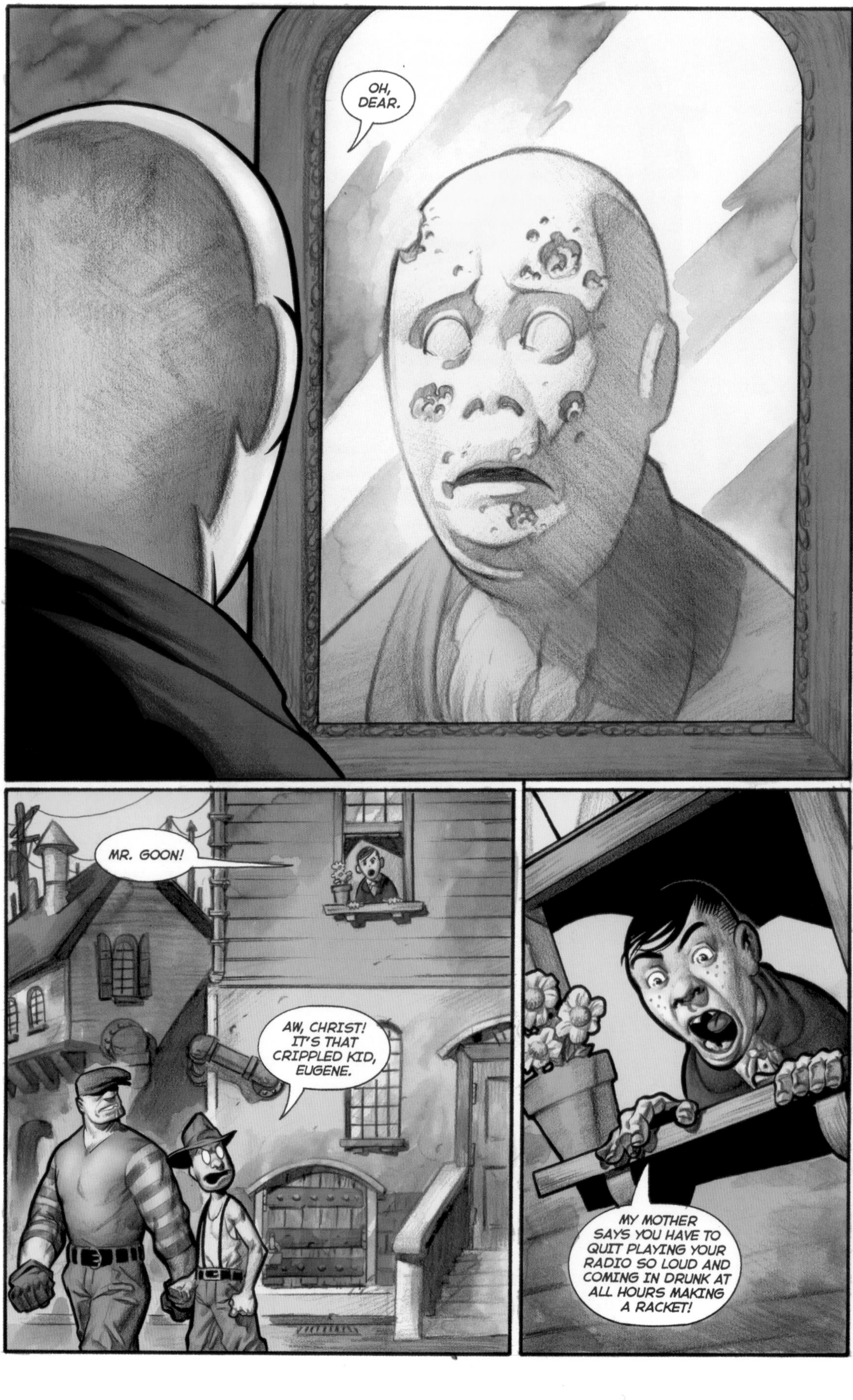
OH, DEAR.
MR. GOON!
AW, CHRIST! IT'S THAT CRIPPLED KID, EUGENE.
MY MOTHER SAYS YOU HAVE TO QUIT PLAYING YOUR RADIO SO LOUD AND COMING IN DRUNK AT ALL HOURS MAKING A RACKET!

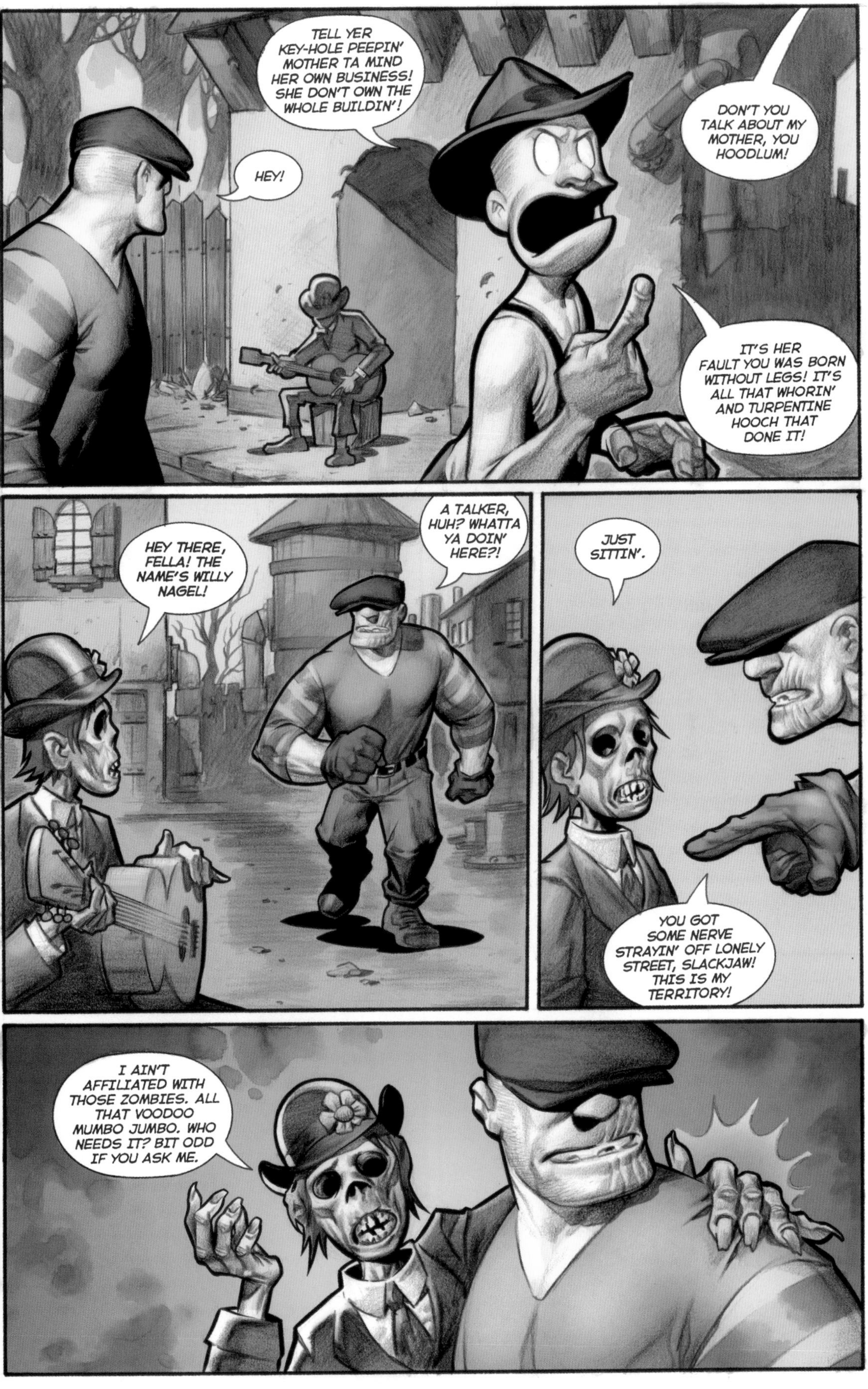

TELL YER KEY-HOLE PEEPIN' MOTHER TA MIND HER OWN BUSINESS! SHE DON'T OWN THE WHOLE BUILDIN'!
HEY!
DON'T YOU TALK ABOUT MY MOTHER, YOU HOODLUM!
IT'S HER FAULT YOU WAS BORN WITHOUT LEGS! IT'S ALL THAT WHORIN' AND TURPENTINE HOOCH THAT DONE IT!
HEY THERE, FELLA! THE NAME'S WILLY NAGEL!
A TALKER, HUH? WHATTA YA DOIN' HERE?!
JUST SITTIN'.
YOU GOT SOME NERVE STRAYIN' OFF LONELY STREET, SLACKJAW! THIS IS MY TERRITORY!
I AIN'T AFFILIATED WITH THOSE ZOMBIES. ALL THAT VOODOO MUMBO JUMBO. WHO NEEDS IT? BIT ODD IF YOU ASK ME.

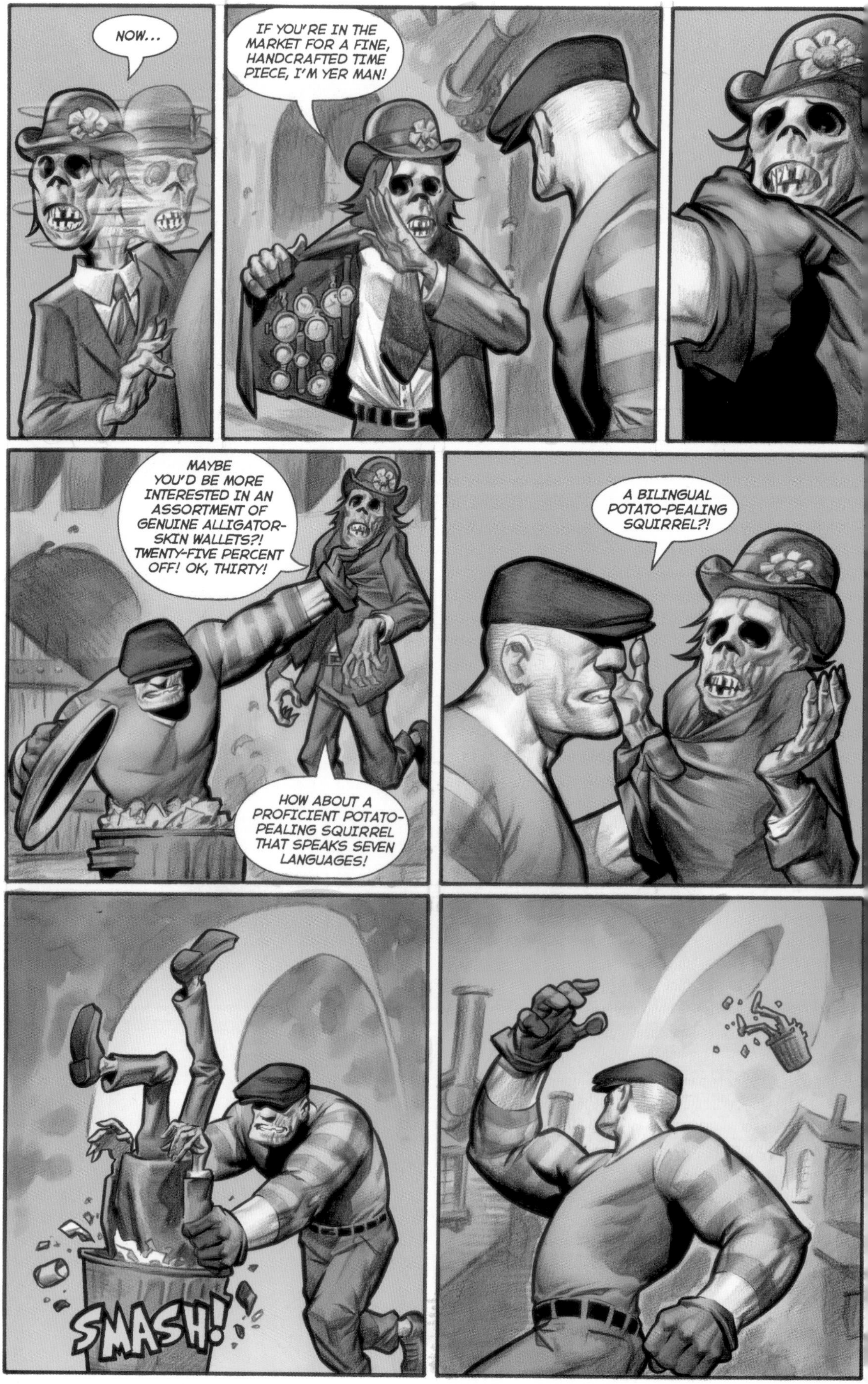
NOW...
IF YOU'RE IN THE MARKET FOR A FINE, HANDCRAFTED TIME PIECE, I'M YER MAN!
MAYBE YOU'D BE MORE INTERESTED IN AN ASSORTMENT OF GENUINE ALLIGATOR-SKIN WALLETS?! TWENTY-FIVE PERCENT OFF! OK, THIRTY!
HOW ABOUT A PROFICIENT POTATO-PEALING SQUIRREL THAT SPEAKS SEVEN LANGUAGES!
A BILINGUAL POTATO-PEALING SQUIRREL?!
SMASH!

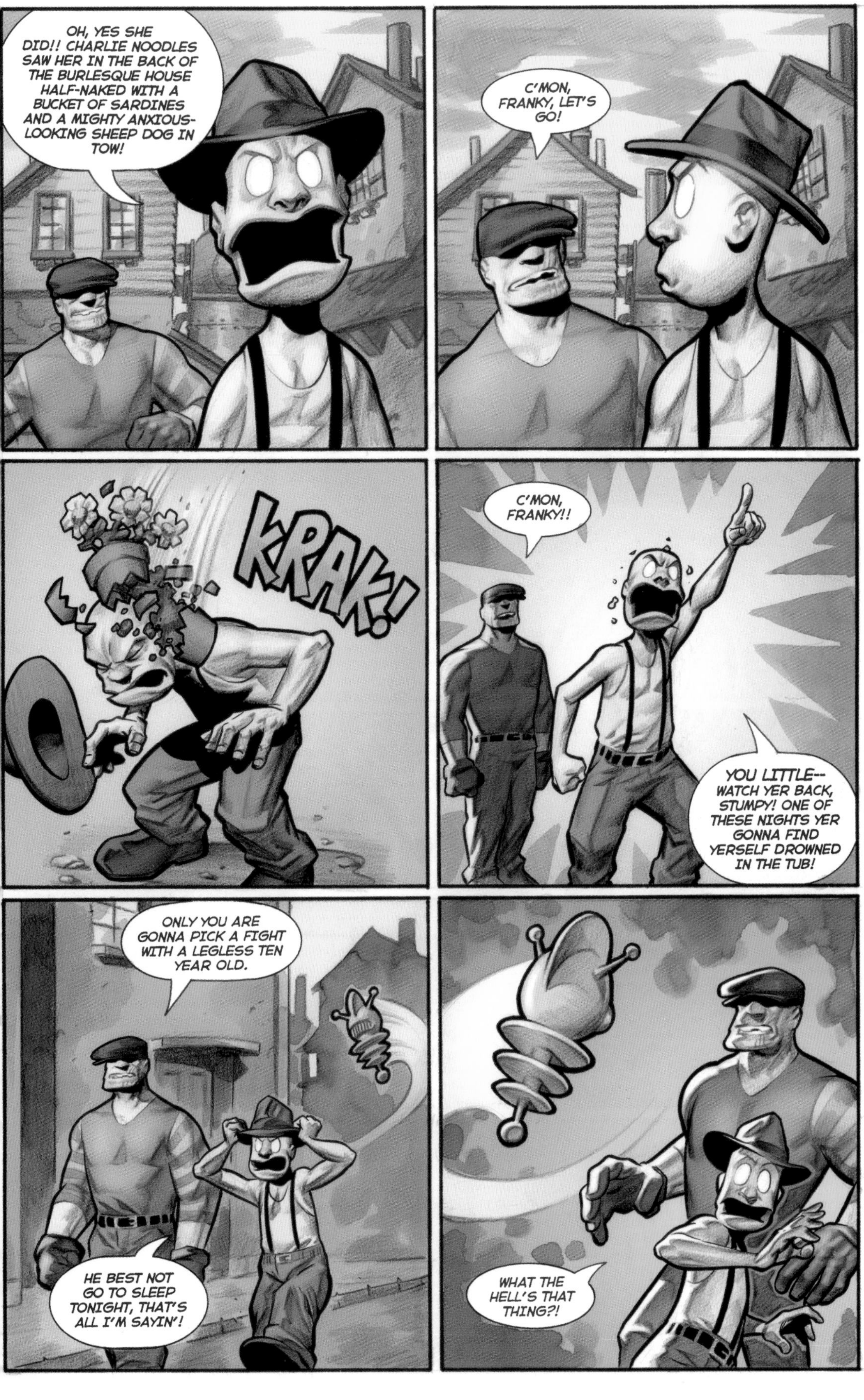
OH, YES SHE DID!! CHARLIE NOODLES SAW HER IN THE BACK OF THE BURLESQUE HOUSE HALF-NAKED WITH A BUCKET OF SARDINES AND A MIGHTY ANXIOUS-LOOKING SHEEP DOG IN TOW!
C'MON, FRANKY, LET'S GO!
KRAK!
C'MON, FRANKY!!
YOU LITTLE-- WATCH YER BACK, STUMPY! ONE OF THESE NIGHTS YER GONNA FIND YERSELF DROWNED IN THE TUB!
ONLY YOU ARE GONNA PICK A FIGHT WITH A LEGLESS TEN YEAR OLD.
HE BEST NOT GO TO SLEEP TONIGHT, THAT'S ALL I'M SAYIN'!
WHAT THE HELL'S THAT THING?!

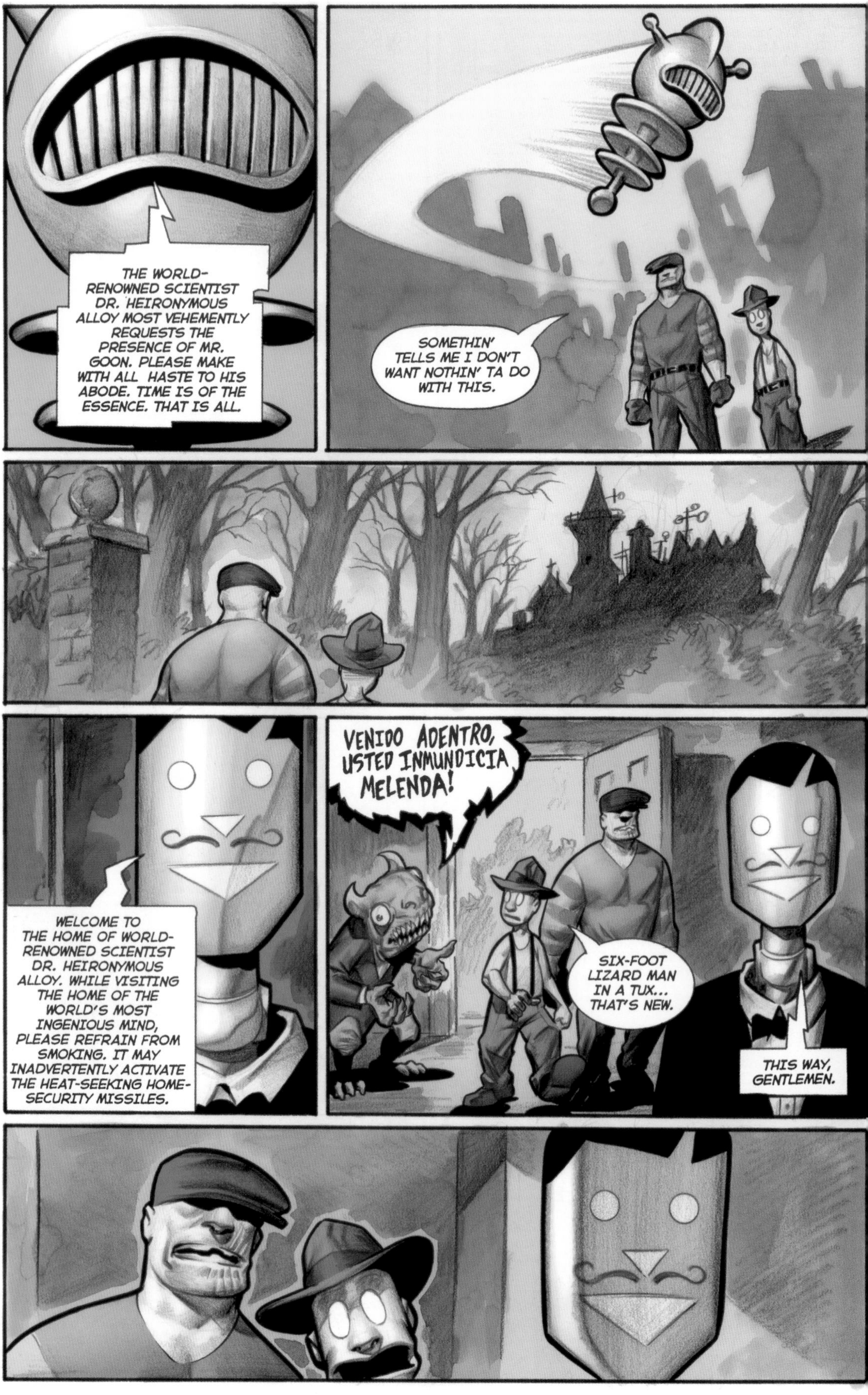
THE WORLD-RENOWNED SCIENTIST DR. HEIRONYMOUS ALLOY MOST VEHEMENTLY REQUESTS THE PRESENCE OF MR. GOON. PLEASE MAKE WITH ALL HASTE TO HIS ABODE. TIME IS OF THE ESSENCE. THAT IS ALL.
SOMETHIN' TELLS ME I DON'T WANT NOTHIN' TA DO WITH THIS.
WELCOME TO THE HOME OF WORLD-RENOWNED SCIENTIST DR. HEIRONYMOUS ALLOY. WHILE VISITING THE HOME OF THE WORLD'S MOST INGENIOUS MIND, PLEASE REFRAIN FROM SMOKING. IT MAY INADVERTENTLY ACTIVATE THE HEAT-SEEKING HOME-SECURITY MISSILES.
VENIDO ADENTRO, USTED INMUNDICIA MELENDA!
SIX-FOOT LIZARD MAN IN A TUX... THAT'S NEW.
THIS WAY, GENTLEMEN.

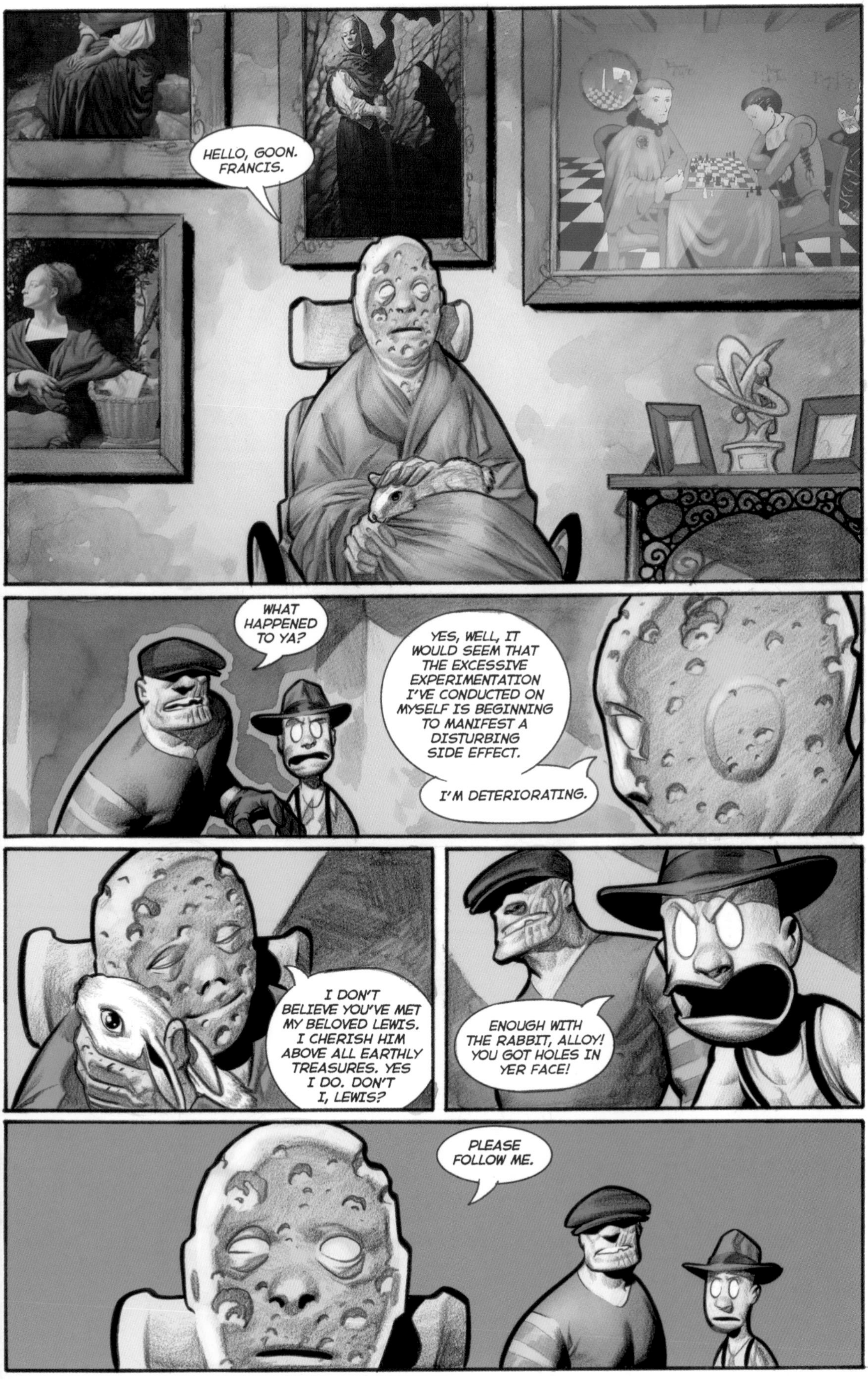
HELLO, GOON. FRANCIS.
WHAT HAPPENED TO YA?
YES, WELL, IT WOULD SEEM THAT THE EXCESSIVE EXPERIMENTATION I'VE CONDUCTED ON MYSELF IS BEGINNING TO MANIFEST A DISTURBING SIDE EFFECT.
I'M DETERIORATING.
I DON'T BELIEVE YOU'VE MET MY BELOVED LEWIS. I CHERISH HIM ABOVE ALL EARTHLY TREASURES. YES I DO. DON'T I, LEWIS?
ENOUGH WITH THE RABBIT, ALLOY! YOU GOT HOLES IN YER FACE!
PLEASE FOLLOW ME.

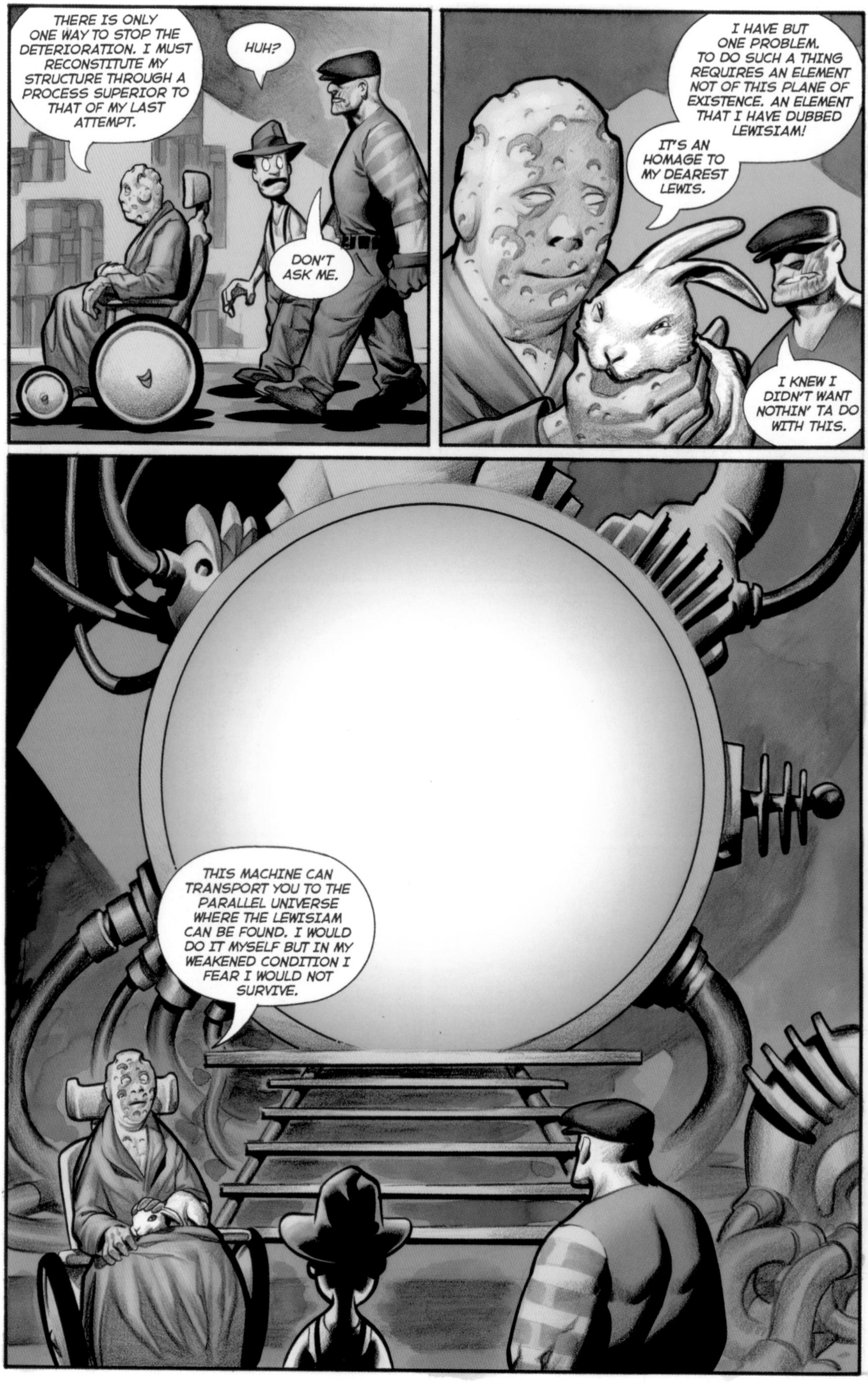
THERE IS ONLY ONE WAY TO STOP THE DETERIORATION. I MUST RECONSTITUTE MY STRUCTURE THROUGH A PROCESS SUPERIOR TO THAT OF MY LAST ATTEMPT.
HUH?
DON'T ASK ME.
I HAVE BUT ONE PROBLEM. TO DO SUCH A THING REQUIRES AN ELEMENT NOT OF THIS PLANE OF EXISTENCE. AN ELEMENT THAT I HAVE DUBBED LEWISIAM!
IT'S AN HOMAGE TO MY DEAREST LEWIS.
I KNEW I DIDN'T WANT NOTHIN' TA DO WITH THIS.
THIS MACHINE CAN TRANSPORT YOU TO THE PARALLEL UNIVERSE WHERE THE LEWISIAM CAN BE FOUND. I WOULD DO IT MYSELF BUT IN MY WEAKENED CONDITION I FEAR I WOULD NOT SURVIVE.

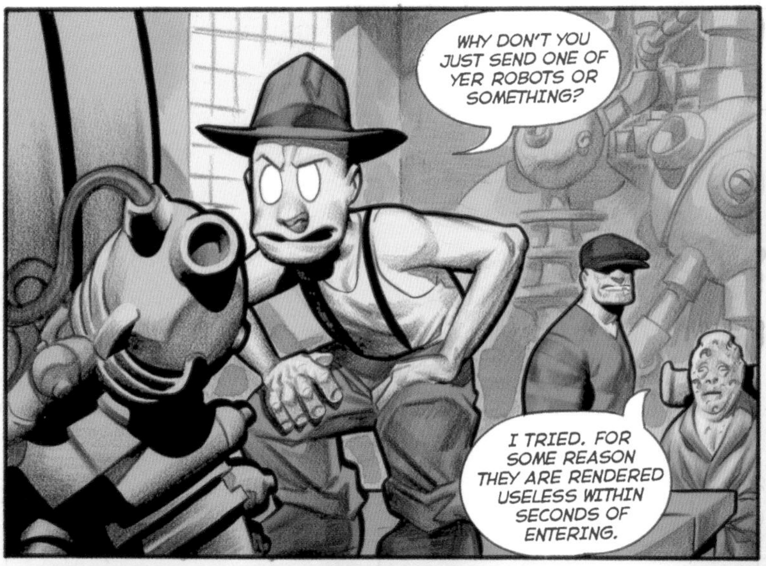
WHY DON'T YOU JUST SEND ONE OF YER ROBOTS OR SOMETHING?
I TRIED. FOR SOME REASON THEY ARE RENDERED USELESS WITHIN SECONDS OF ENTERING.

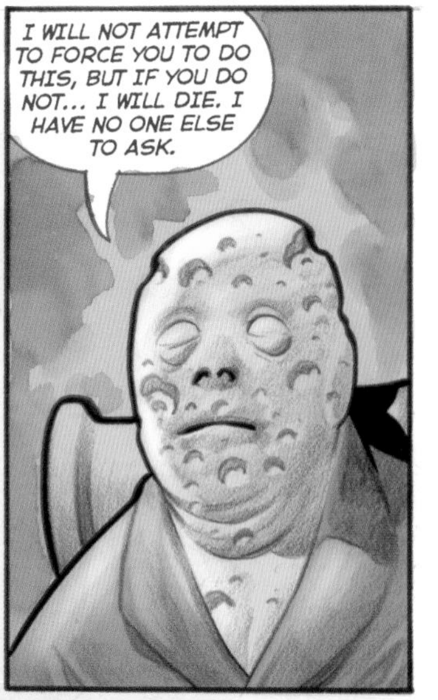
I WILL NOT ATTEMPT TO FORCE YOU TO DO THIS, BUT IF YOU DO NOT... I WILL DIE. I HAVE NO ONE ELSE TO ASK.

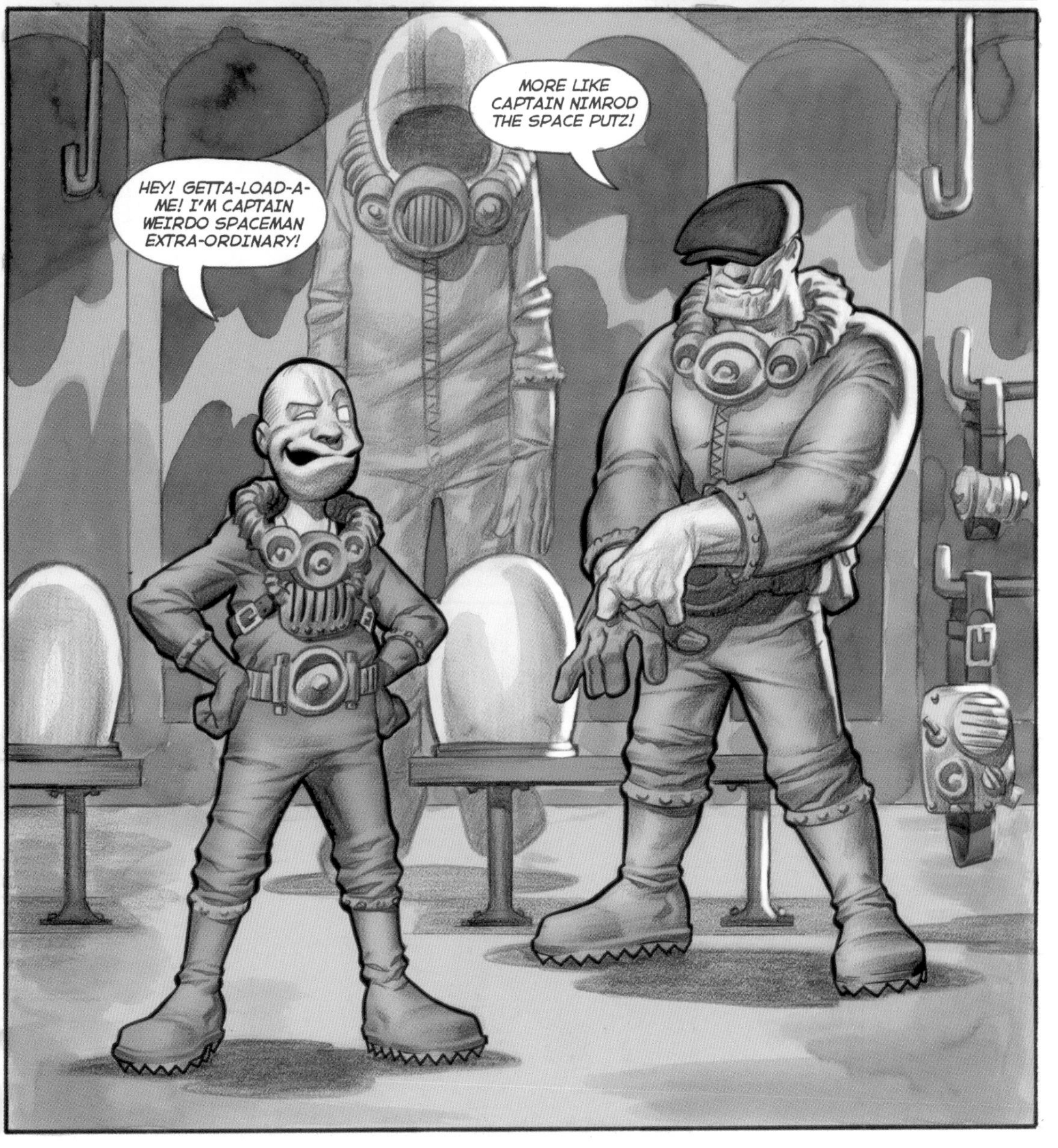
HEY! GETTA-LOAD-A-ME! I'M CAPTAIN WEIRDO SPACEMAN EXTRA-ORDINARY!
MORE LIKE CAPTAIN NIMROD THE SPACE PUTZ!

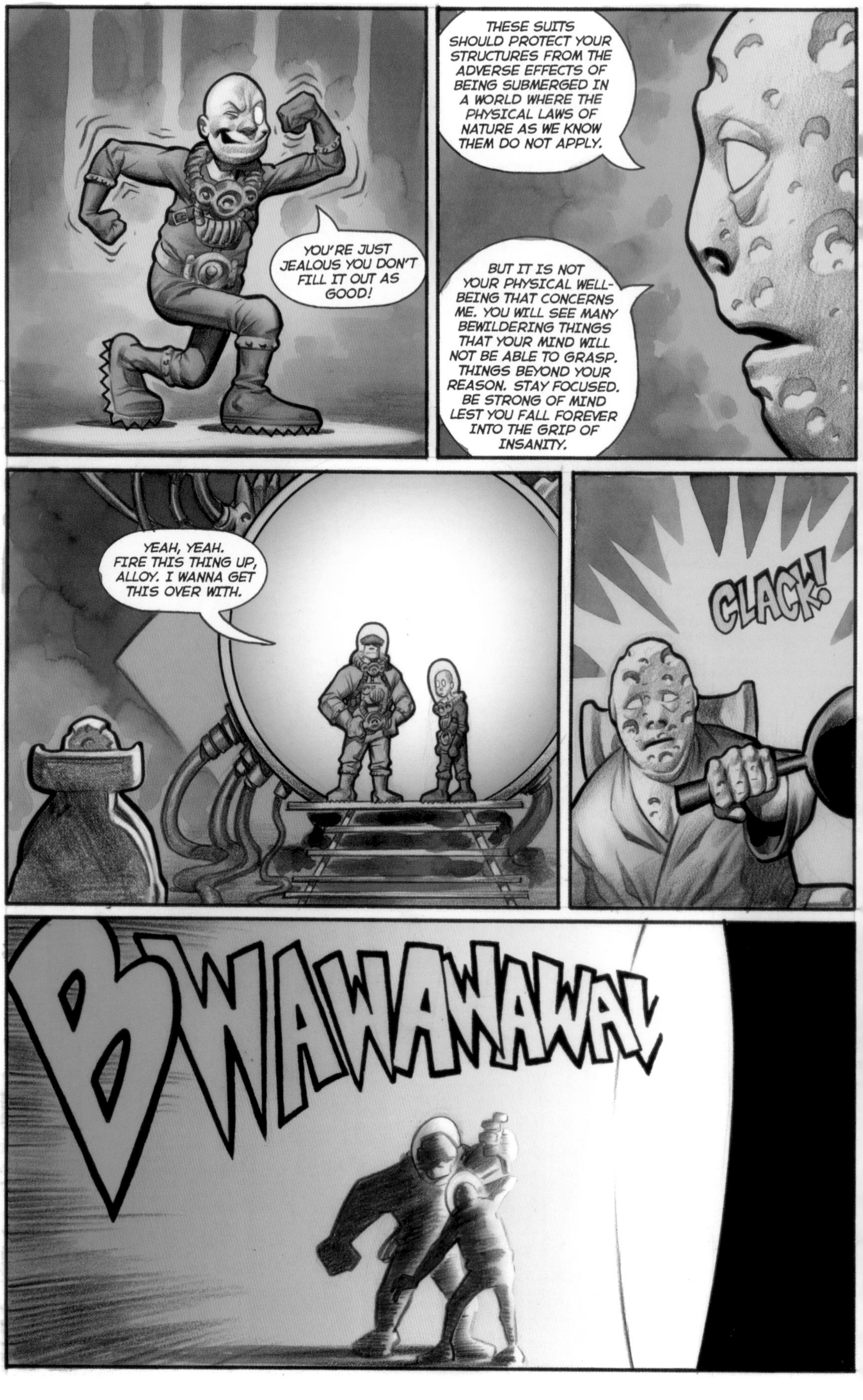
YOU'RE JUST JEALOUS YOU DON'T FILL IT OUT AS GOOD!
THESE SUITS SHOULD PROTECT YOUR STRUCTURES FROM THE ADVERSE EFFECTS OF BEING SUBMERGED IN A WORLD WHERE THE PHYSICAL LAWS OF NATURE AS WE KNOW THEM DO NOT APPLY.
BUT IT IS NOT YOUR PHYSICAL WELL-BEING THAT CONCERNS ME. YOU WILL SEE MANY BEWILDERING THINGS THAT YOUR MIND WILL NOT BE ABLE TO GRASP. THINGS BEYOND YOUR REASON. STAY FOCUSED. BE STRONG OF MIND LEST YOU FALL FOREVER INTO THE GRIP OF INSANITY.
YEAH, YEAH. FIRE THIS THING UP, ALLOY. I WANNA GET THIS OVER WITH.
CLACK!
BWAWAWAWAWA

GULP!

THE DEVICE ON YOUR BELT WILL LEAD YOU DIRECTLY TO THE LEWISIAM!

WHEN YOU HAVE FOUND IT AND ARE READY TO RETURN, SIMPLY PRESS THE BUTTONS ON YOUR CHEST PLATES IN UNISON AND THE PAIR OF YOU WILL INSTANTANEOUSLY RETURN HERE. IT WILL NOT WORK UNLESS YOU PRESS THEM IN UNISON!

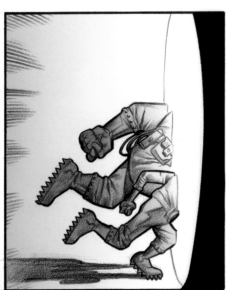

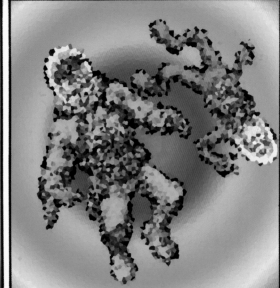

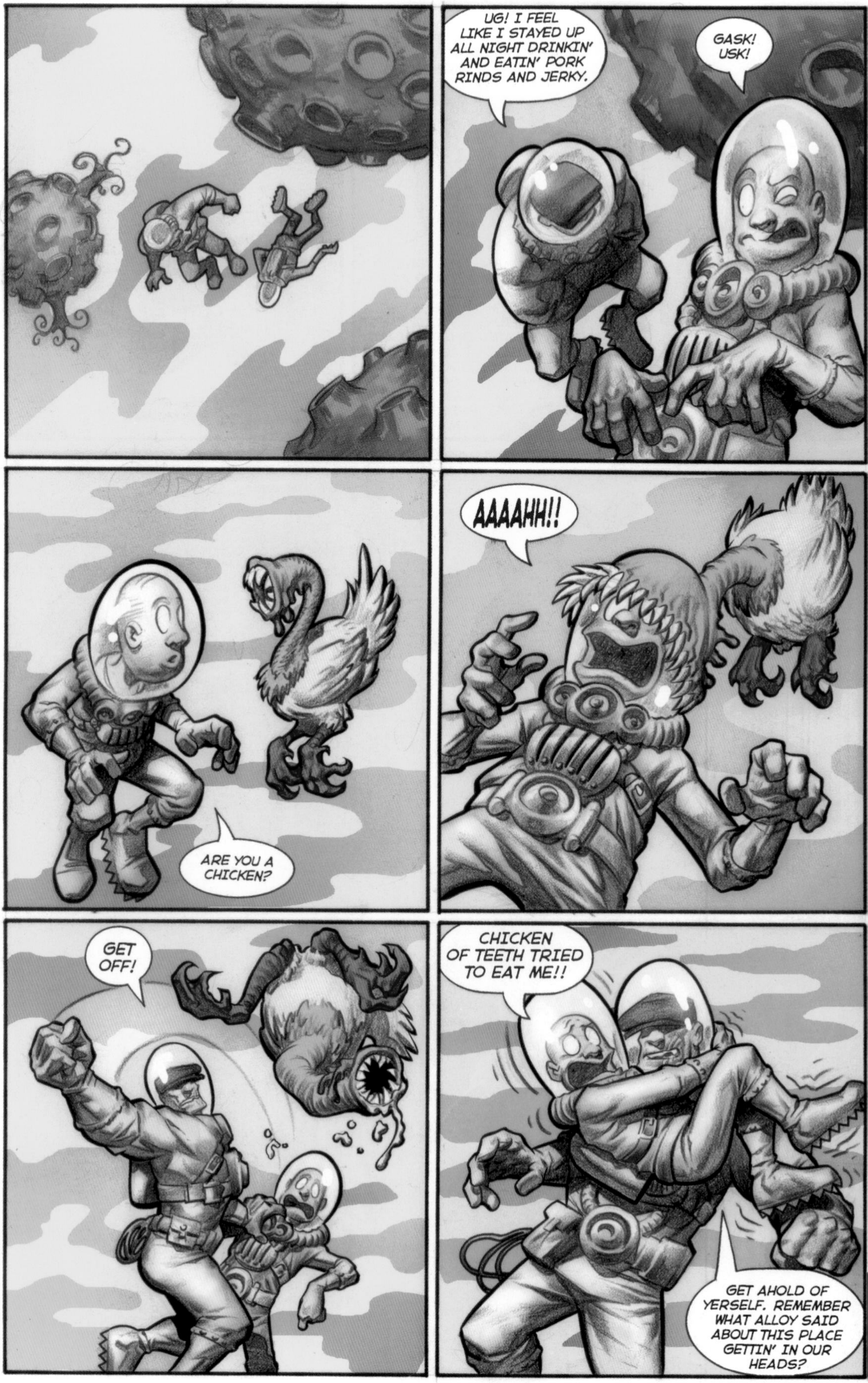
UG! I FEEL LIKE I STAYED UP ALL NIGHT DRINKIN' AND EATIN' PORK RINDS AND JERKY.
GASK! USK!
ARE YOU A CHICKEN?
AAAAHH!!
GET OFF!
CHICKEN OF TEETH TRIED TO EAT ME!!
GET AHOLD OF YERSELF. REMEMBER WHAT ALLOY SAID ABOUT THIS PLACE GETTIN' IN OUR HEADS?

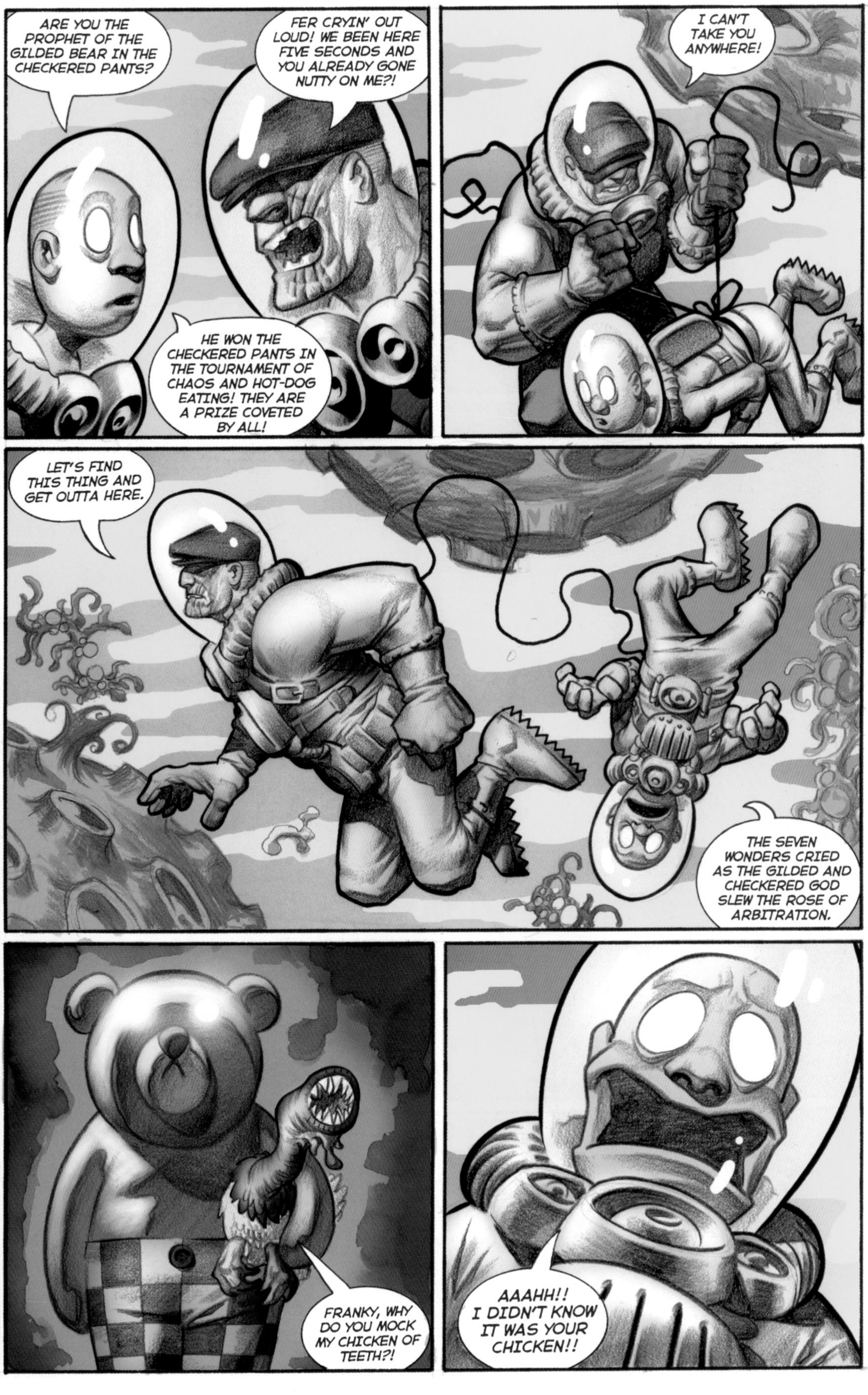
ARE YOU THE PROPHET OF THE GILDED BEAR IN THE CHECKERED PANTS?
FER CRYIN' OUT LOUD! WE BEEN HERE FIVE SECONDS AND YOU ALREADY GONE NUTTY ON ME?!
HE WON THE CHECKERED PANTS IN THE TOURNAMENT OF CHAOS AND HOT-DOG EATING! THEY ARE A PRIZE COVETED BY ALL!
I CAN'T TAKE YOU ANYWHERE!
LET'S FIND THIS THING AND GET OUTTA HERE.
THE SEVEN WONDERS CRIED AS THE GILDED AND CHECKERED GOD SLEW THE ROSE OF ARBITRATION.
FRANKY, WHY DO YOU MOCK MY CHICKEN OF TEETH?!
AAAHH!! I DIDN'T KNOW IT WAS YOUR CHICKEN!!

LAGARTO! I DO NOT FEEL WELL!
AHH! NO! MY MIND! IT IS EATING INTO MY GLORIOUS MIND!!
¡CESTE GRINGO BRILLANTE ES TERRIBLE INSANO!
NOT MY INGENIOUS MIND!! YOU MUST HURRY, GOON!

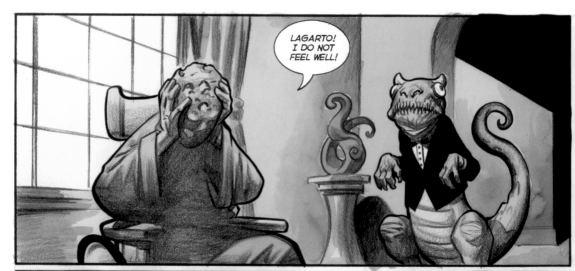

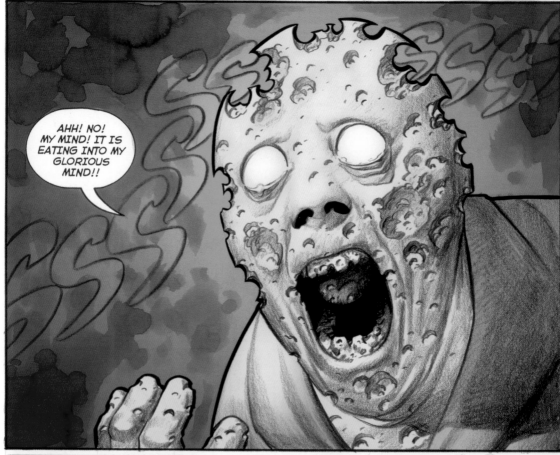

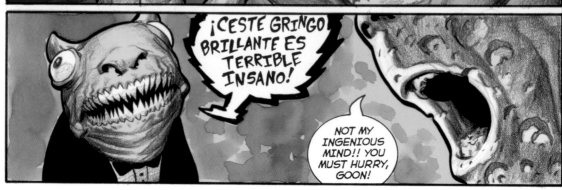

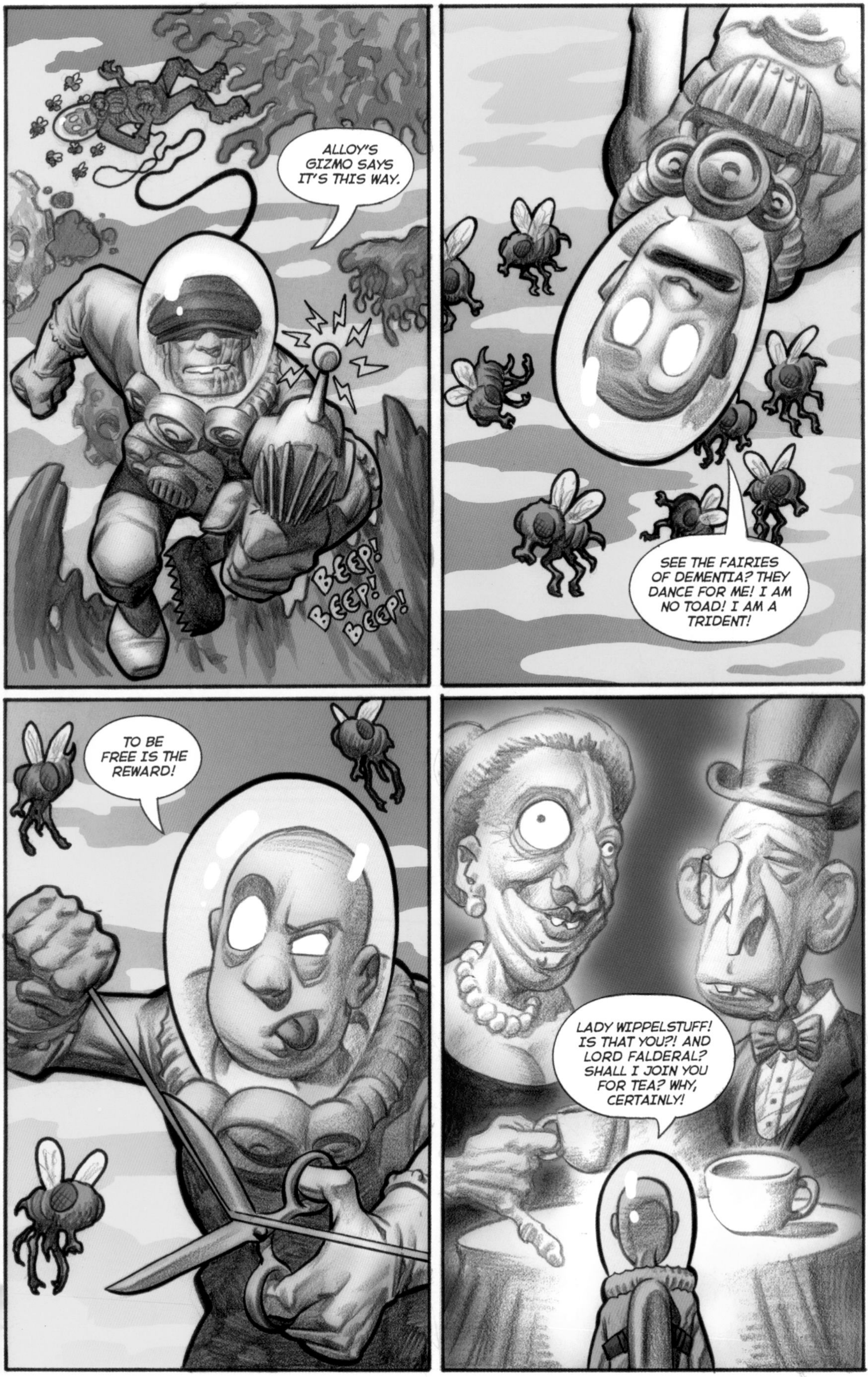
ALLOY'S GIZMO SAYS IT'S THIS WAY.
BEEP! BEEP! BEEP!
SEE THE FAIRIES OF DEMENTIA? THEY DANCE FOR ME! I AM NO TOAD! I AM A TRIDENT!
TO BE FREE IS THE REWARD!
LADY WIPPELSTUFF! IS THAT YOU?! AND LORD FALDERAL? SHALL I JOIN YOU FOR TEA? WHY, CERTAINLY!

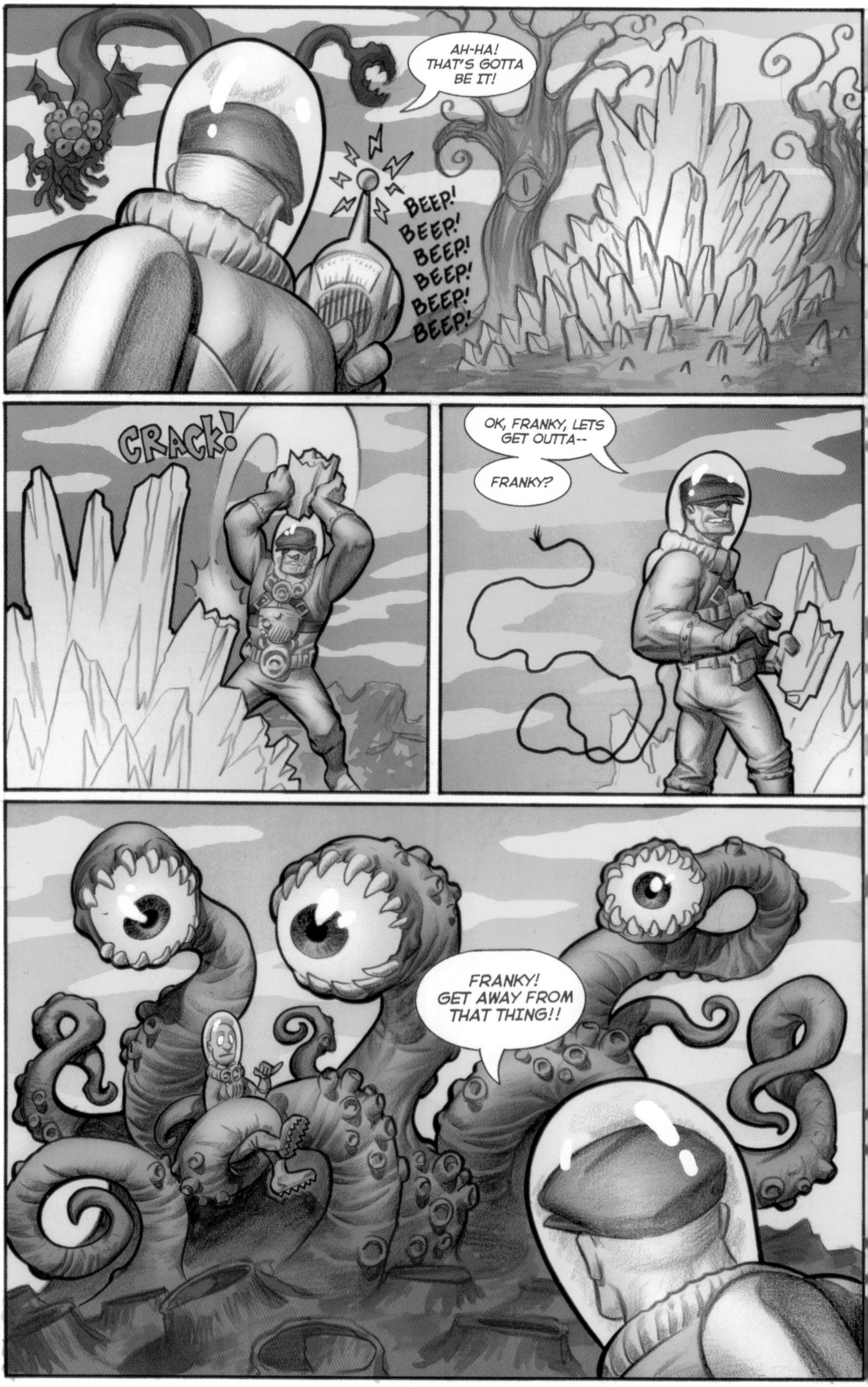
AH-HA! THAT'S GOTTA BE IT!
BEEP! BEEP! BEEP! BEEP! BEEP! BEEP!
CRACK!
OK, FRANKY, LETS GET OUTTA--
FRANKY?
FRANKY! GET AWAY FROM THAT THING!!

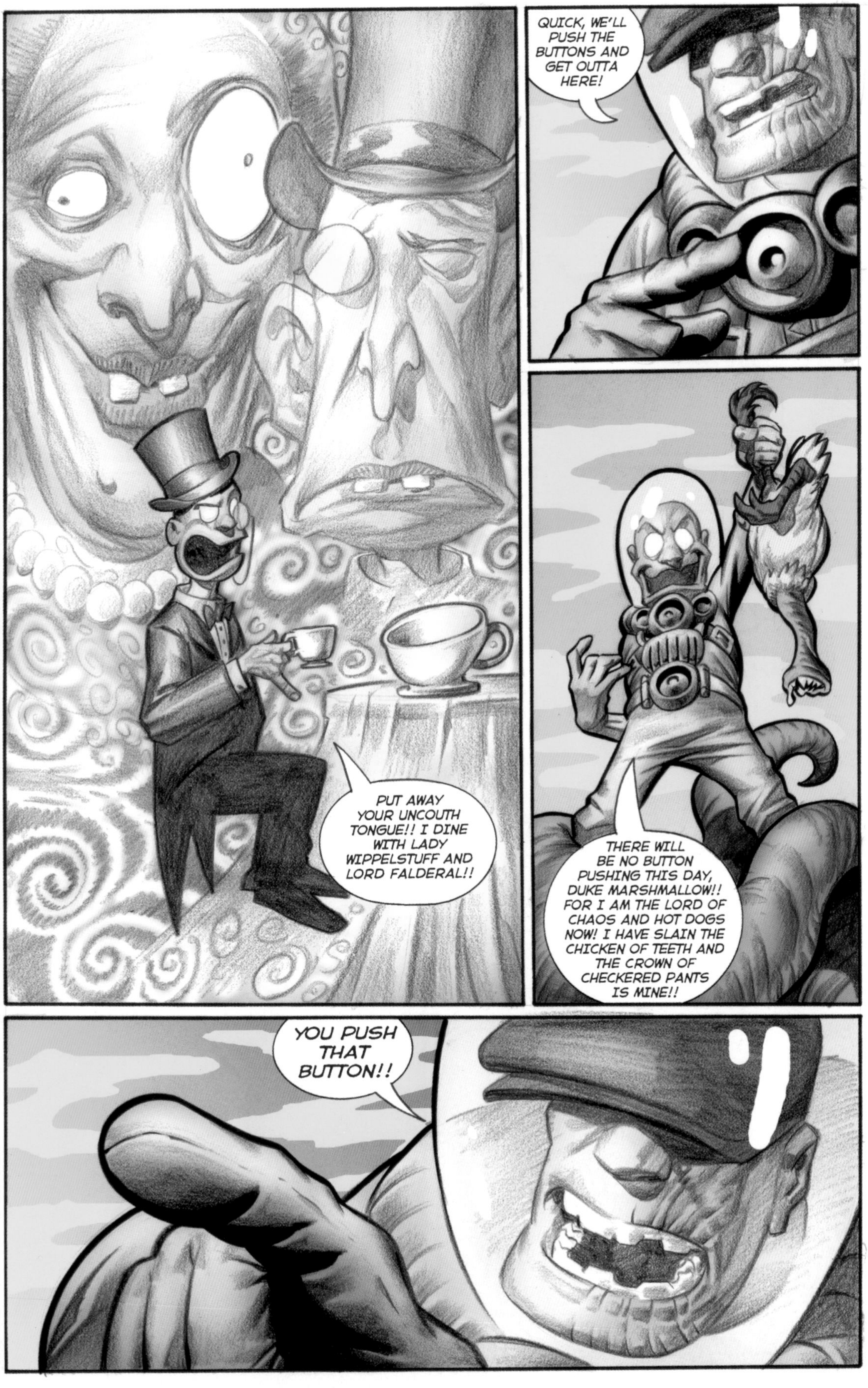
QUICK, WE'LL PUSH THE BUTTONS AND GET OUTTA HERE!
PUT AWAY YOUR UNCOUTH TONGUE!! I DINE WITH LADY WIPPELSTUFF AND LORD FALDERAL!!
THERE WILL BE NO BUTTON PUSHING THIS DAY, DUKE MARSHMALLOW!! FOR I AM THE LORD OF CHAOS AND HOT DOGS NOW! I HAVE SLAIN THE CHICKEN OF TEETH AND THE CROWN OF CHECKERED PANTS IS MINE!!
YOU PUSH THAT BUTTON!!

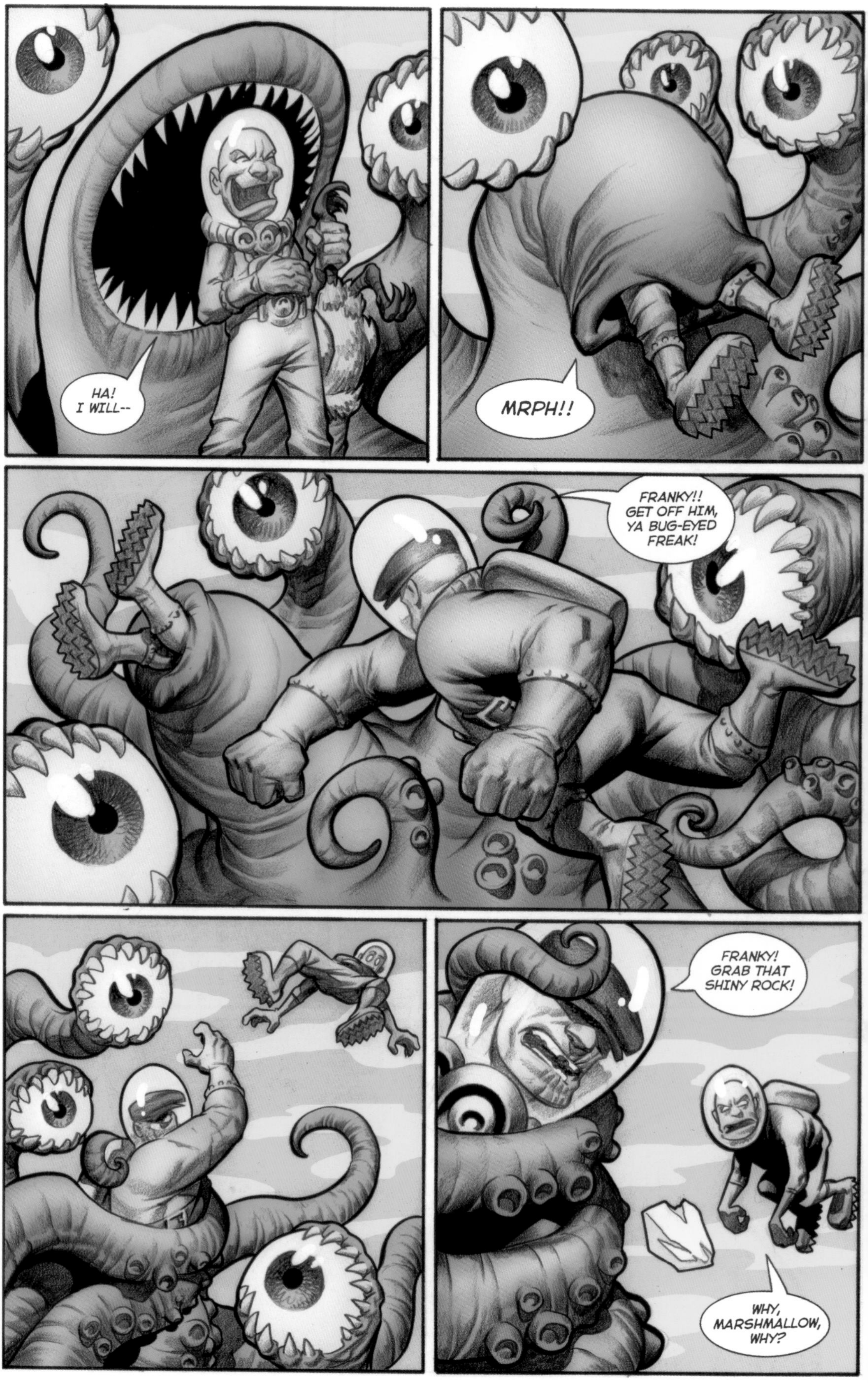
HA! I WILL--
MRPH!!
FRANKY!! GET OFF HIM, YA BUG-EYED FREAK!
FRANKY! GRAB THAT SHINY ROCK!
WHY, MARSHMALLOW, WHY?

YOU CAN DO THAT?

UH... BECAUSE... BECAUSE IF YOU DON'T, I'LL RESTORE THE GILDED BEAR TO POWER AND INCREASE THE CHICKEN OF TEETH BY TEN FOLD!!

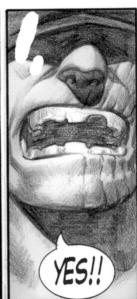

YES!!

AAAHHH!!!

I GOT IT!

NOW PUSH THE BUTTON!!

CLICK!

CLICK!

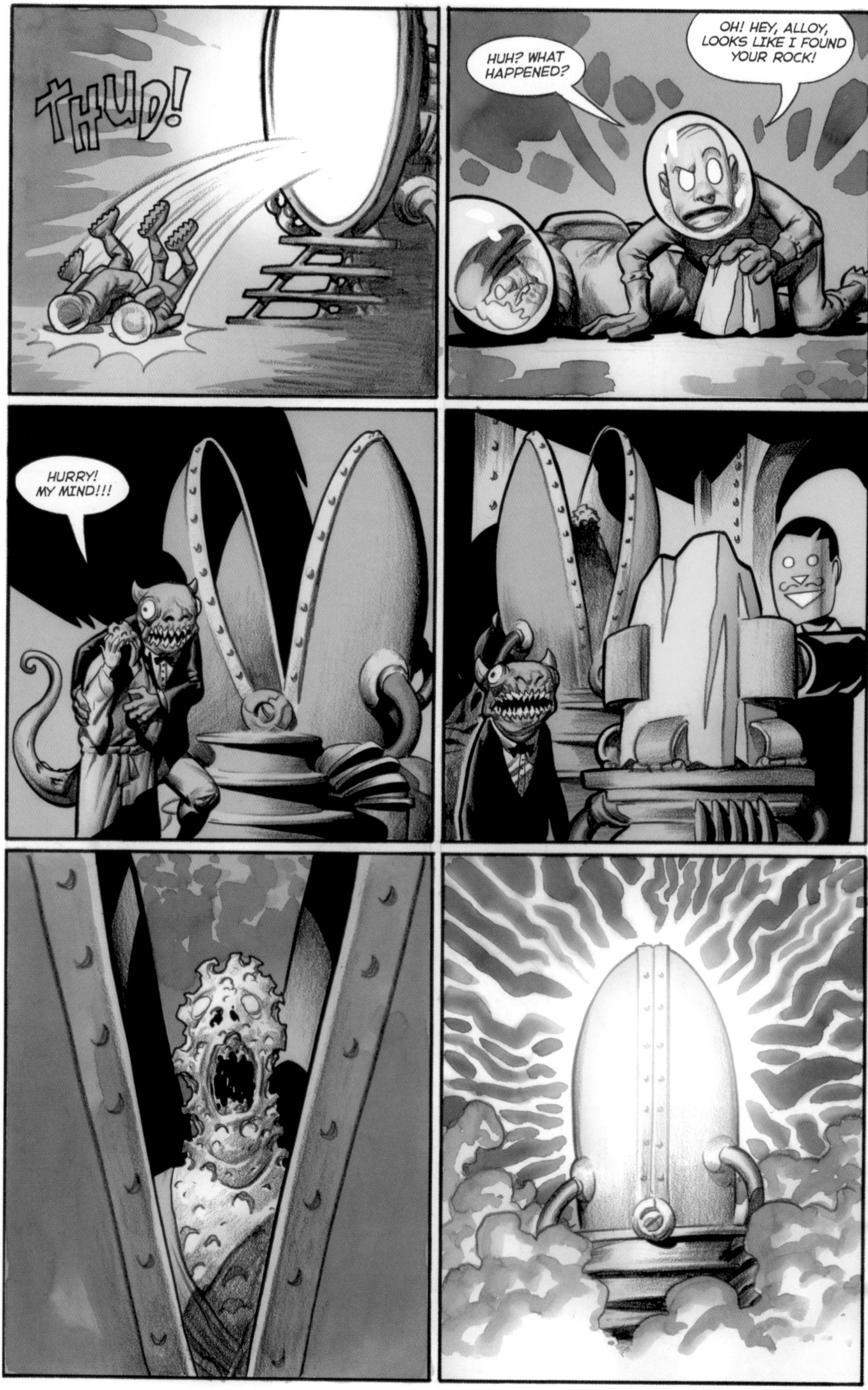
THUD!
HUH? WHAT HAPPENED?
OH! HEY, ALLOY, LOOKS LIKE I FOUND YOUR ROCK!
HURRY! MY MIND!!!

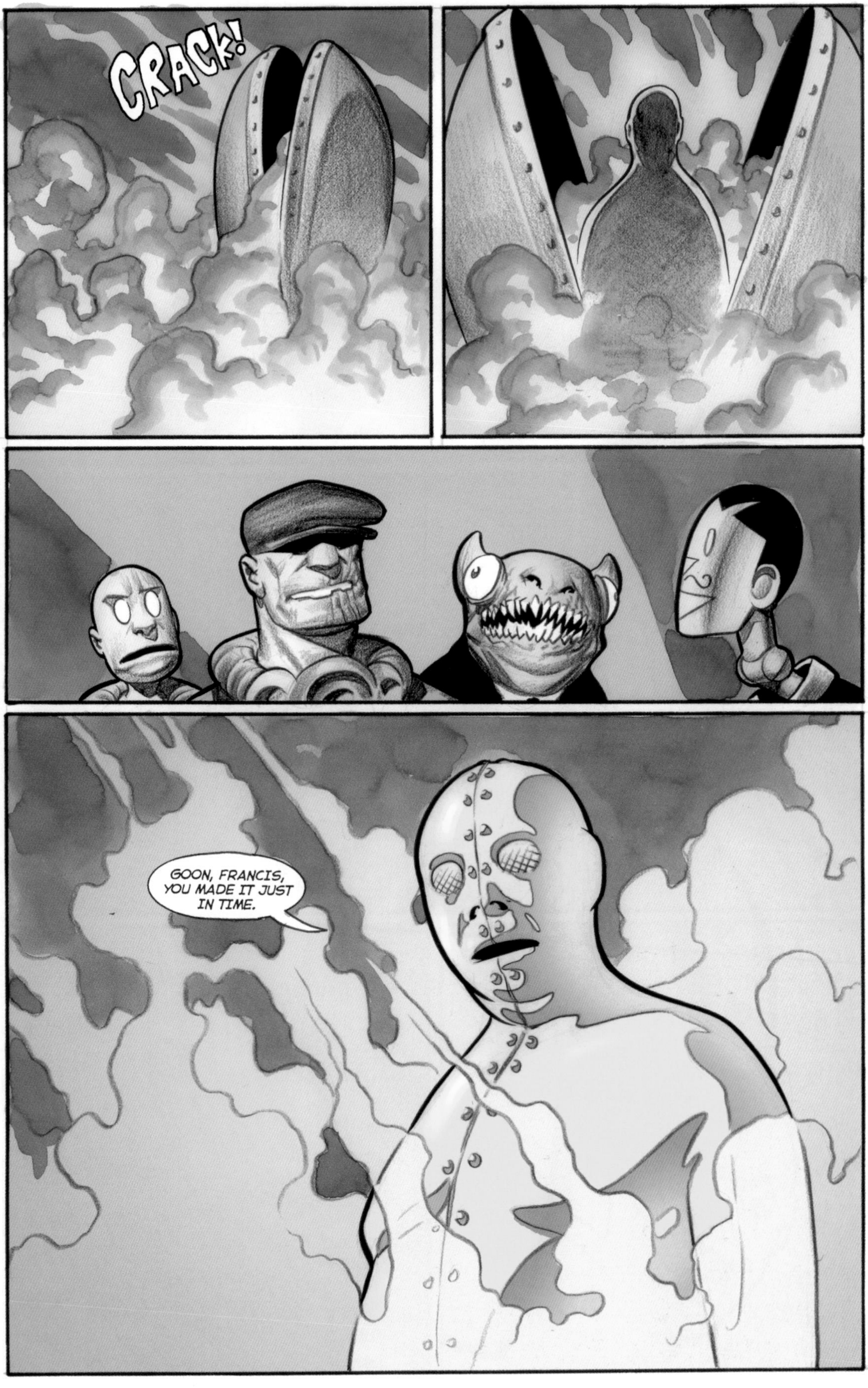
CRACK!
GOON, FRANCIS, YOU MADE IT JUST IN TIME.

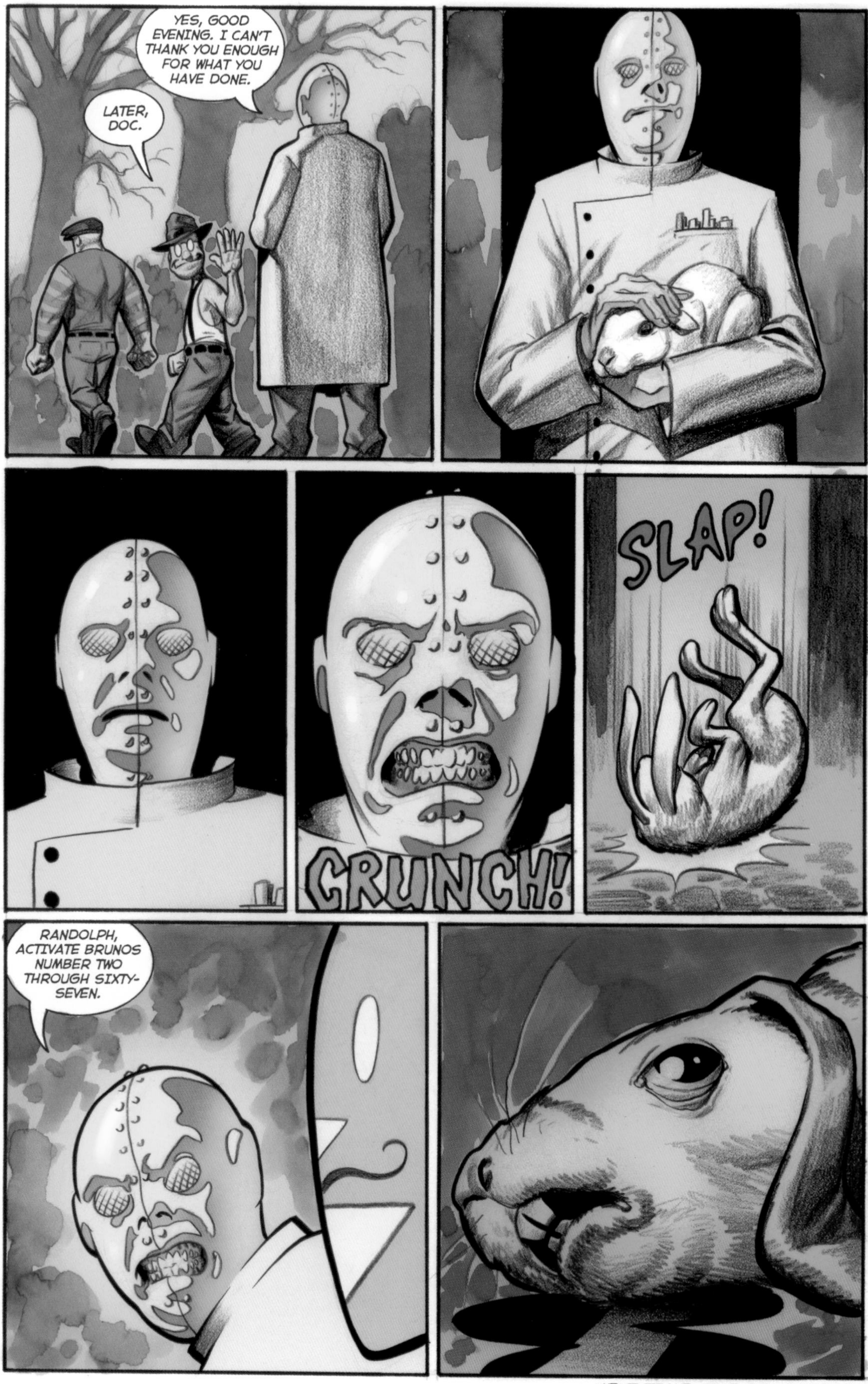
YES, GOOD EVENING. I CAN'T THANK YOU ENOUGH FOR WHAT YOU HAVE DONE.
LATER, DOC.
CRUNCH!
SLAP!
RANDOLPH, ACTIVATE BRUNOS NUMBER TWO THROUGH SIXTY-SEVEN.

NEXT TIME: THE DIABOLICAL DR. ALLOY RISES AGAIN!

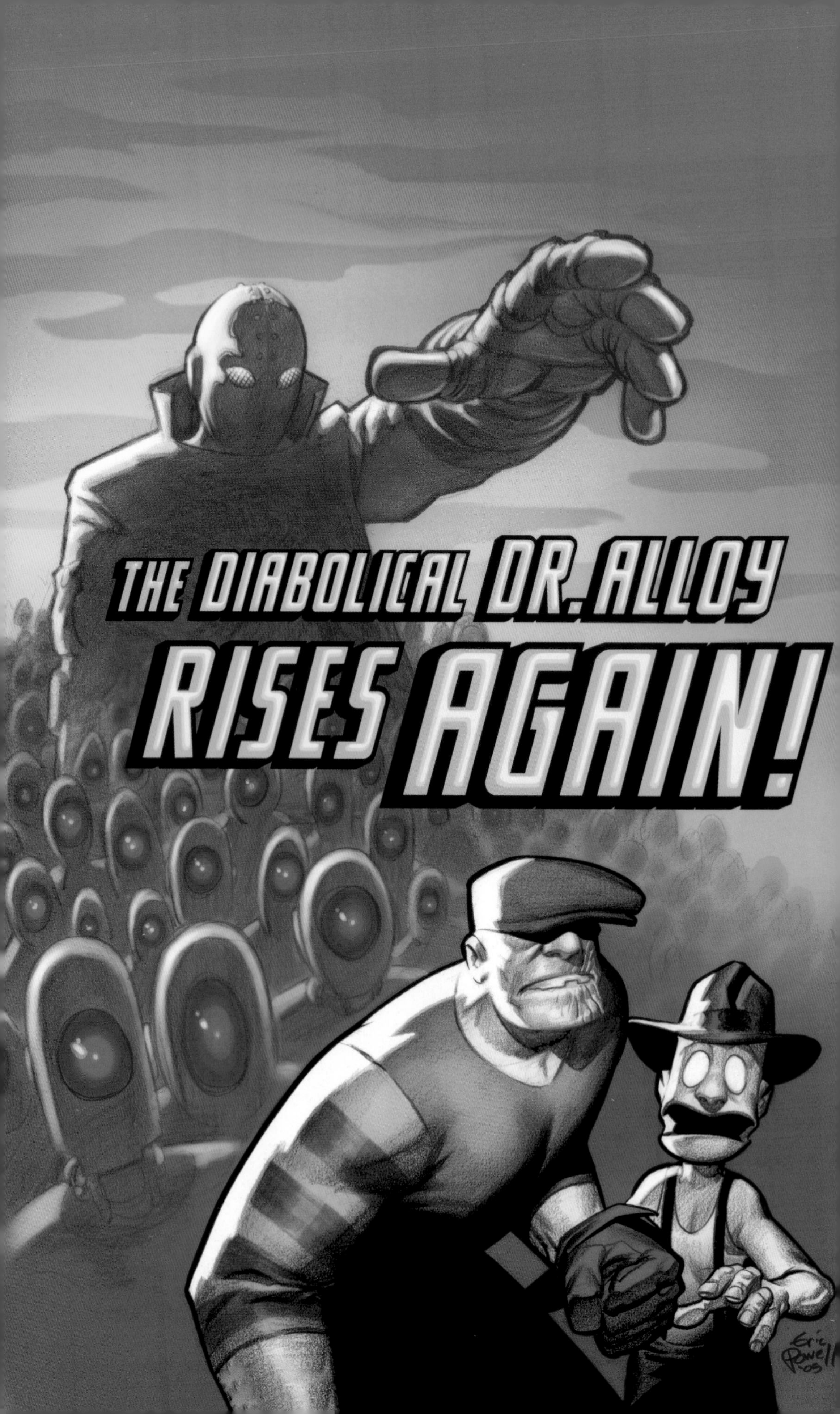
THE DIABOLICAL DR. ALLOY
RISES AGAIN!
Eric Powell '05

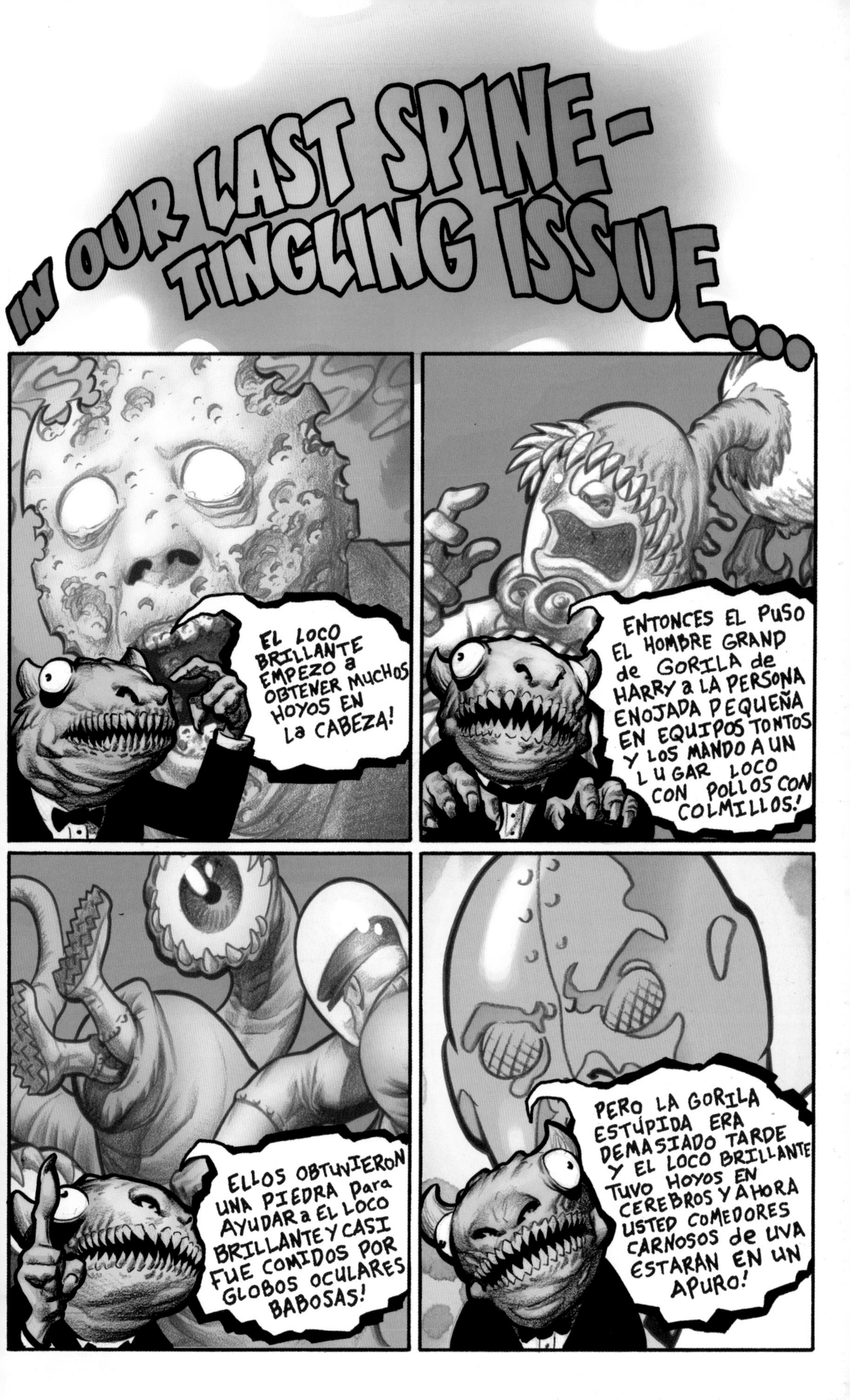
IN OUR LAST SPINE-TINGLING ISSUE....
EL LOCO BRILLANTE EMPEZO a OBTENER MUCHOS HOYOS EN La CABEZA!
ENTONCES EL PUSO EL HOMBRE GRAND de GORILA de HARRY a LA PERSONA ENOJADA PEQUEÑA EN EQUIPOS TONTOS Y LOS MANDO A UN LUGAR LOCO CON POLLOS CON COLMILLOS!
ELLOS OBTUVIERON UNA PIEDRA Para AYUDAR a EL LOCO BRILLANTE Y CASI FUE COMIDOS POR GLOBOS OCULARES BABOSAS!
PERO LA GORILA ESTÚPIDA ERA DEMASIADO TARDE Y EL LOCO BRILLANTE TUVO HOYOS EN CEREBROS Y AHORA USTED COMEDORES CARNOSOS de UVA ESTARAN EN UN APURO!

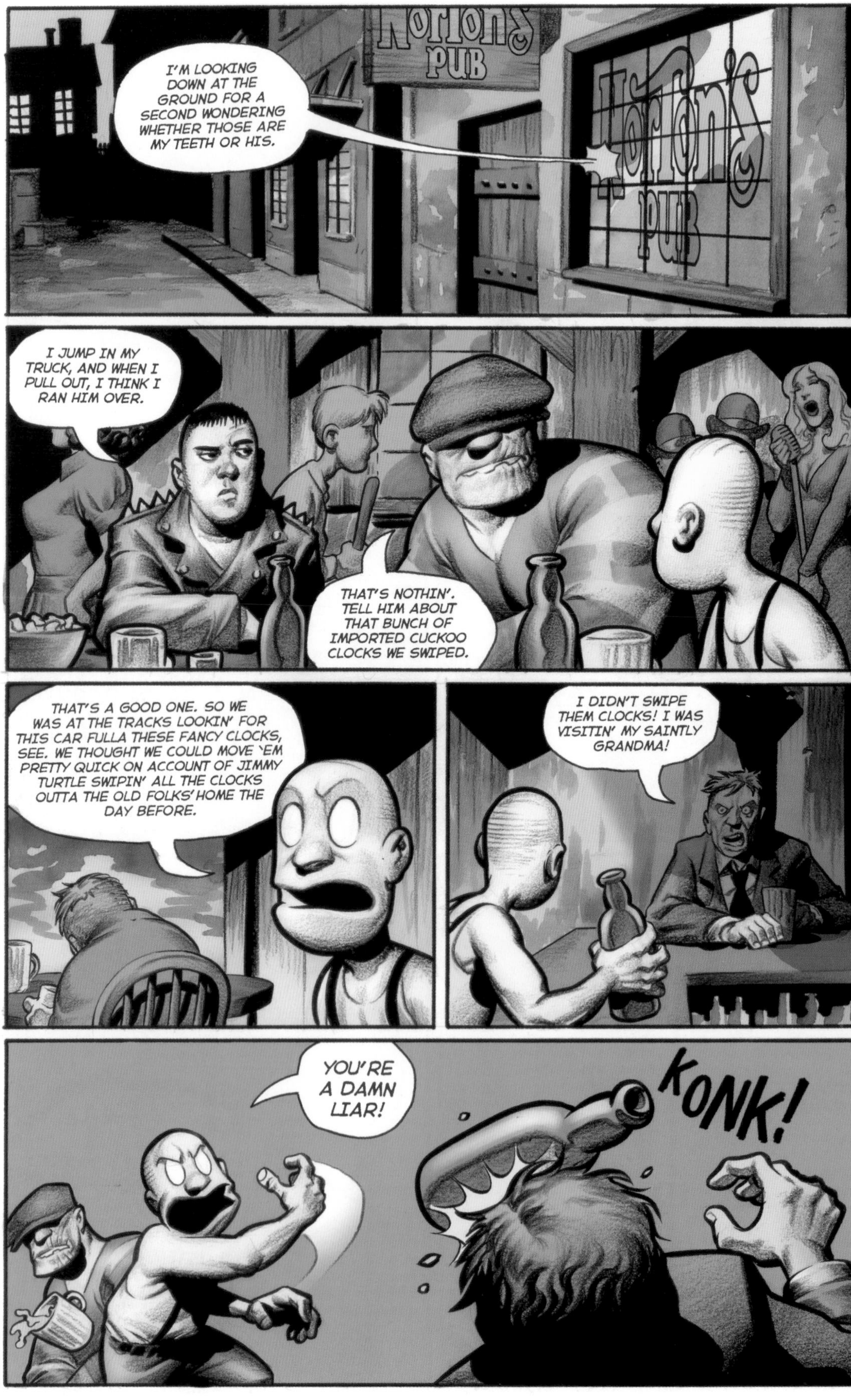
NORTON'S PUB
I'M LOOKING DOWN AT THE GROUND FOR A SECOND WONDERING WHETHER THOSE ARE MY TEETH OR HIS.
NORTON'S PUB
I JUMP IN MY TRUCK, AND WHEN I PULL OUT, I THINK I RAN HIM OVER.
THAT'S NOTHIN'. TELL HIM ABOUT THAT BUNCH OF IMPORTED CUCKOO CLOCKS WE SWIPED.
THAT'S A GOOD ONE. SO WE WAS AT THE TRACKS LOOKIN' FOR THIS CAR FULLA THESE FANCY CLOCKS, SEE. WE THOUGHT WE COULD MOVE 'EM PRETTY QUICK ON ACCOUNT OF JIMMY TURTLE SWIPIN' ALL THE CLOCKS OUTTA THE OLD FOLKS' HOME THE DAY BEFORE.
I DIDN'T SWIPE THEM CLOCKS! I WAS VISITIN' MY SAINTLY GRANDMA!
YOU'RE A DAMN LIAR!
KONK!

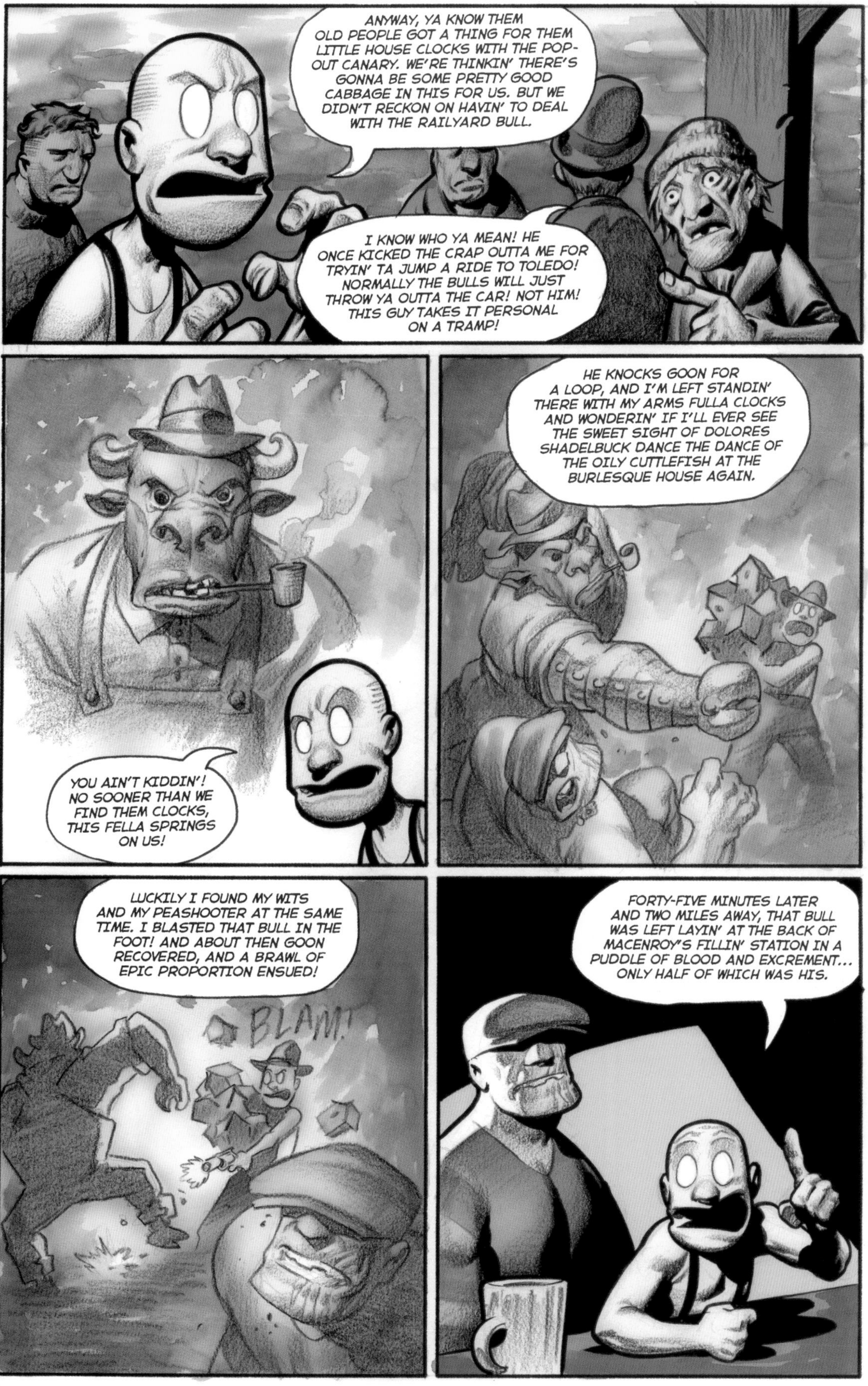
ANYWAY, YA KNOW THEM OLD PEOPLE GOT A THING FOR THEM LITTLE HOUSE CLOCKS WITH THE POP-OUT CANARY. WE'RE THINKIN' THERE'S GONNA BE SOME PRETTY GOOD CABBAGE IN THIS FOR US. BUT WE DIDN'T RECKON ON HAVIN' TO DEAL WITH THE RAILYARD BULL.
I KNOW WHO YA MEAN! HE ONCE KICKED THE CRAP OUTTA ME FOR TRYIN' TA JUMP A RIDE TO TOLEDO! NORMALLY THE BULLS WILL JUST THROW YA OUTTA THE CAR! NOT HIM! THIS GUY TAKES IT PERSONAL ON A TRAMP!
YOU AIN'T KIDDIN'! NO SOONER THAN WE FIND THEM CLOCKS, THIS FELLA SPRINGS ON US!
HE KNOCKS GOON FOR A LOOP, AND I'M LEFT STANDIN' THERE WITH MY ARMS FULLA CLOCKS AND WONDERIN' IF I'LL EVER SEE THE SWEET SIGHT OF DOLORES SHADELBUCK DANCE THE DANCE OF THE OILY CUTTLEFISH AT THE BURLESQUE HOUSE AGAIN.
LUCKILY I FOUND MY WITS AND MY PEASHOOTER AT THE SAME TIME. I BLASTED THAT BULL IN THE FOOT! AND ABOUT THEN GOON RECOVERED, AND A BRAWL OF EPIC PROPORTION ENSUED!
BLAM!
FORTY-FIVE MINUTES LATER AND TWO MILES AWAY, THAT BULL WAS LEFT LAYIN' AT THE BACK OF MACENROY'S FILLIN' STATION IN A PUDDLE OF BLOOD AND EXCREMENT... ONLY HALF OF WHICH WAS HIS.

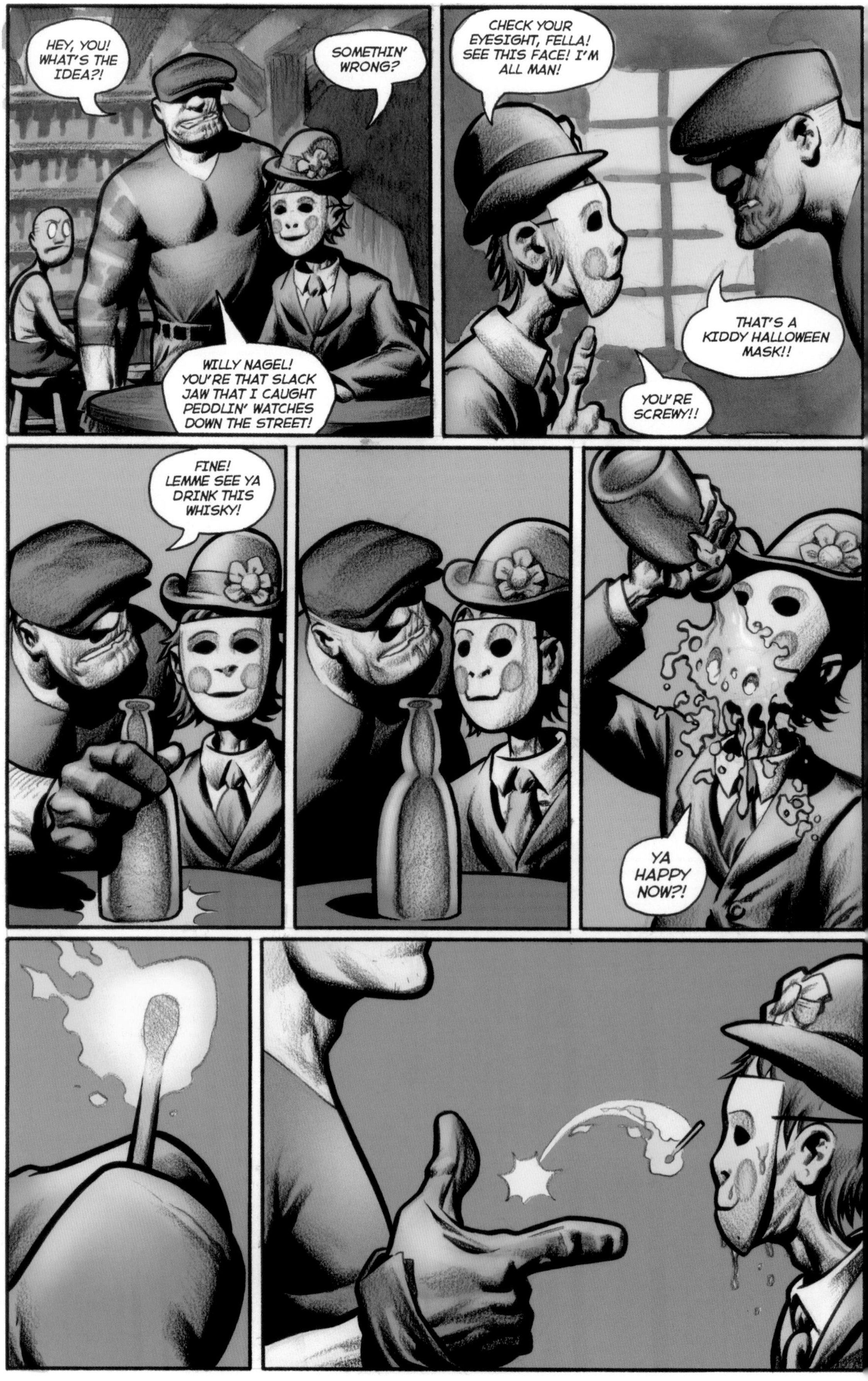
HEY, YOU! WHAT'S THE IDEA?!
SOMETHIN' WRONG?
WILLY NAGEL! YOU'RE THAT SLACK JAW THAT I CAUGHT PEDDLIN' WATCHES DOWN THE STREET!
CHECK YOUR EYESIGHT, FELLA! SEE THIS FACE! I'M ALL MAN!
THAT'S A KIDDY HALLOWEEN MASK!!
YOU'RE SCREWY!!
FINE! LEMME SEE YA DRINK THIS WHISKY!
YA HAPPY NOW?!

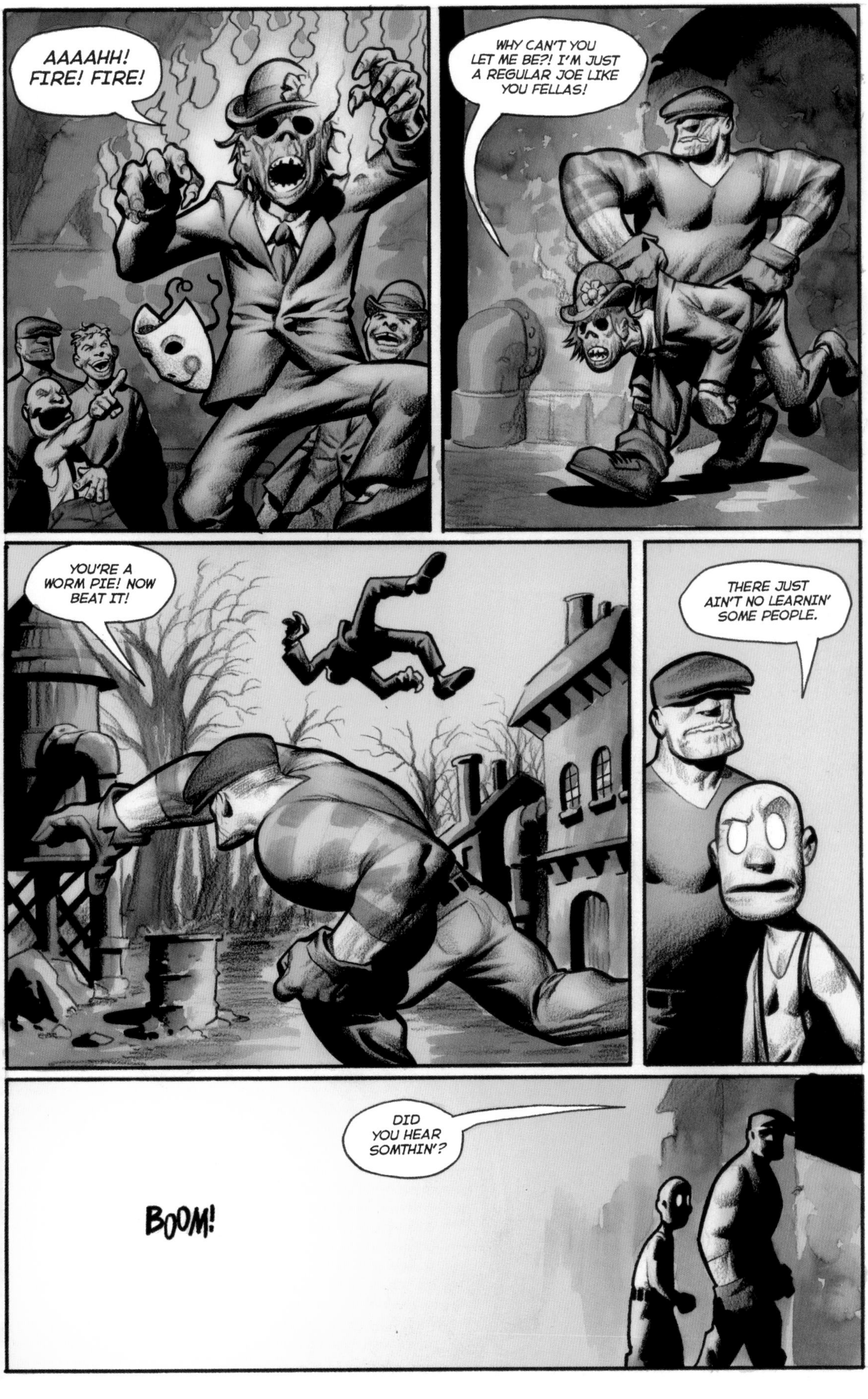
AAAAHH! FIRE! FIRE!
WHY CAN'T YOU LET ME BE?! I'M JUST A REGULAR JOE LIKE YOU FELLAS!
YOU'RE A WORM PIE! NOW BEAT IT!
THERE JUST AIN'T NO LEARNIN' SOME PEOPLE.
DID YOU HEAR SOMTHIN'?
BOOM!

NO, I--

BOOM!
BOOM!

BOOM! BOOM! BOOM!

SAY, WHAT IS THAT?

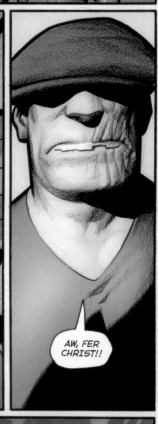

AW, FER CHRIST!!

NO LONGER WILL I STAND IDLY BY AND WATCH YOU PRIMITIVES BASK IN THE SINS OF IGNORANCE! YOU LECHES! YOU HEATHENS OF INTELLECT!!

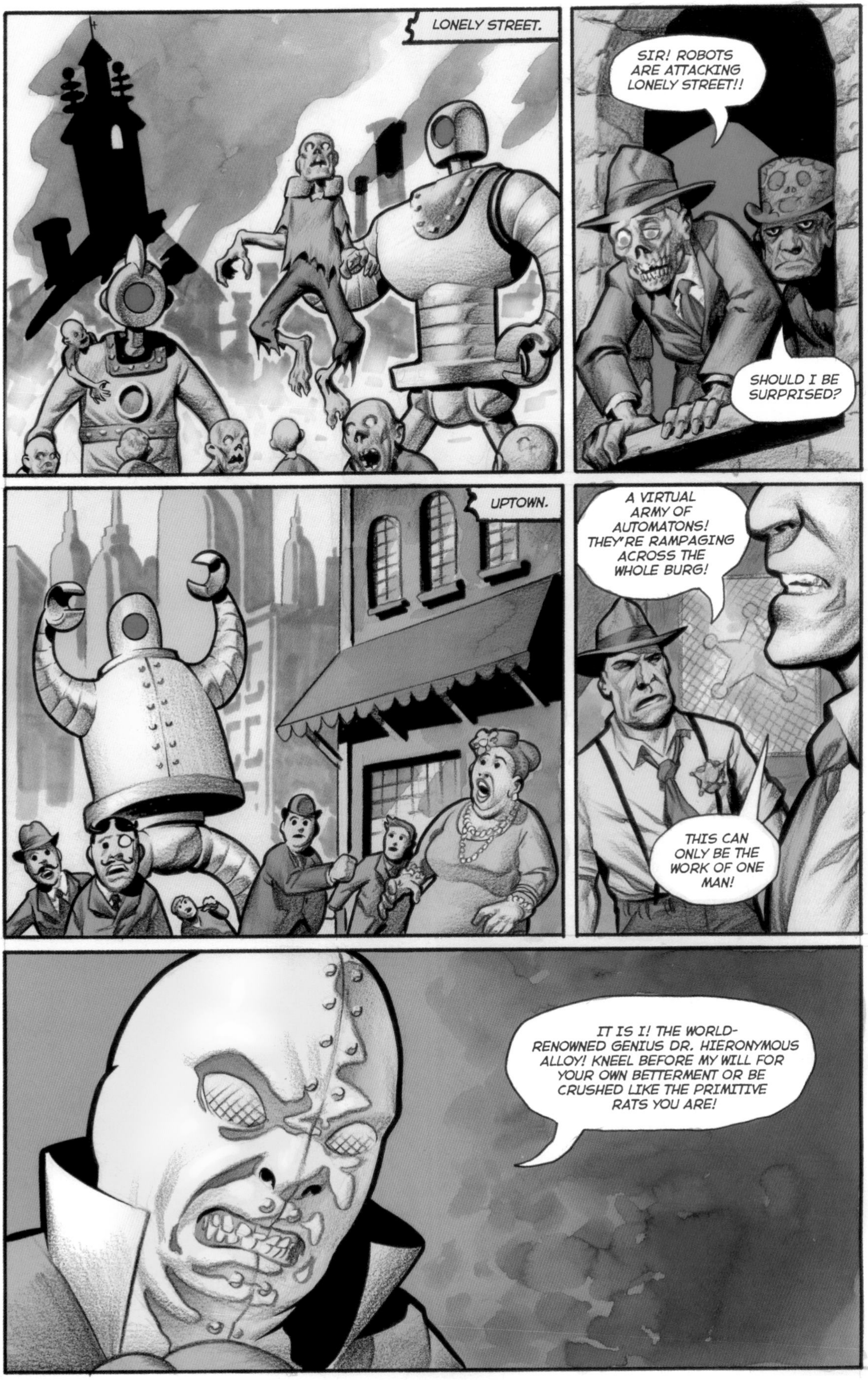
LONELY STREET.
SIR! ROBOTS ARE ATTACKING LONELY STREET!!
SHOULD I BE SURPRISED?
UPTOWN.
A VIRTUAL ARMY OF AUTOMATONS! THEY'RE RAMPAGING ACROSS THE WHOLE BURG!
THIS CAN ONLY BE THE WORK OF ONE MAN!
IT IS I! THE WORLD-RENOWNED GENIUS DR. HIERONYMOUS ALLOY! KNEEL BEFORE MY WILL FOR YOUR OWN BETTERMENT OR BE CRUSHED LIKE THE PRIMITIVE RATS YOU ARE!

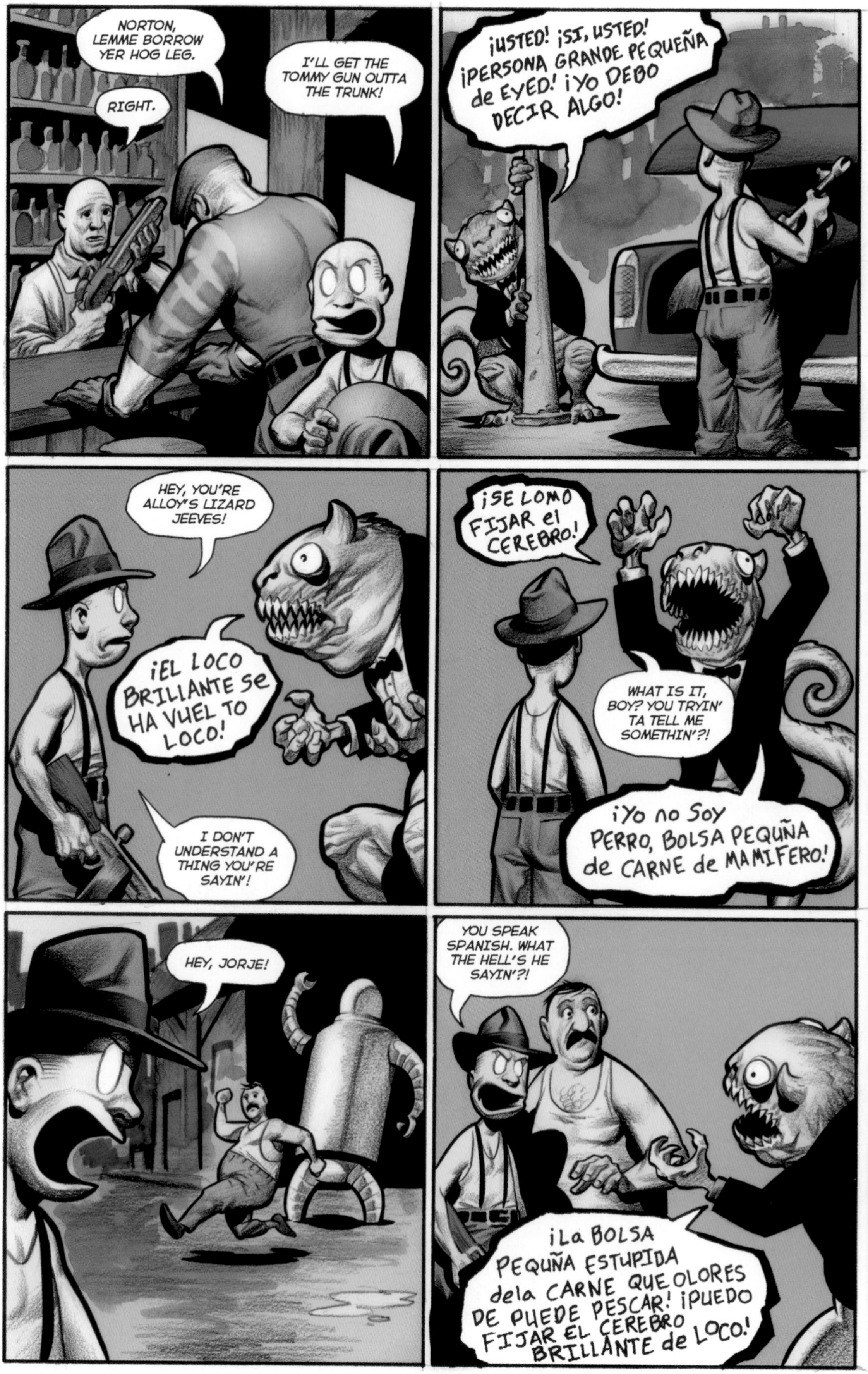
NORTON, LEMME BORROW YER HOG LEG.
RIGHT.
I'LL GET THE TOMMY GUN OUTTA THE TRUNK!
¡USTED! ¡SI, USTED! ¡PERSONA GRANDE PEQUEÑA de EYED! ¡YO DEBO DECIR ALGO!
HEY, YOU'RE ALLOY'S LIZARD JEEVES!
¡EL LOCO BRILLANTE SE HA VUELTO LOCO!
I DON'T UNDERSTAND A THING YOU'RE SAYIN'!
¡SE LOMO FIJAR el CEREBRO!
WHAT IS IT, BOY? YOU TRYIN' TA TELL ME SOMETHIN'?!
¡YO no SOY PERRO, BOLSA PEQUÑA de CARNE de MAMIFERO!
HEY, JORJE!
YOU SPEAK SPANISH. WHAT THE HELL'S HE SAYIN'?!
¡La BOLSA PEQUÑA ESTUPIDA dela CARNE QUE OLORES DE PUEDE PESCAR! ¡PUEDO FIJAR EL CEREBRO BRILLANTE de LOCO!

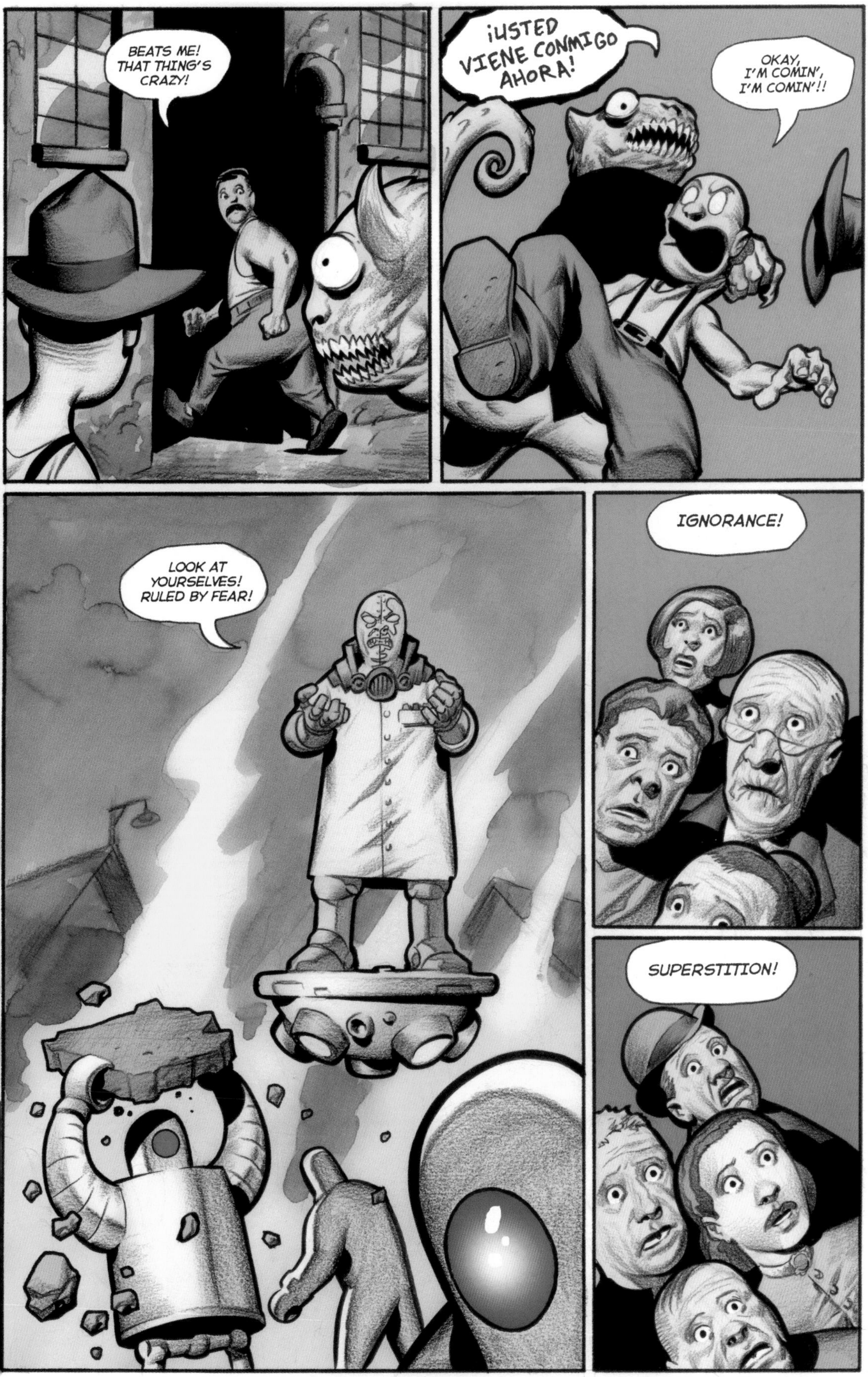
BEATS ME! THAT THING'S CRAZY!
¡USTED VIENE CONMIGO AHORA!
OKAY, I'M COMIN', I'M COMIN'!!
LOOK AT YOURSELVES! RULED BY FEAR!
IGNORANCE!
SUPERSTITION!

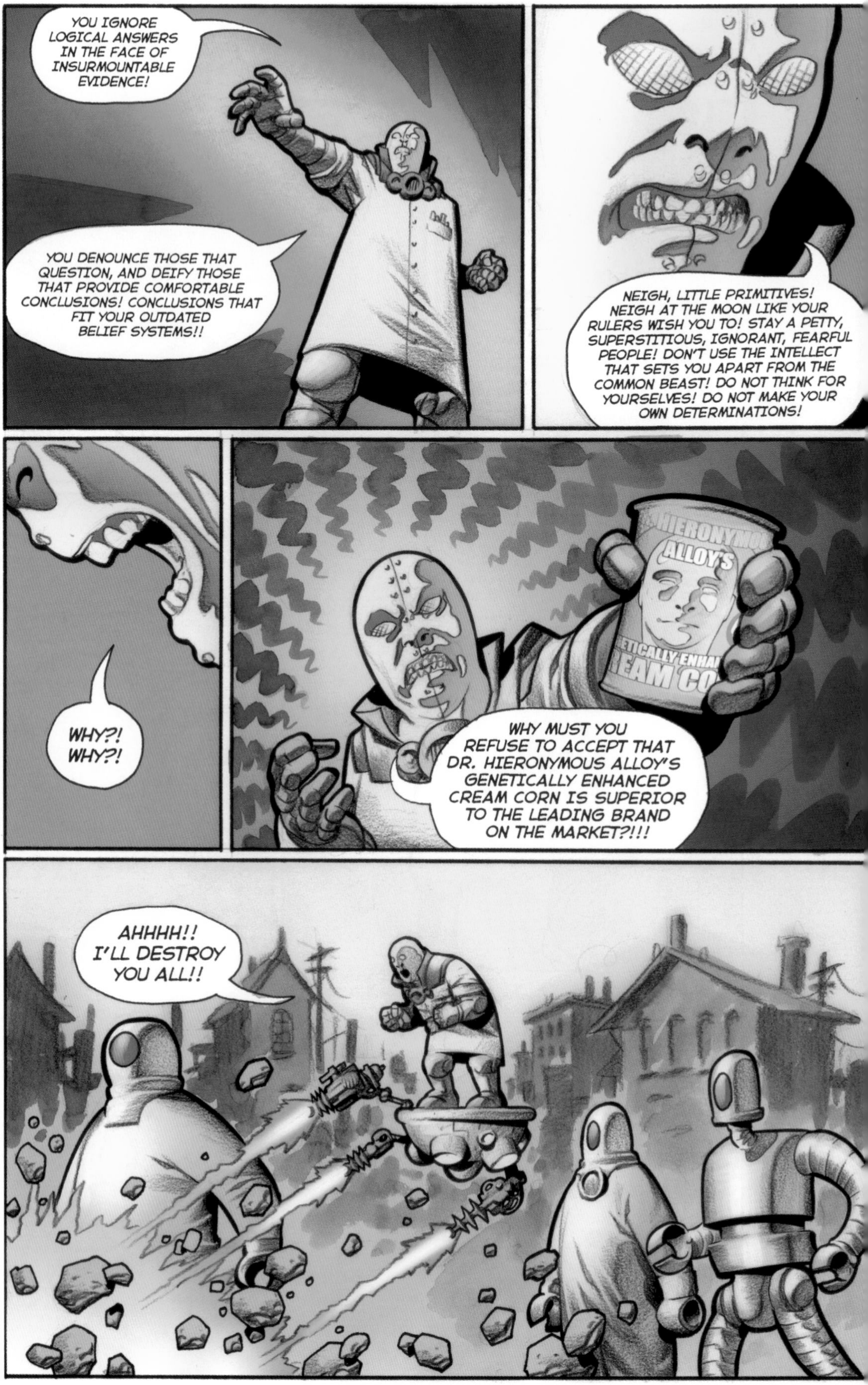
YOU IGNORE LOGICAL ANSWERS IN THE FACE OF INSURMOUNTABLE EVIDENCE!
YOU DENOUNCE THOSE THAT QUESTION, AND DEIFY THOSE THAT PROVIDE COMFORTABLE CONCLUSIONS! CONCLUSIONS THAT FIT YOUR OUTDATED BELIEF SYSTEMS!!
NEIGH, LITTLE PRIMITIVES! NEIGH AT THE MOON LIKE YOUR RULERS WISH YOU TO! STAY A PETTY, SUPERSTITIOUS, IGNORANT, FEARFUL PEOPLE! DON'T USE THE INTELLECT THAT SETS YOU APART FROM THE COMMON BEAST! DO NOT THINK FOR YOURSELVES! DO NOT MAKE YOUR OWN DETERMINATIONS!
WHY?! WHY?!
ALLOY'S
WHY MUST YOU REFUSE TO ACCEPT THAT DR. HIERONYMOUS ALLOY'S GENETICALLY ENHANCED CREAM CORN IS SUPERIOR TO THE LEADING BRAND ON THE MARKET?!!!
AHHHH!! I'LL DESTROY YOU ALL!!

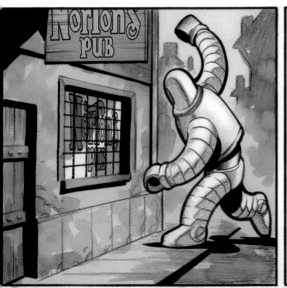

BLAM!

BACK OFF THERE, LUG NUT! AIN'T NO BAG OF BOLTS TAKIN' POTSHOTS AT MY FAVORITE DIVE!

GOON!

RELINQUISH TO ME OR BE OBLITERATED, OAFISH BRUTE!

WHAT THE HELL'S WRONG WITH YOU, ALLOY?! IF I KNEW'D YOU WAS GONNA GO LOONY ON ME, I WOULD HAVE LET YA MELT!!

YOU SUGGEST THAT I AM INSANE?! YOU ARE THE DEFECTIVES! HOW DO YOU PEOPLE STAND LIVING WITH YOUR OWN IGNORANCE?! SURRENDER TO MY WILL OR BE DESTROYED! YOU COULDN'T BEST ONE OF MY ROBOTS! WHAT MAKES YOU THINK YOU COULD OVERCOME AN ARMY OF THEM?!

BLAM!

JUST STUPID, I GUESS.

DESTROY HIM!!

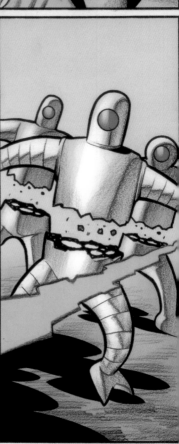

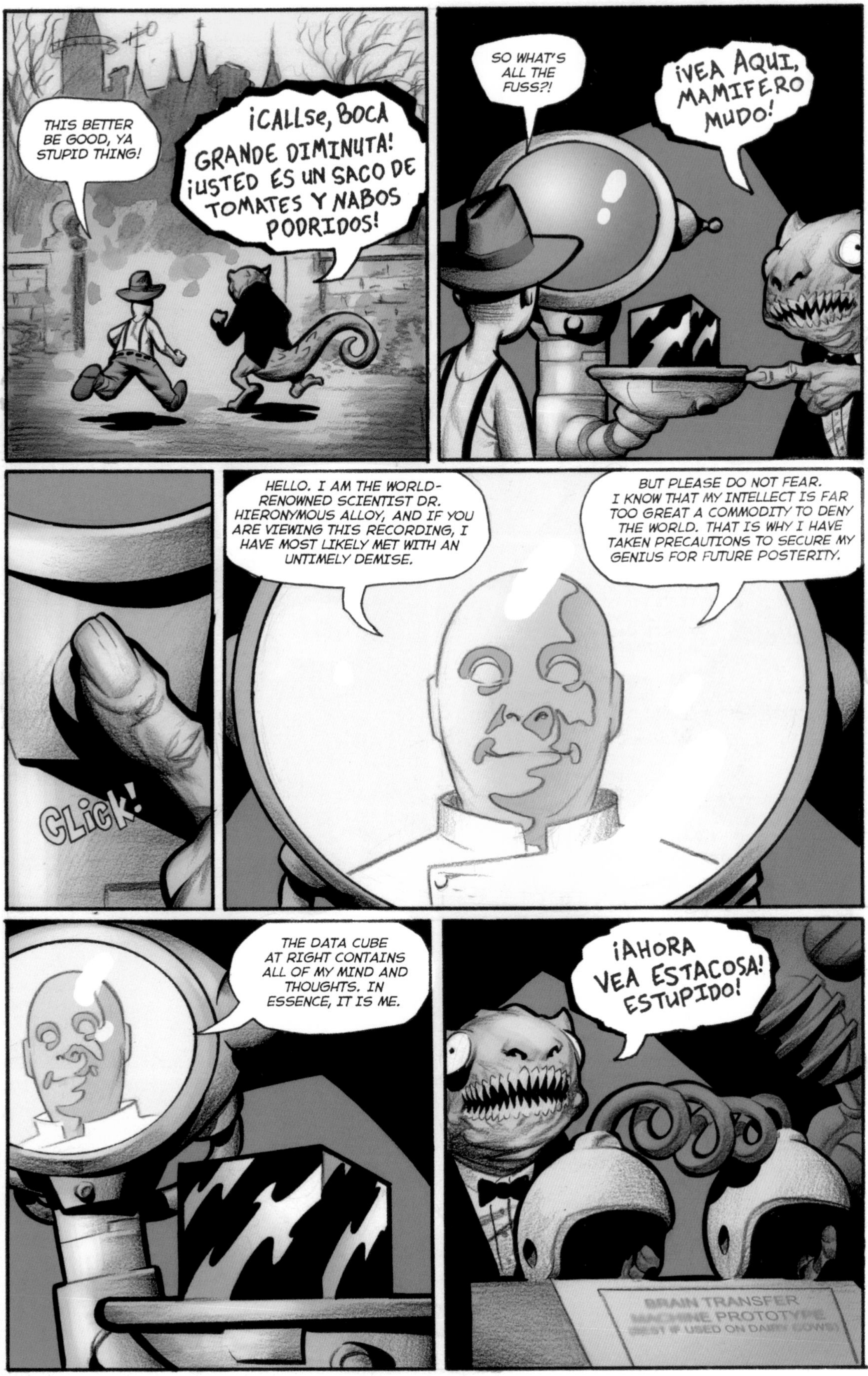
THIS BETTER BE GOOD, YA STUPID THING!
¡CALLSe, BOCA GRANDE DIMINUTA! ¡USTED ES UN SACO DE TOMATES Y NABOS PODRIDOS!
SO WHAT'S ALL THE FUSS?!
¡VEA AQUI, MAMIFERO MUDO!
CLICK!
HELLO. I AM THE WORLD-RENOWNED SCIENTIST DR. HIERONYMOUS ALLOY, AND IF YOU ARE VIEWING THIS RECORDING, I HAVE MOST LIKELY MET WITH AN UNTIMELY DEMISE.
BUT PLEASE DO NOT FEAR. I KNOW THAT MY INTELLECT IS FAR TOO GREAT A COMMODITY TO DENY THE WORLD. THAT IS WHY I HAVE TAKEN PRECAUTIONS TO SECURE MY GENIUS FOR FUTURE POSTERITY.
THE DATA CUBE AT RIGHT CONTAINS ALL OF MY MIND AND THOUGHTS. IN ESSENCE, IT IS ME.
¡AHORA VEA ESTACOSA! ESTUPIDO!
BRAIN TRANSFER
MACHINE PROTOTYPE

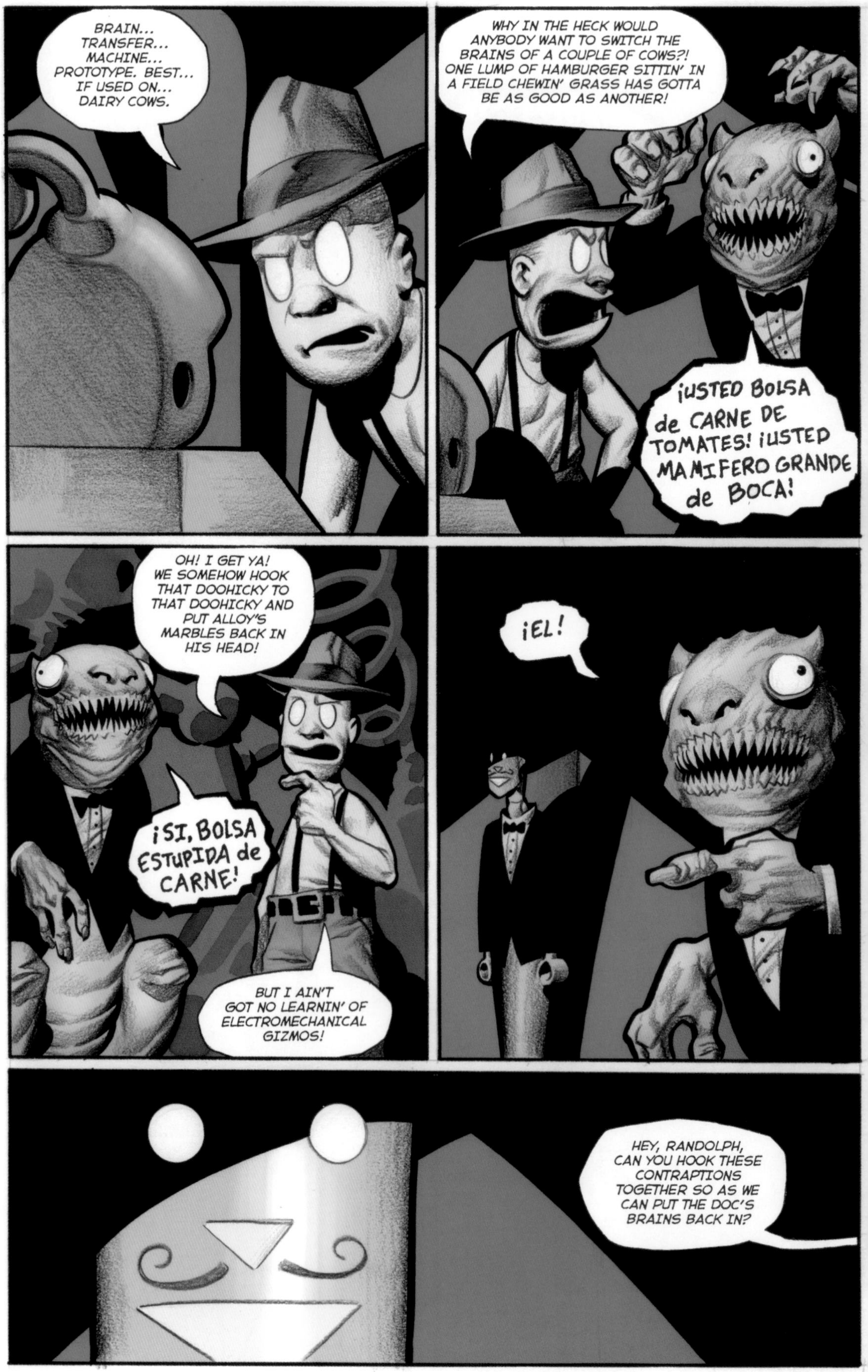
BRAIN... TRANSFER... MACHINE... PROTOTYPE. BEST... IF USED ON... DAIRY COWS.
WHY IN THE HECK WOULD ANYBODY WANT TO SWITCH THE BRAINS OF A COUPLE OF COWS?! ONE LUMP OF HAMBURGER SITTIN' IN A FIELD CHEWIN' GRASS HAS GOTTA BE AS GOOD AS ANOTHER!
¡USTED BOLSA de CARNE DE TOMATES! ¡USTED MAMIFERO GRANDE de BOCA!
OH! I GET YA! WE SOMEHOW HOOK THAT DOOHICKY TO THAT DOOHICKY AND PUT ALLOY'S MARBLES BACK IN HIS HEAD!
¡SI, BOLSA ESTUPIDA de CARNE!
BUT I AIN'T GOT NO LEARNIN' OF ELECTROMECHANICAL GIZMOS!
¡EL!
HEY, RANDOLPH, CAN YOU HOOK THESE CONTRAPTIONS TOGETHER SO AS WE CAN PUT THE DOC'S BRAINS BACK IN?

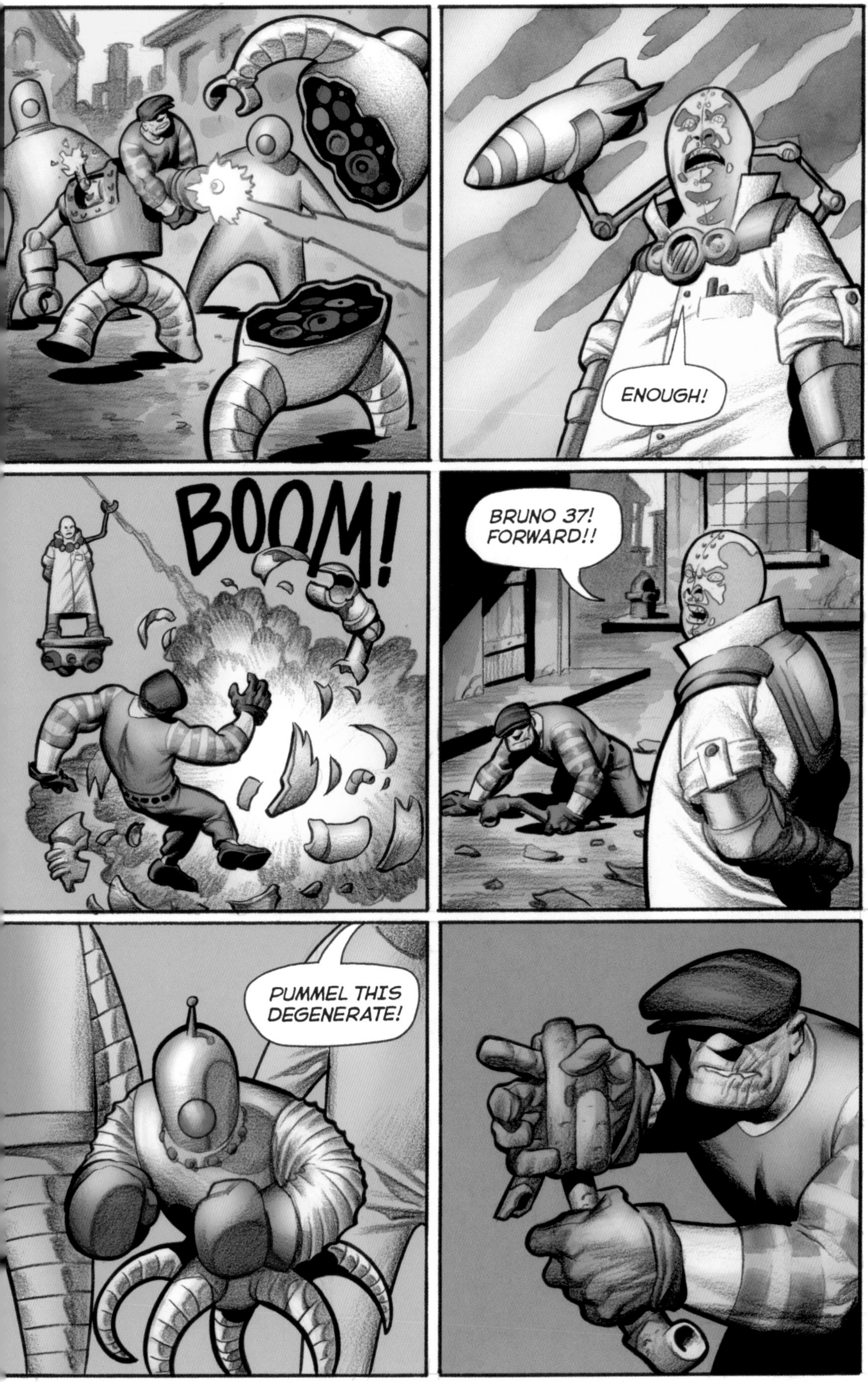
ENOUGH!
BOOM!
BRUNO 37! FORWARD!!
PUMMEL THIS DEGENERATE!

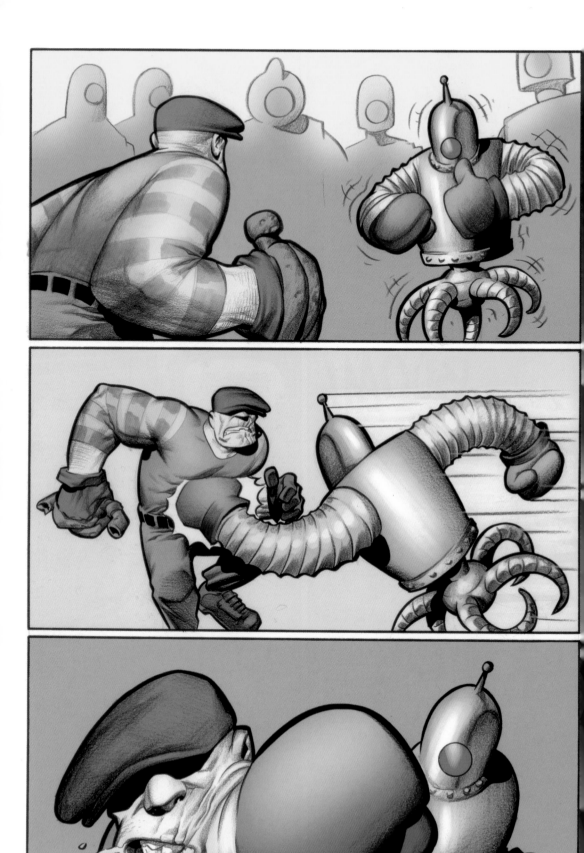

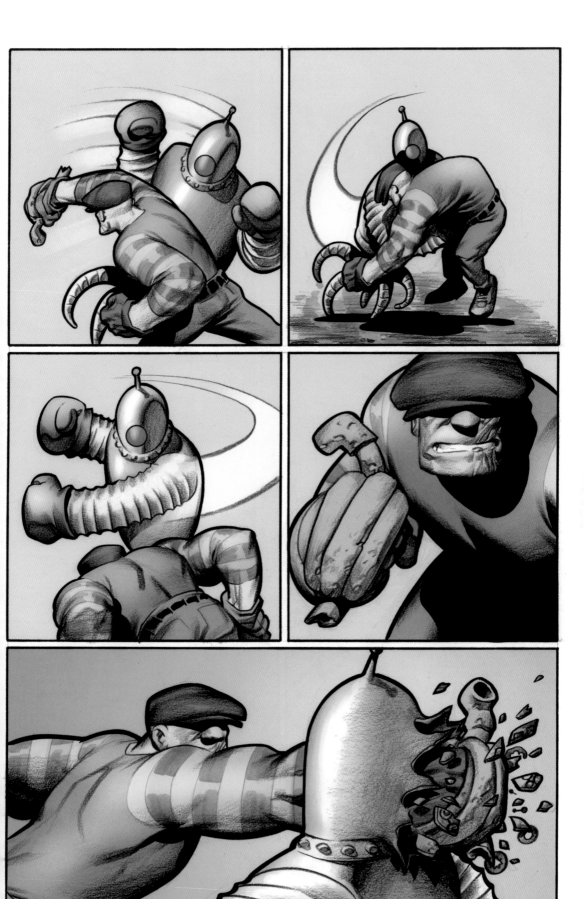

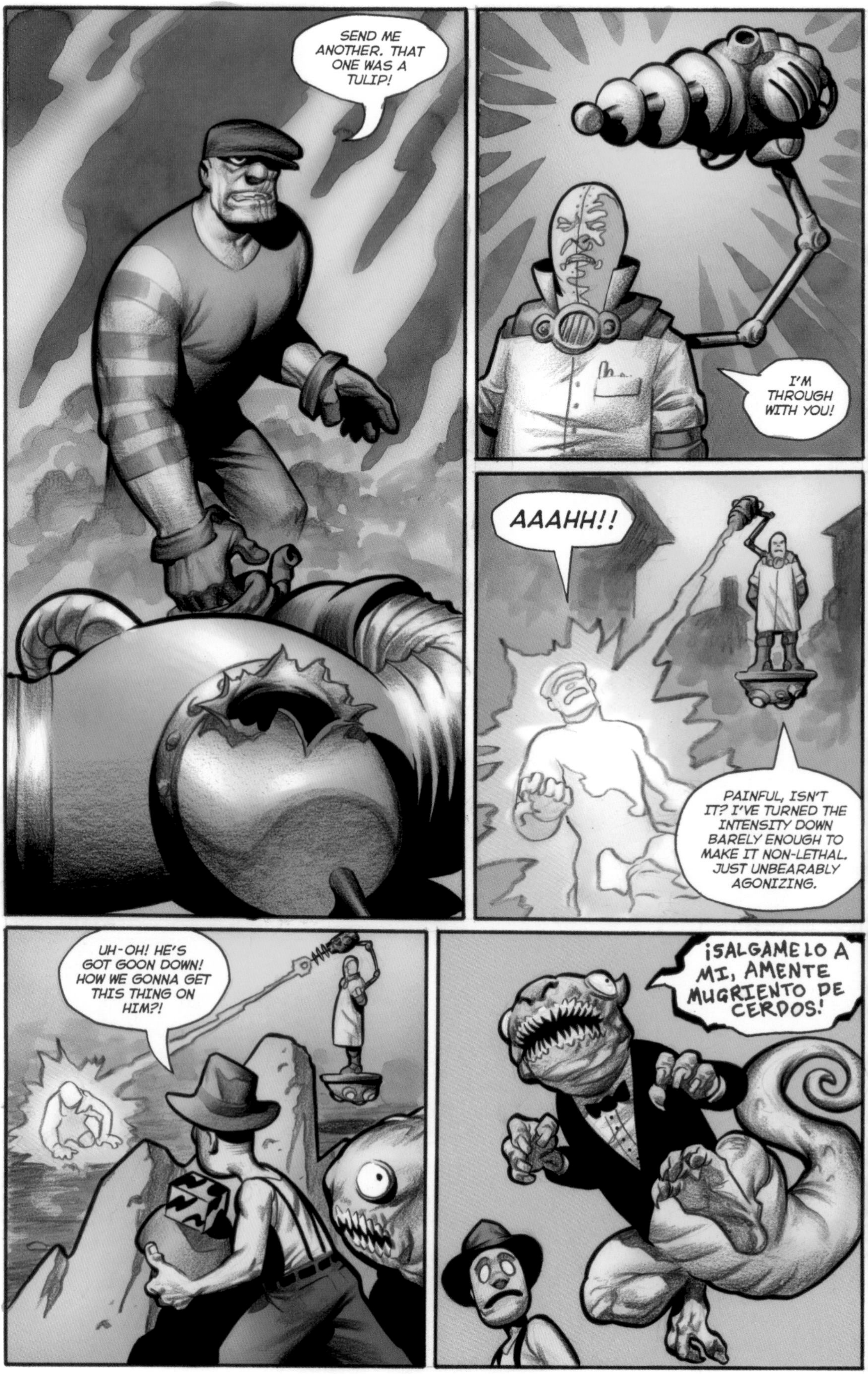
SEND ME ANOTHER. THAT ONE WAS A TULIP!
I'M THROUGH WITH YOU!
AAAHH!!
PAINFUL, ISN'T IT? I'VE TURNED THE INTENSITY DOWN BARELY ENOUGH TO MAKE IT NON-LETHAL. JUST UNBEARABLY AGONIZING.
UH-OH! HE'S GOT GOON DOWN! HOW WE GONNA GET THIS THING ON HIM?!
¡SALGAMELO A MI, AMENTE MUGRIENTO DE CERDOS!

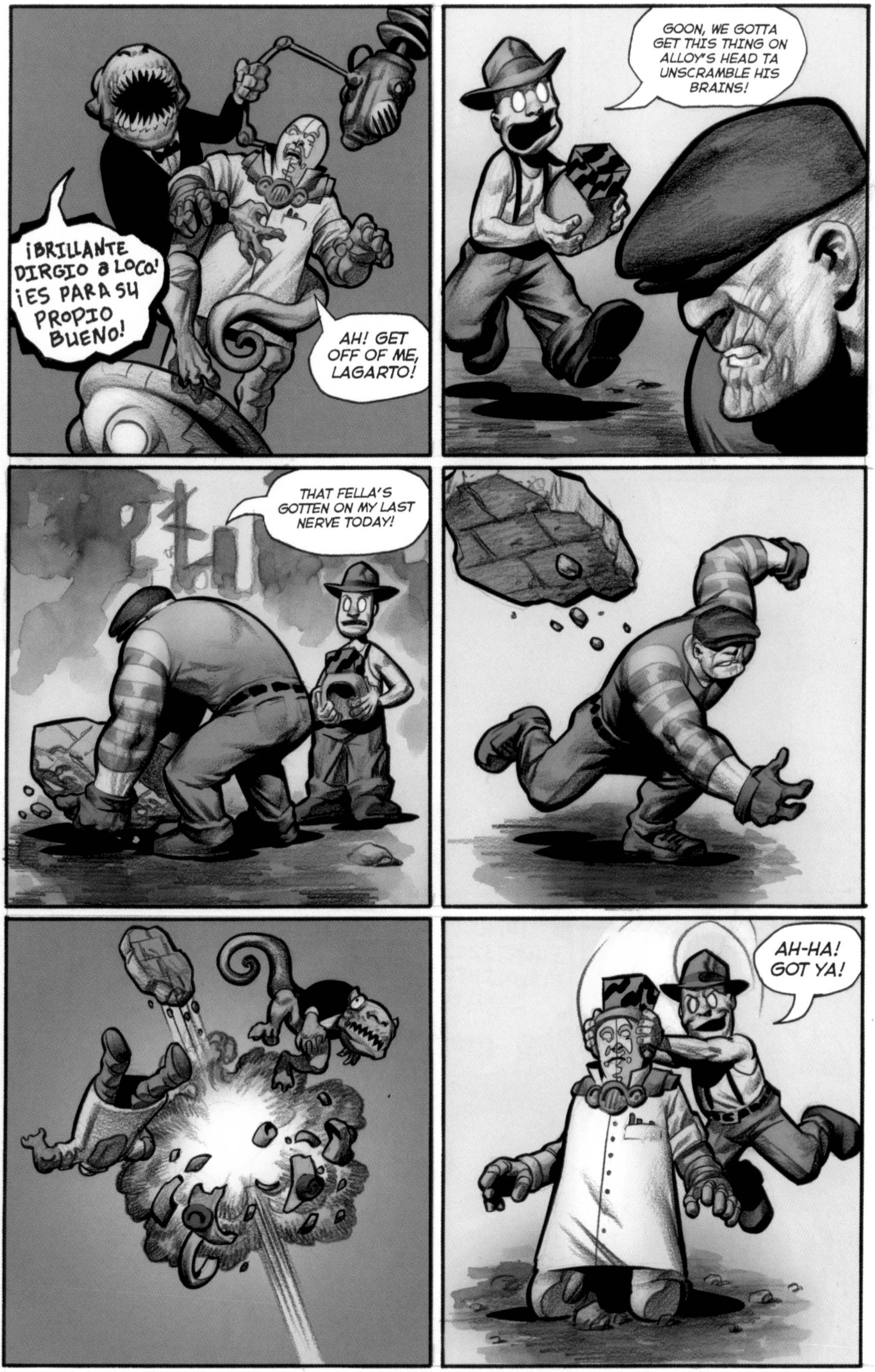
¡BRILLANTE DIRGIO a LOCO! ¡ES PARA SU PROPIO BUENO!
AH! GET OFF OF ME, LAGARTO!
GOON, WE GOTTA GET THIS THING ON ALLOY'S HEAD TA UNSCRAMBLE HIS BRAINS!
THAT FELLA'S GOTTEN ON MY LAST NERVE TODAY!
AH-HA! GOT YA!

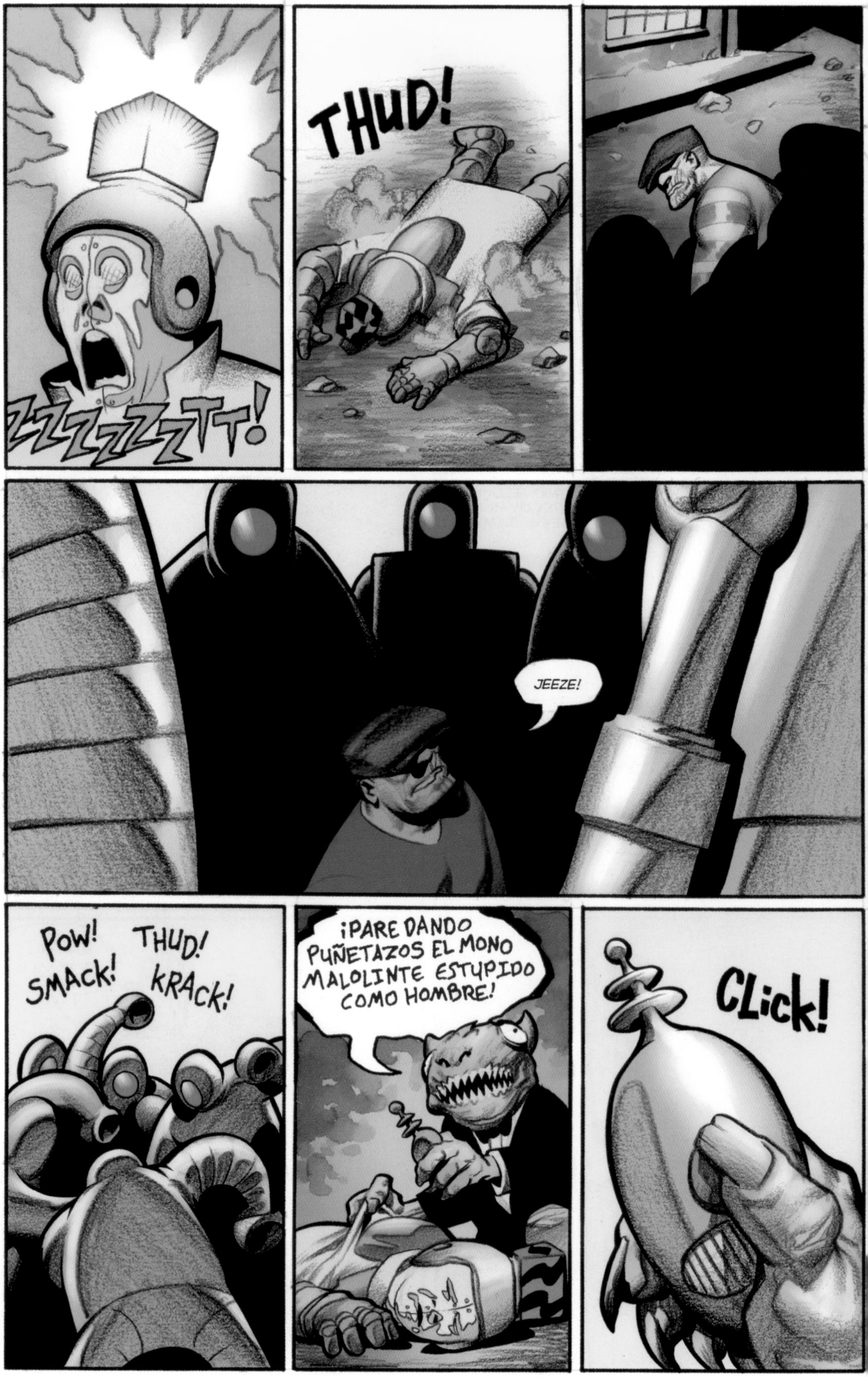
ZZZZZZZZTT!
THUD!
JEEZE!
POW!
THUD!
SMACK!
KRACK!
¡PARE DANDO PUÑETAZOS EL MONO MALOLINTE ESTUPIDO COMO HOMBRE!
CLick!

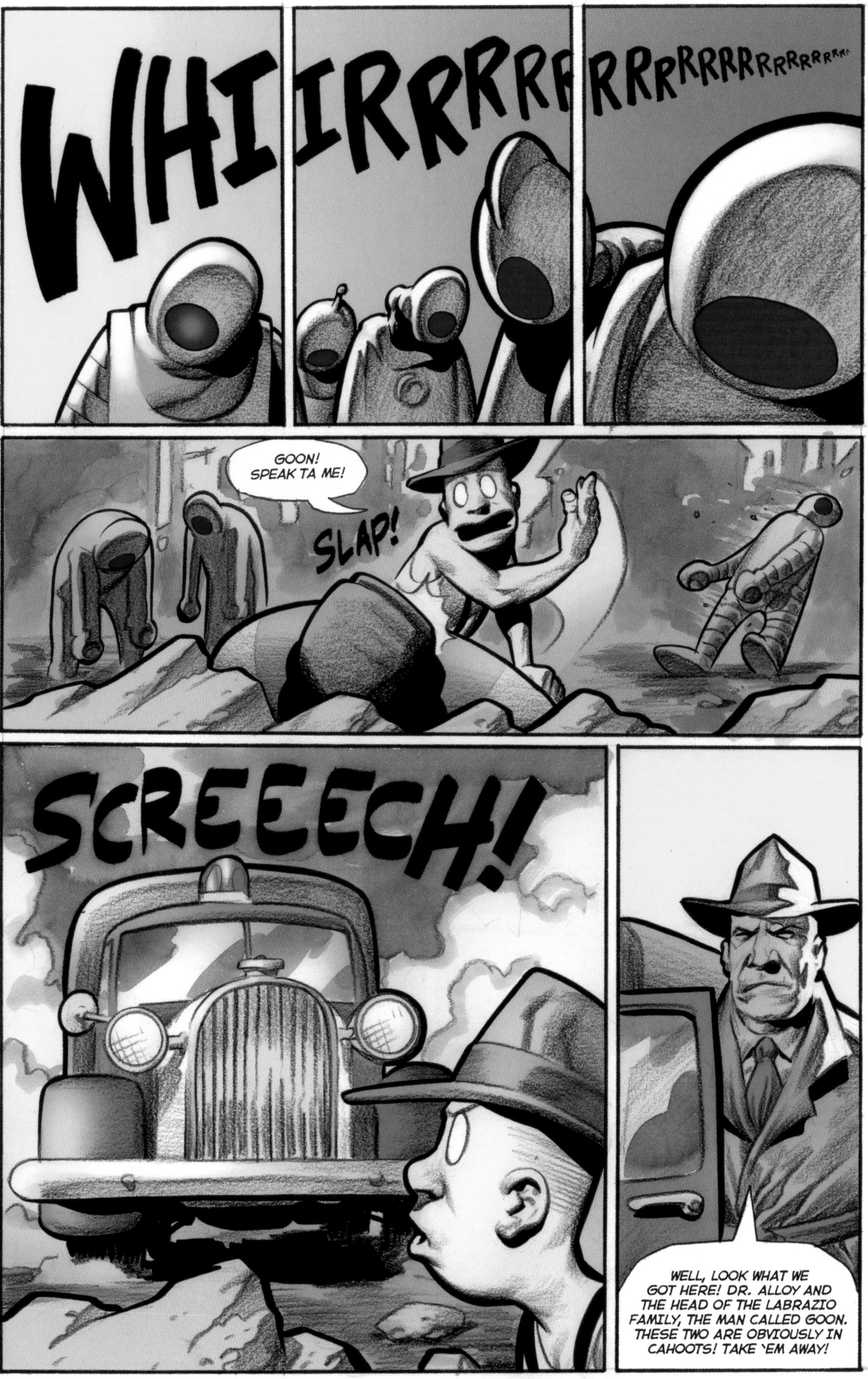

WHIRRRRRRRRRRRRRRRR
GOON! SPEAK TA ME!
SLAP!
SCREEECH!
WELL, LOOK WHAT WE GOT HERE! DR. ALLOY AND THE HEAD OF THE LABRAZIO FAMILY, THE MAN CALLED GOON. THESE TWO ARE OBVIOUSLY IN CAHOOTS! TAKE 'EM AWAY!

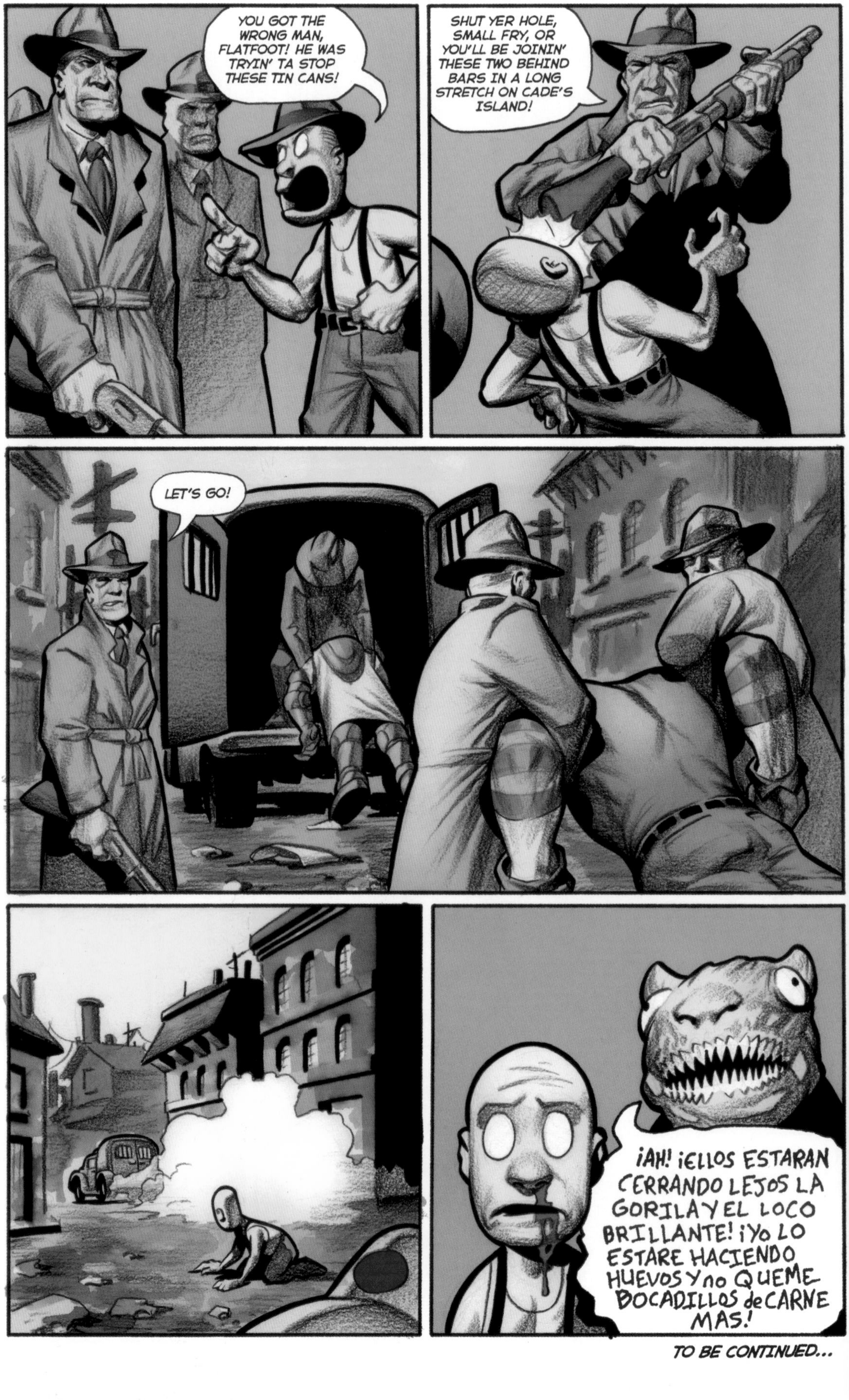
YOU GOT THE WRONG MAN, FLATFOOT! HE WAS TRYIN' TA STOP THESE TIN CANS!
SHUT YER HOLE, SMALL FRY, OR YOU'LL BE JOININ' THESE TWO BEHIND BARS IN A LONG STRETCH ON CADE'S ISLAND!
LET'S GO!
¡AH! ¡ELLOS ESTARAN CERRANDO LEJOS LA GORILA Y EL LOCO BRILLANTE! ¡YO LO ESTARE HACIENDO HUEVOS Y no QUEME BOCADILLOS de CARNE MAS!

TO BE CONTINUED...

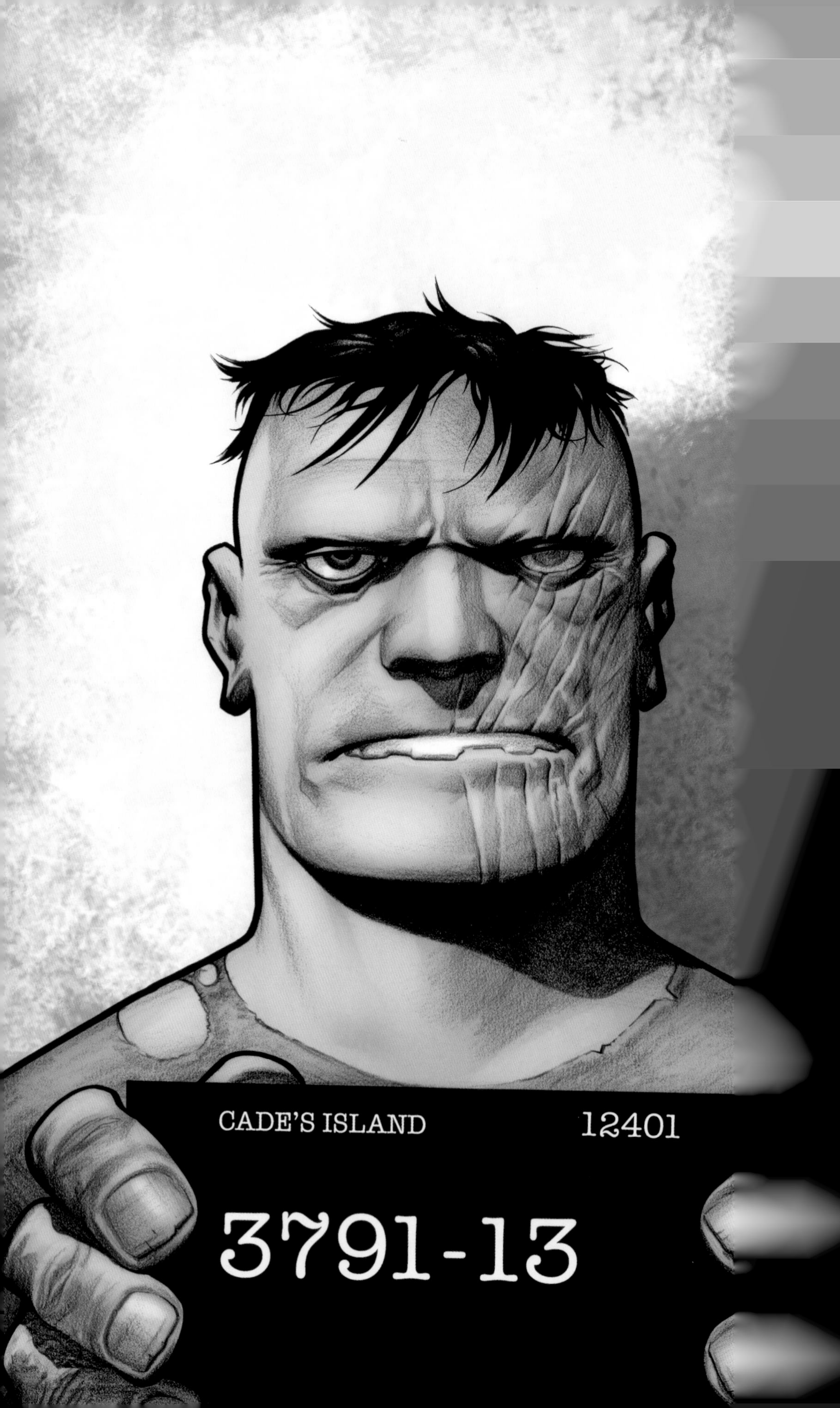
CADE'S ISLAND
12401
3791-13

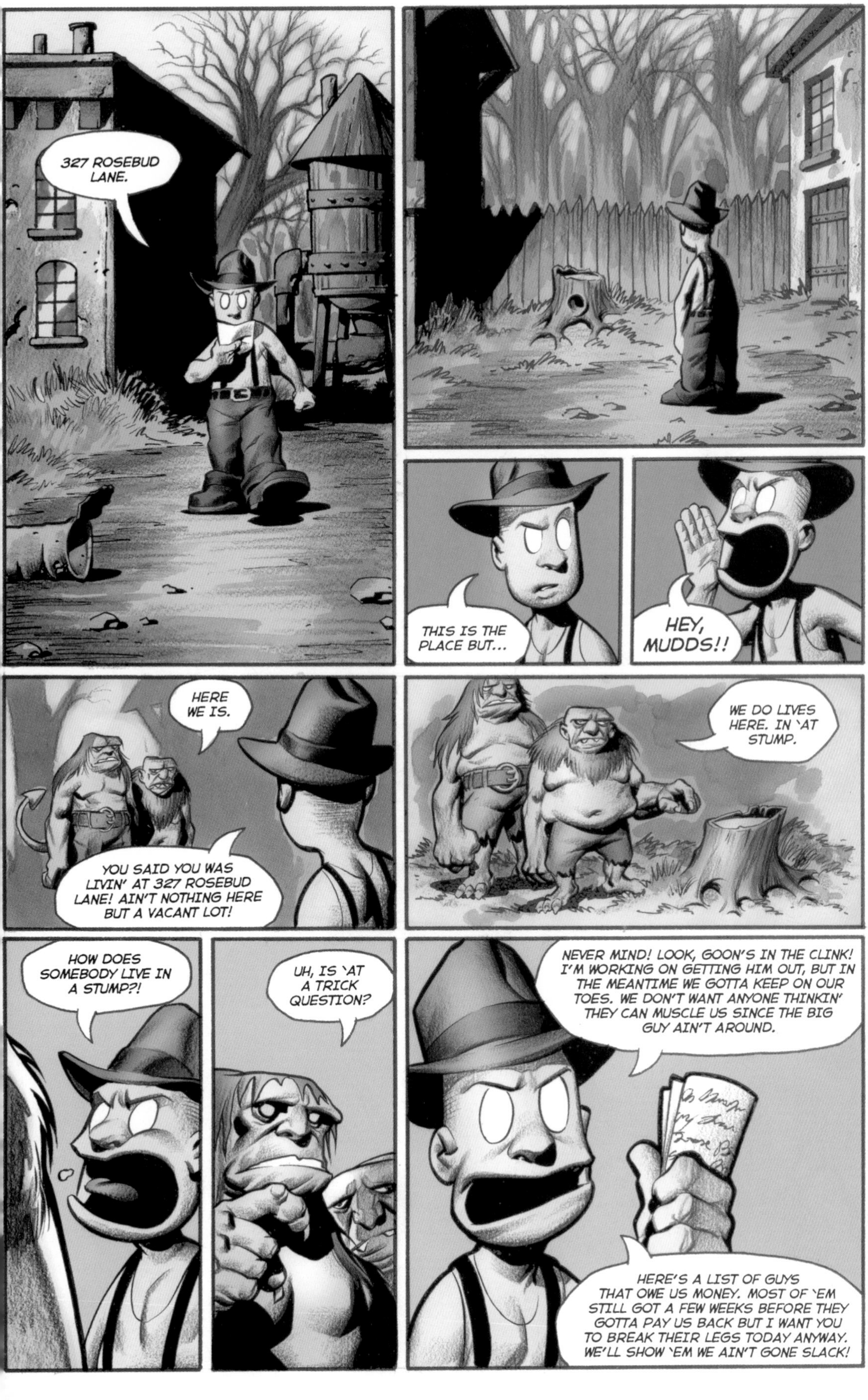
327 ROSEBUD LANE.
THIS IS THE PLACE BUT...
HEY, MUDDS!!
HERE WE IS.
YOU SAID YOU WAS LIVIN' AT 327 ROSEBUD LANE! AIN'T NOTHING HERE BUT A VACANT LOT!
WE DO LIVES HERE. IN 'AT STUMP.
HOW DOES SOMEBODY LIVE IN A STUMP?!
UH, IS 'AT A TRICK QUESTION?
NEVER MIND! LOOK, GOON'S IN THE CLINK! I'M WORKING ON GETTING HIM OUT, BUT IN THE MEANTIME WE GOTTA KEEP ON OUR TOES. WE DON'T WANT ANYONE THINKIN' THEY CAN MUSCLE US SINCE THE BIG GUY AIN'T AROUND.
HERE'S A LIST OF GUYS THAT OWE US MONEY. MOST OF 'EM STILL GOT A FEW WEEKS BEFORE THEY GOTTA PAY US BACK BUT I WANT YOU TO BREAK THEIR LEGS TODAY ANYWAY. WE'LL SHOW 'EM WE AIN'T GONE SLACK!

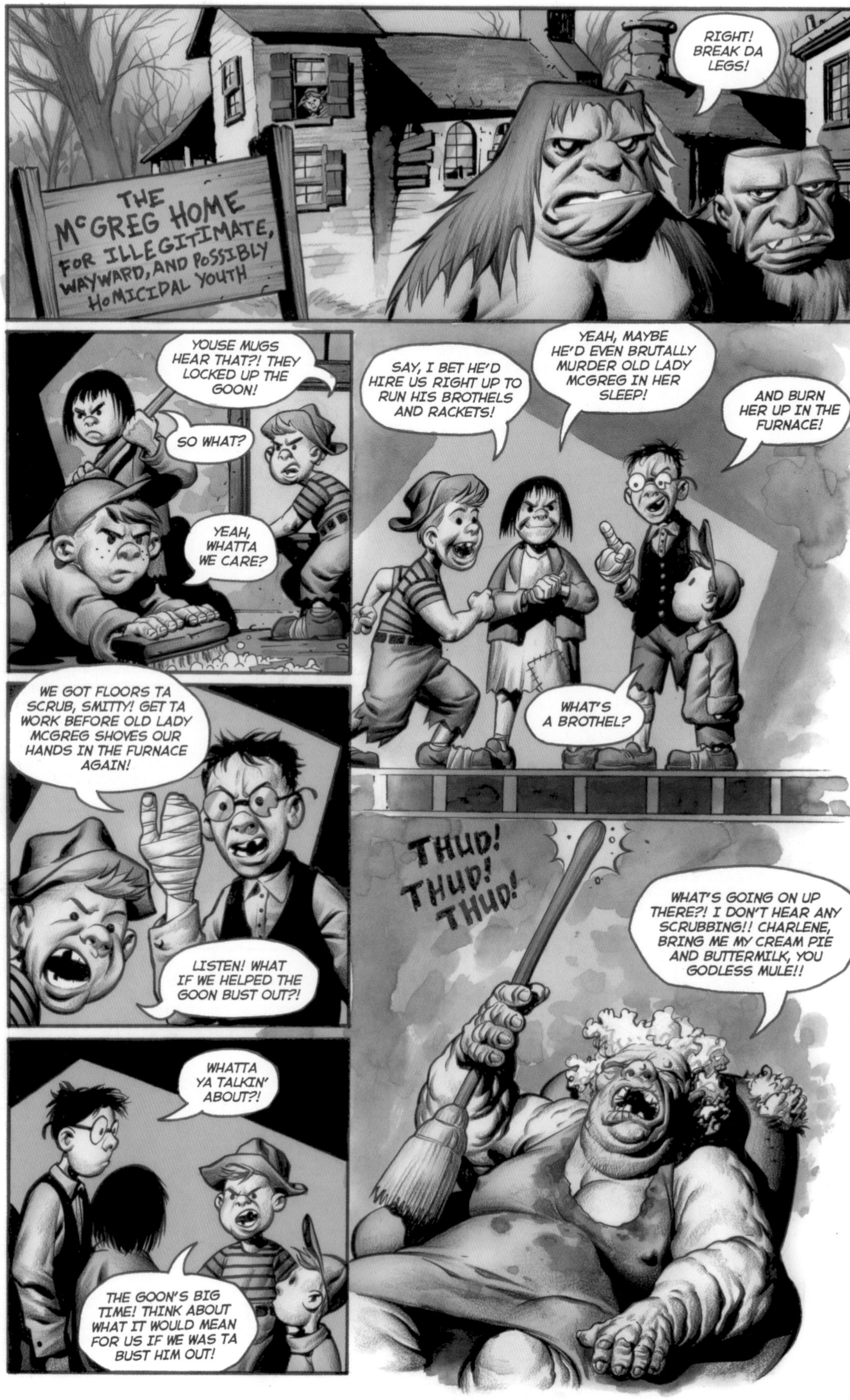
THE McGREG HOME FOR ILLEGITIMATE, WAYWARD, AND POSSIBLY HOMICIDAL YOUTH
RIGHT! BREAK DA LEGS!
YOUSE MUGS HEAR THAT?! THEY LOCKED UP THE GOON!
SO WHAT?
YEAH, WHATTA WE CARE?
WE GOT FLOORS TA SCRUB, SMITTY! GET TA WORK BEFORE OLD LADY MCGREG SHOVES OUR HANDS IN THE FURNACE AGAIN!
LISTEN! WHAT IF WE HELPED THE GOON BUST OUT?!
WHATTA YA TALKIN' ABOUT?!
THE GOON'S BIG TIME! THINK ABOUT WHAT IT WOULD MEAN FOR US IF WE WAS TA BUST HIM OUT!
SAY, I BET HE'D HIRE US RIGHT UP TO RUN HIS BROTHELS AND RACKETS!
YEAH, MAYBE HE'D EVEN BRUTALLY MURDER OLD LADY MCGREG IN HER SLEEP!
AND BURN HER UP IN THE FURNACE!
WHAT'S A BROTHEL?
THUD! THUD! THUD!
WHAT'S GOING ON UP THERE?! I DON'T HEAR ANY SCRUBBING!! CHARLENE, BRING ME MY CREAM PIE AND BUTTERMILK, YOU GODLESS MULE!!

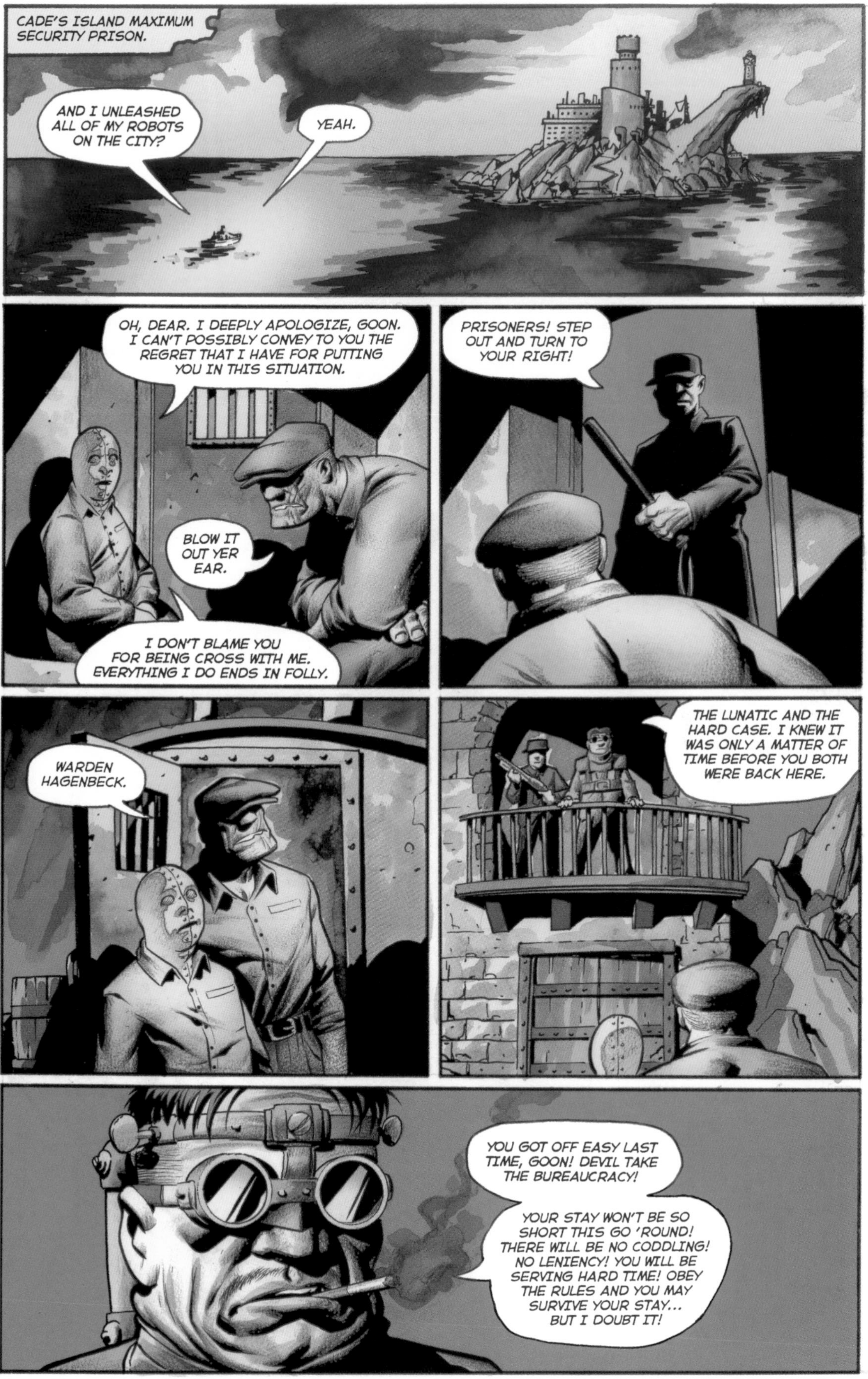
CADE'S ISLAND MAXIMUM SECURITY PRISON.
AND I UNLEASHED ALL OF MY ROBOTS ON THE CITY?
YEAH.
OH, DEAR. I DEEPLY APOLOGIZE, GOON. I CAN'T POSSIBLY CONVEY TO YOU THE REGRET THAT I HAVE FOR PUTTING YOU IN THIS SITUATION.
BLOW IT OUT YER EAR.
I DON'T BLAME YOU FOR BEING CROSS WITH ME. EVERYTHING I DO ENDS IN FOLLY.
PRISONERS! STEP OUT AND TURN TO YOUR RIGHT!
WARDEN HAGENBECK.
THE LUNATIC AND THE HARD CASE. I KNEW IT WAS ONLY A MATTER OF TIME BEFORE YOU BOTH WERE BACK HERE.
YOU GOT OFF EASY LAST TIME, GOON! DEVIL TAKE THE BUREAUCRACY!
YOUR STAY WON'T BE SO SHORT THIS GO 'ROUND! THERE WILL BE NO CODDLING! NO LENIENCY! YOU WILL BE SERVING HARD TIME! OBEY THE RULES AND YOU MAY SURVIVE YOUR STAY... BUT I DOUBT IT!

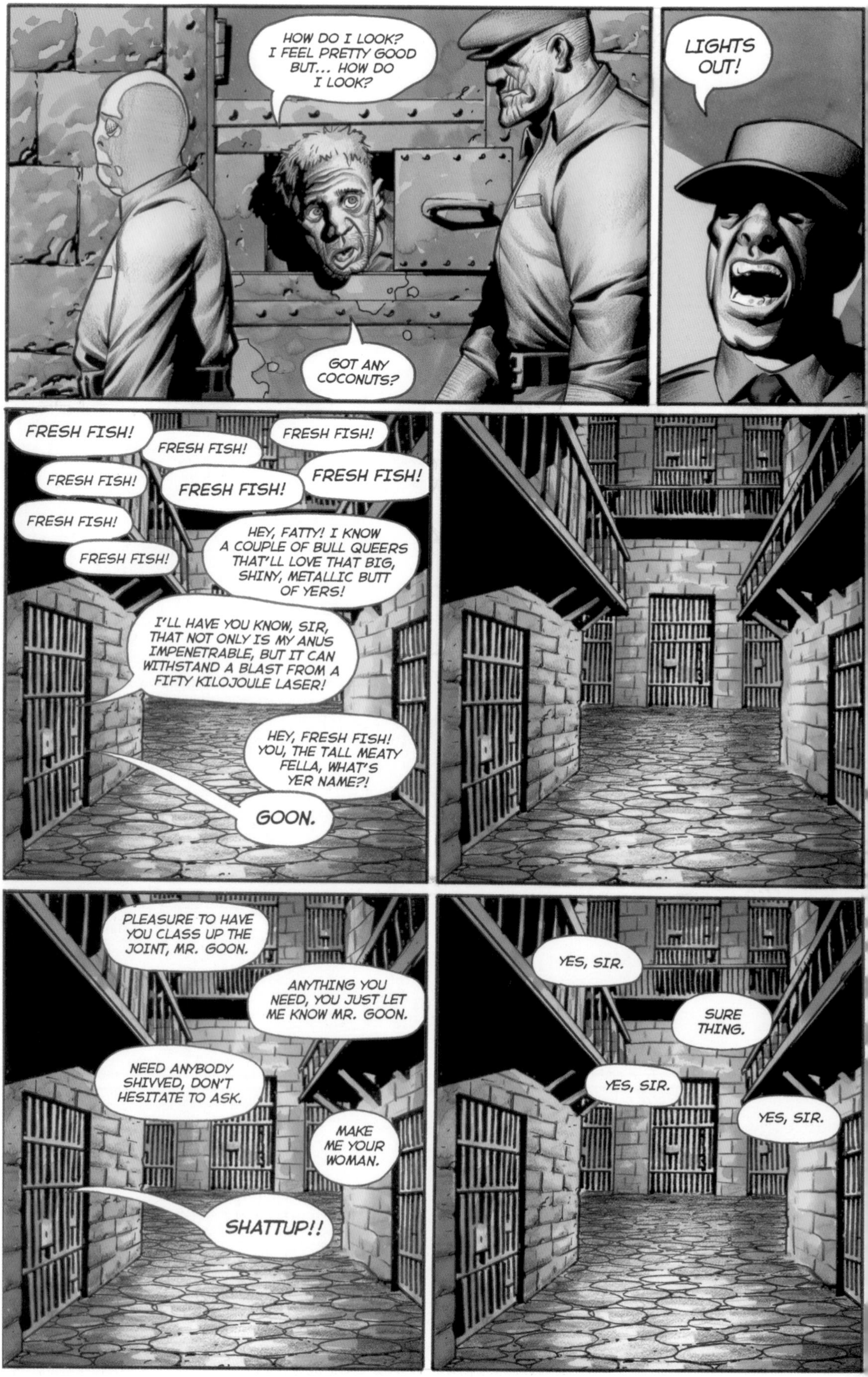
HOW DO I LOOK? I FEEL PRETTY GOOD BUT... HOW DO I LOOK?
GOT ANY COCONUTS?
LIGHTS OUT!
FRESH FISH!
FRESH FISH!
FRESH FISH!
FRESH FISH!
FRESH FISH!
FRESH FISH!
FRESH FISH!
FRESH FISH!
HEY, FATTY! I KNOW A COUPLE OF BULL QUEERS THAT'LL LOVE THAT BIG, SHINY, METALLIC BUTT OF YERS!
I'LL HAVE YOU KNOW, SIR, THAT NOT ONLY IS MY ANUS IMPENETRABLE, BUT IT CAN WITHSTAND A BLAST FROM A FIFTY KILOJOULE LASER!
HEY, FRESH FISH! YOU, THE TALL MEATY FELLA, WHAT'S YER NAME?!
GOON.
PLEASURE TO HAVE YOU CLASS UP THE JOINT, MR. GOON.
ANYTHING YOU NEED, YOU JUST LET ME KNOW MR. GOON.
NEED ANYBODY SHIVVED, DON'T HESITATE TO ASK.
MAKE ME YOUR WOMAN.
SHATTUP!!
YES, SIR.
SURE THING.
YES, SIR.
YES, SIR.

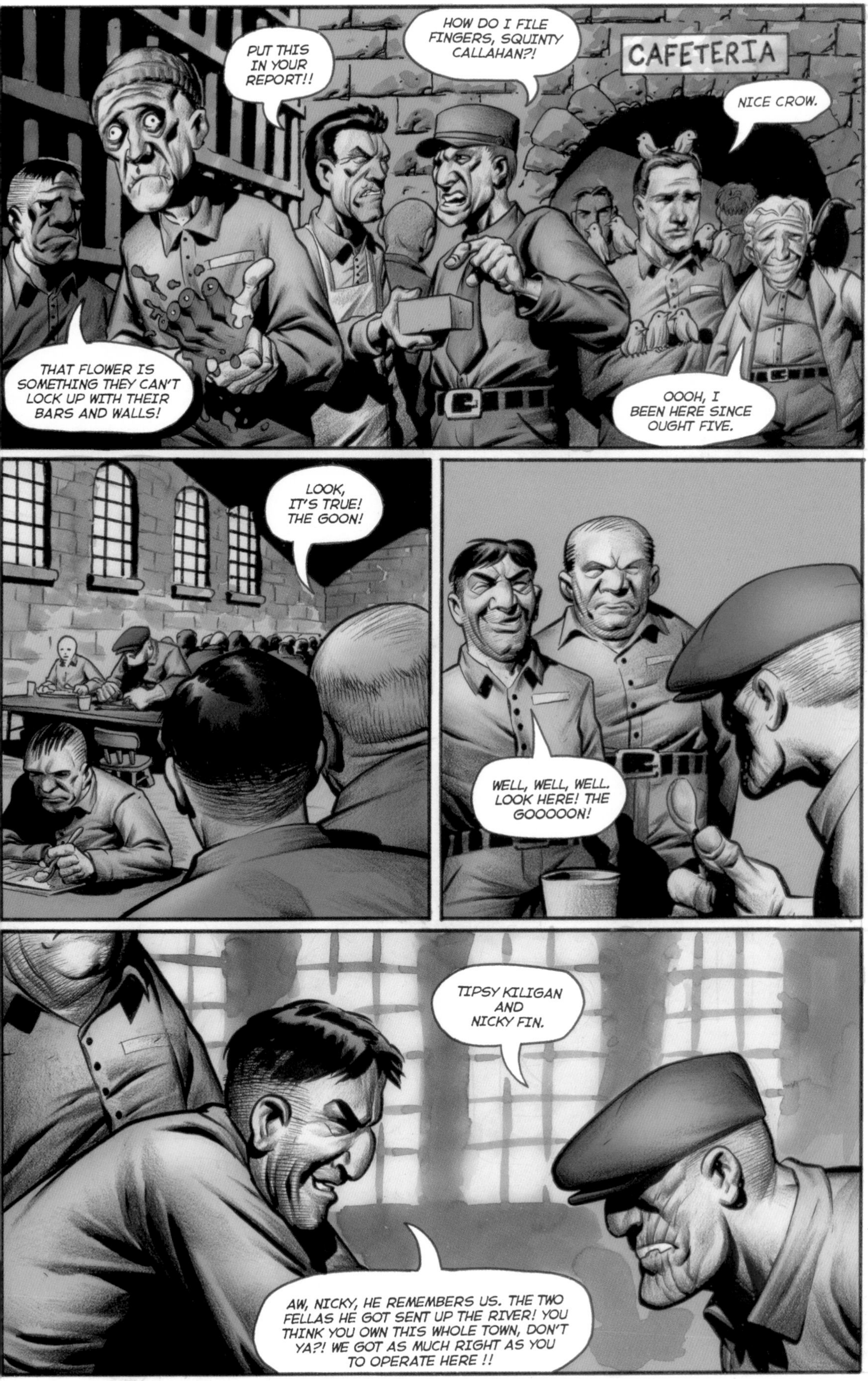

PUT THIS IN YOUR REPORT!!
HOW DO I FILE FINGERS, SQUINTY CALLAHAN?!
CAFETERIA
NICE CROW.
THAT FLOWER IS SOMETHING THEY CAN'T LOCK UP WITH THEIR BARS AND WALLS!
OOOH, I BEEN HERE SINCE OUGHT FIVE.
LOOK, IT'S TRUE! THE GOON!
WELL, WELL, WELL. LOOK HERE! THE GOOOOON!
TIPSY KILIGAN AND NICKY FIN.
AW, NICKY, HE REMEMBERS US. THE TWO FELLAS HE GOT SENT UP THE RIVER! YOU THINK YOU OWN THIS WHOLE TOWN, DON'T YA?! WE GOT AS MUCH RIGHT AS YOU TO OPERATE HERE !!

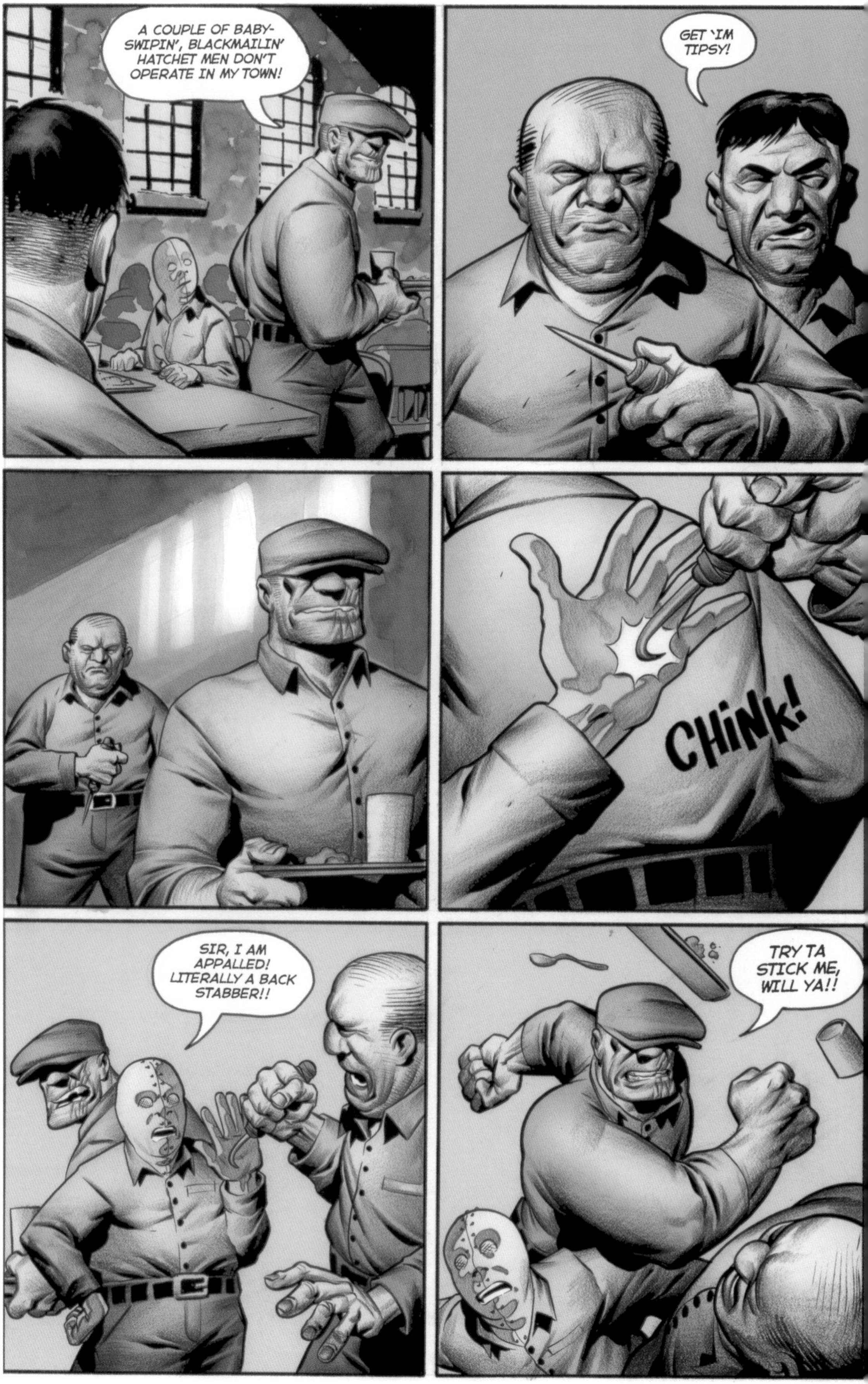
A COUPLE OF BABY-SWIPIN', BLACKMAILIN' HATCHET MEN DON'T OPERATE IN MY TOWN!
GET 'IM TIPSY!
CHINK!
SIR, I AM APPALLED! LITERALLY A BACK STABBER!!
TRY TA STICK ME, WILL YA!!

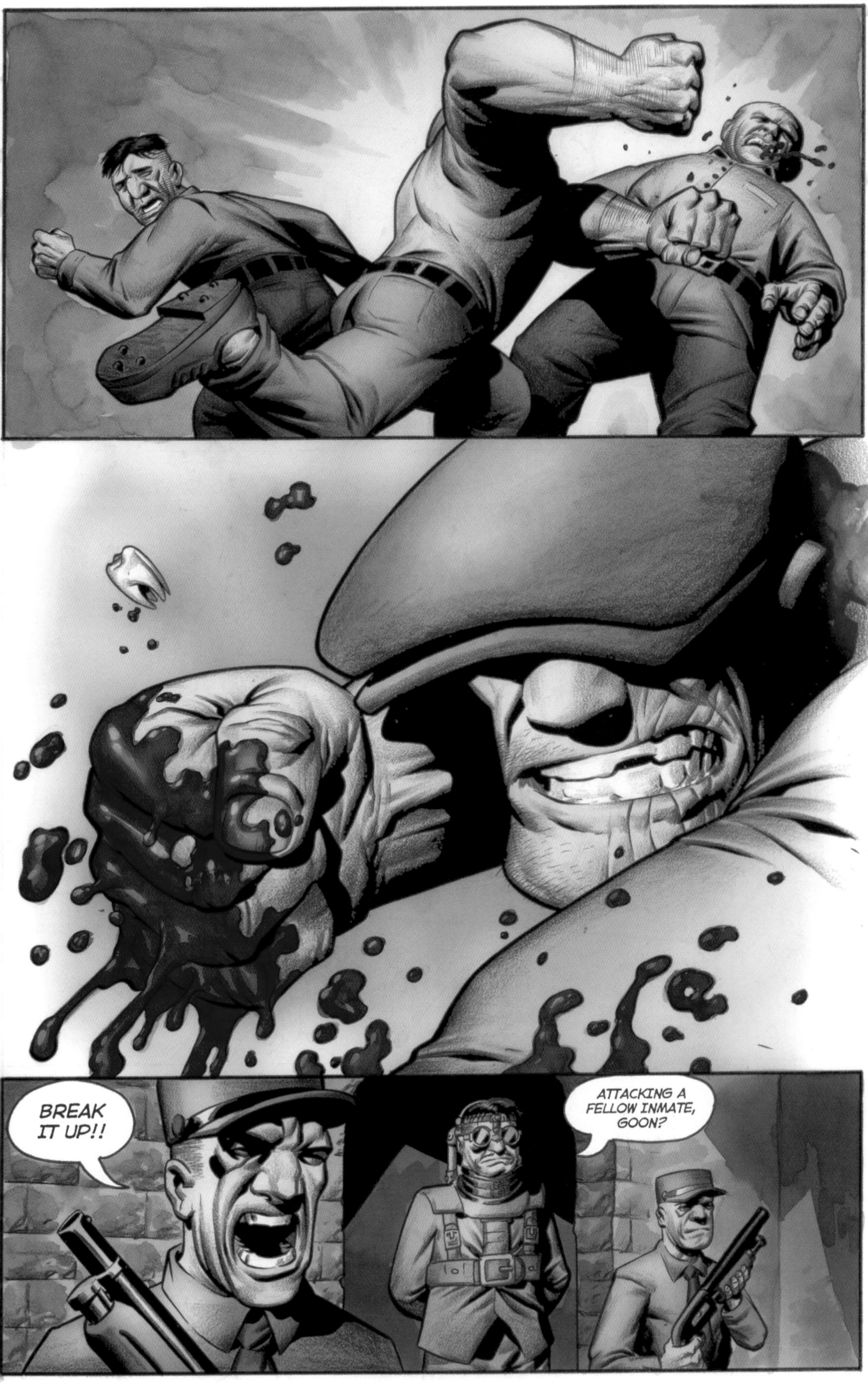
BREAK IT UP!!
ATTACKING A FELLOW INMATE, GOON?

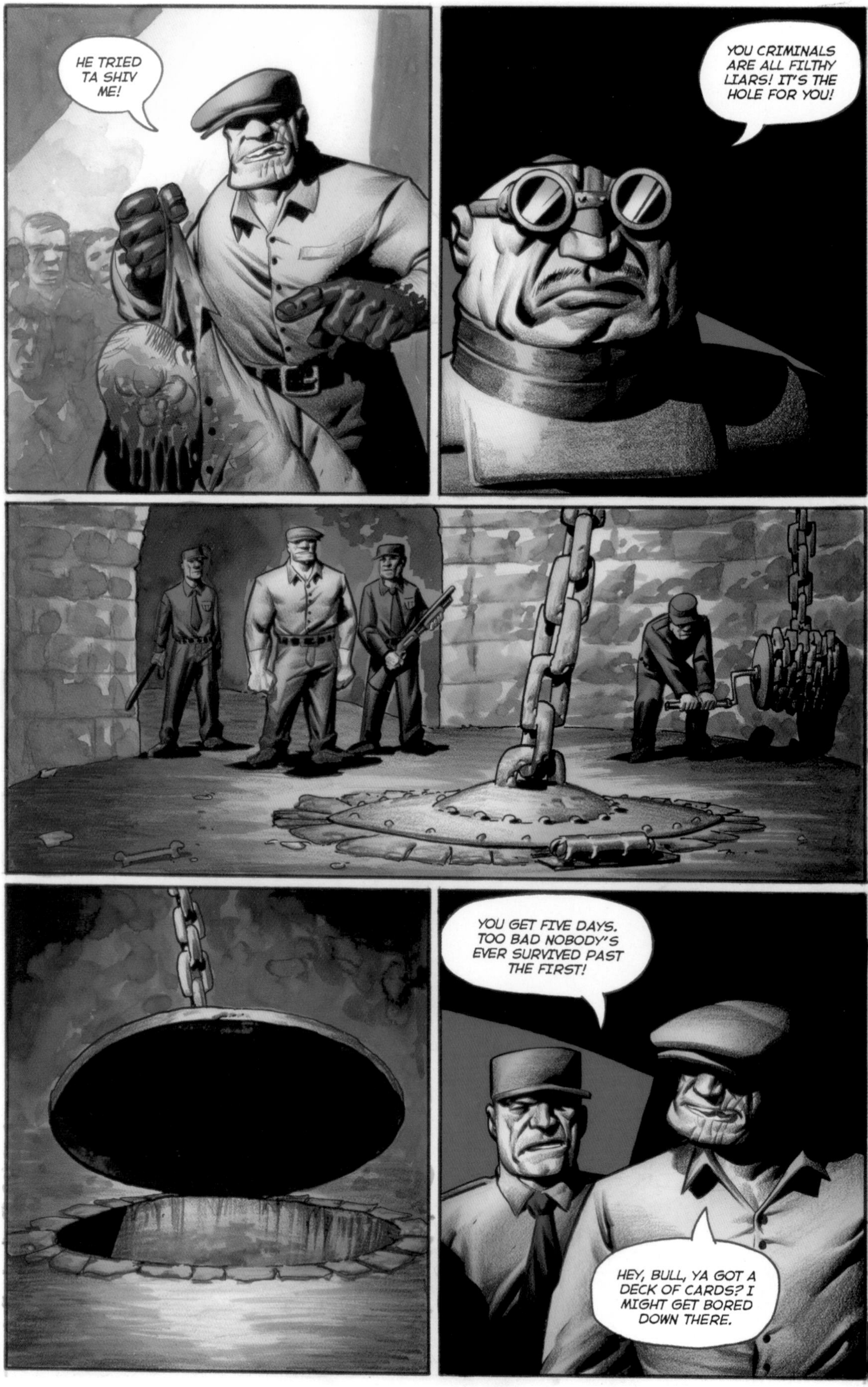
HE TRIED TA SHIV ME!
YOU CRIMINALS ARE ALL FILTHY LIARS! IT'S THE HOLE FOR YOU!
YOU GET FIVE DAYS. TOO BAD NOBODY'S EVER SURVIVED PAST THE FIRST!
HEY, BULL, YA GOT A DECK OF CARDS? I MIGHT GET BORED DOWN THERE.

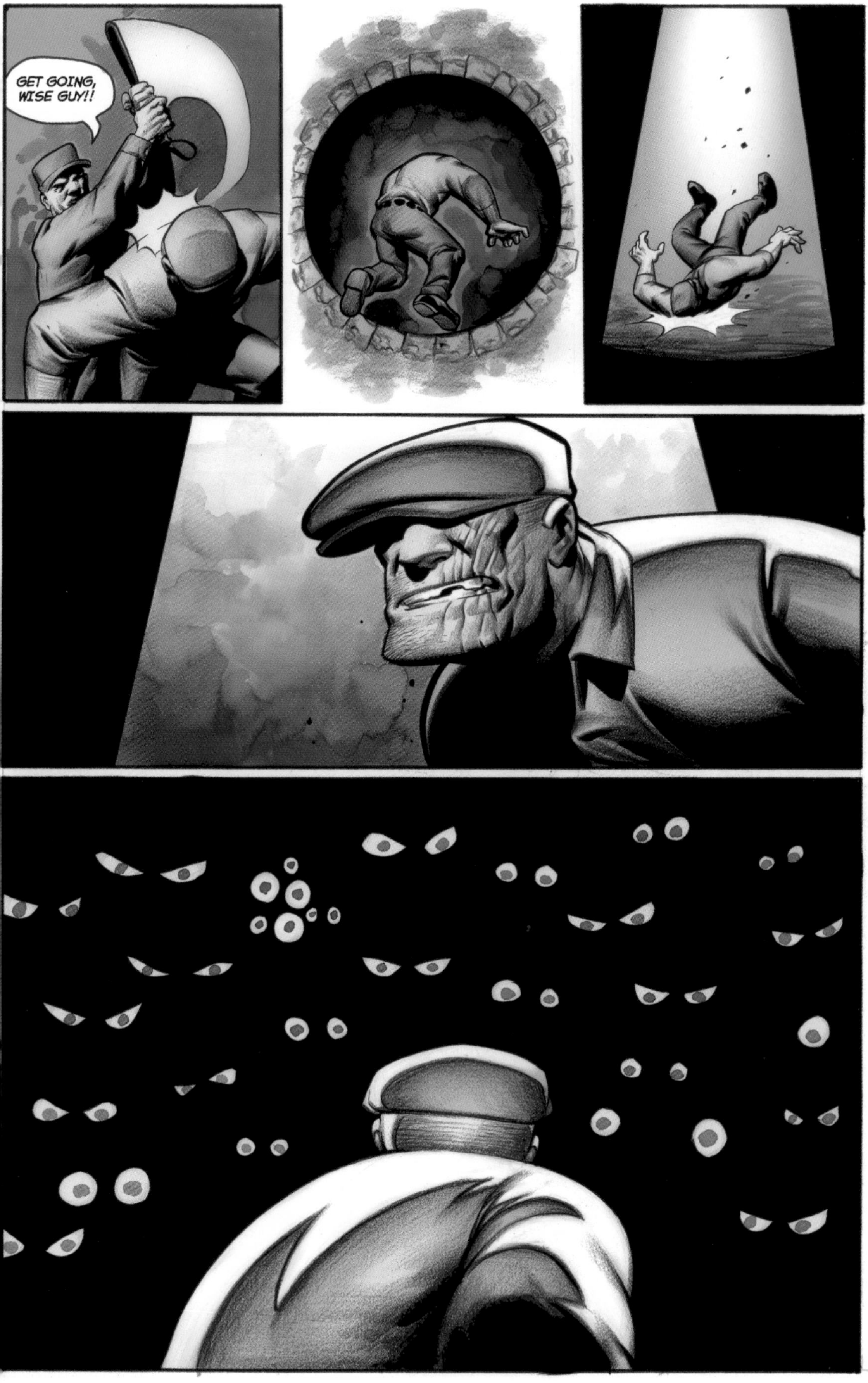
GET GOING,
WISE GUY!!

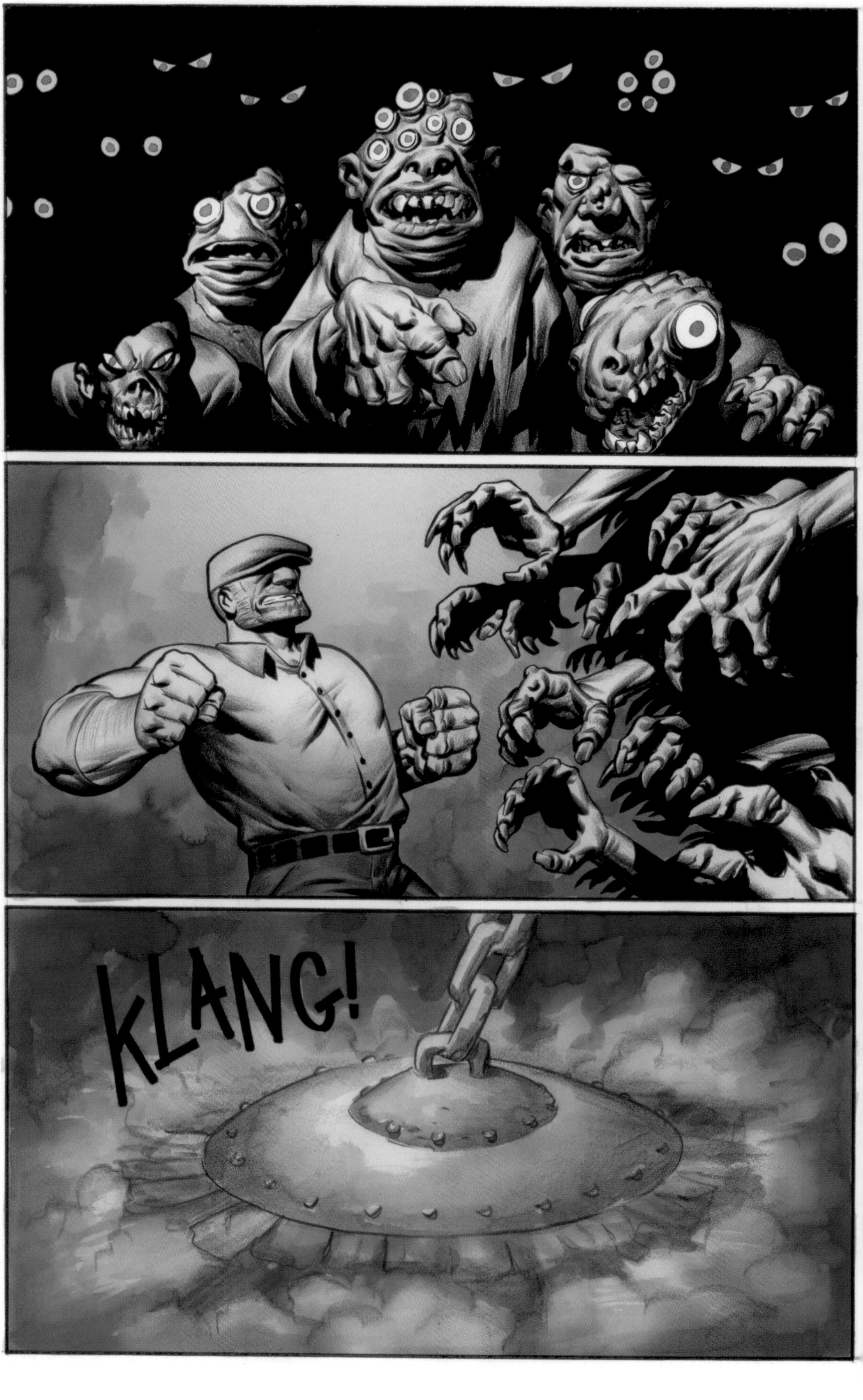
KLANG!

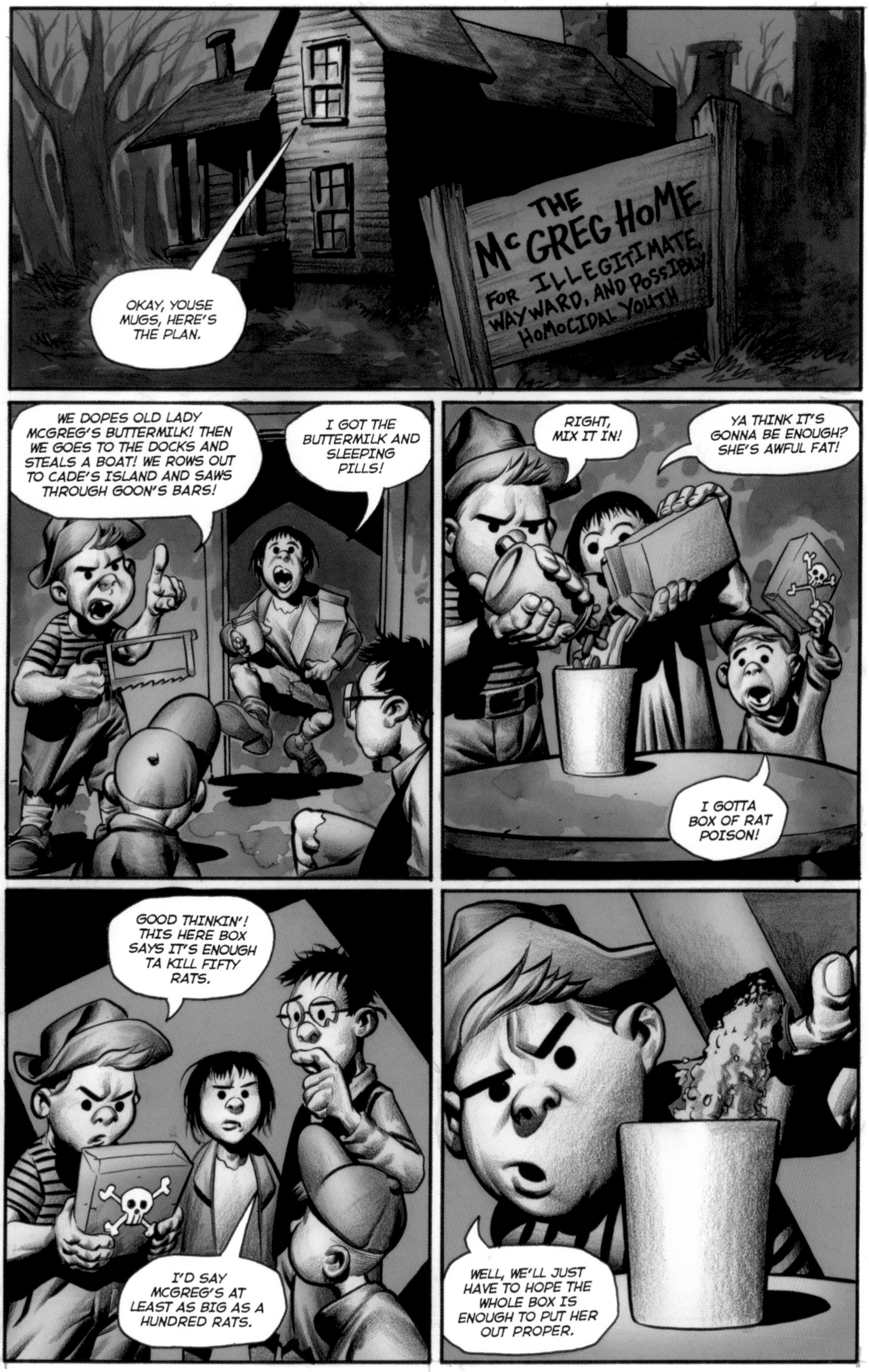
THE McGREG HOME FOR ILLEGITIMATE, WAYWARD, AND POSSIBLY HOMOCIDAL YOUTH
OKAY, YOUSE MUGS, HERE'S THE PLAN.
WE DOPES OLD LADY MCGREG'S BUTTERMILK! THEN WE GOES TO THE DOCKS AND STEALS A BOAT! WE ROWS OUT TO CADE'S ISLAND AND SAWS THROUGH GOON'S BARS!
I GOT THE BUTTERMILK AND SLEEPING PILLS!
RIGHT, MIX IT IN!
YA THINK IT'S GONNA BE ENOUGH? SHE'S AWFUL FAT!
I GOTTA BOX OF RAT POISON!
GOOD THINKIN'! THIS HERE BOX SAYS IT'S ENOUGH TA KILL FIFTY RATS.
I'D SAY MCGREG'S AT LEAST AS BIG AS A HUNDRED RATS.
WELL, WE'LL JUST HAVE TO HOPE THE WHOLE BOX IS ENOUGH TO PUT HER OUT PROPER.

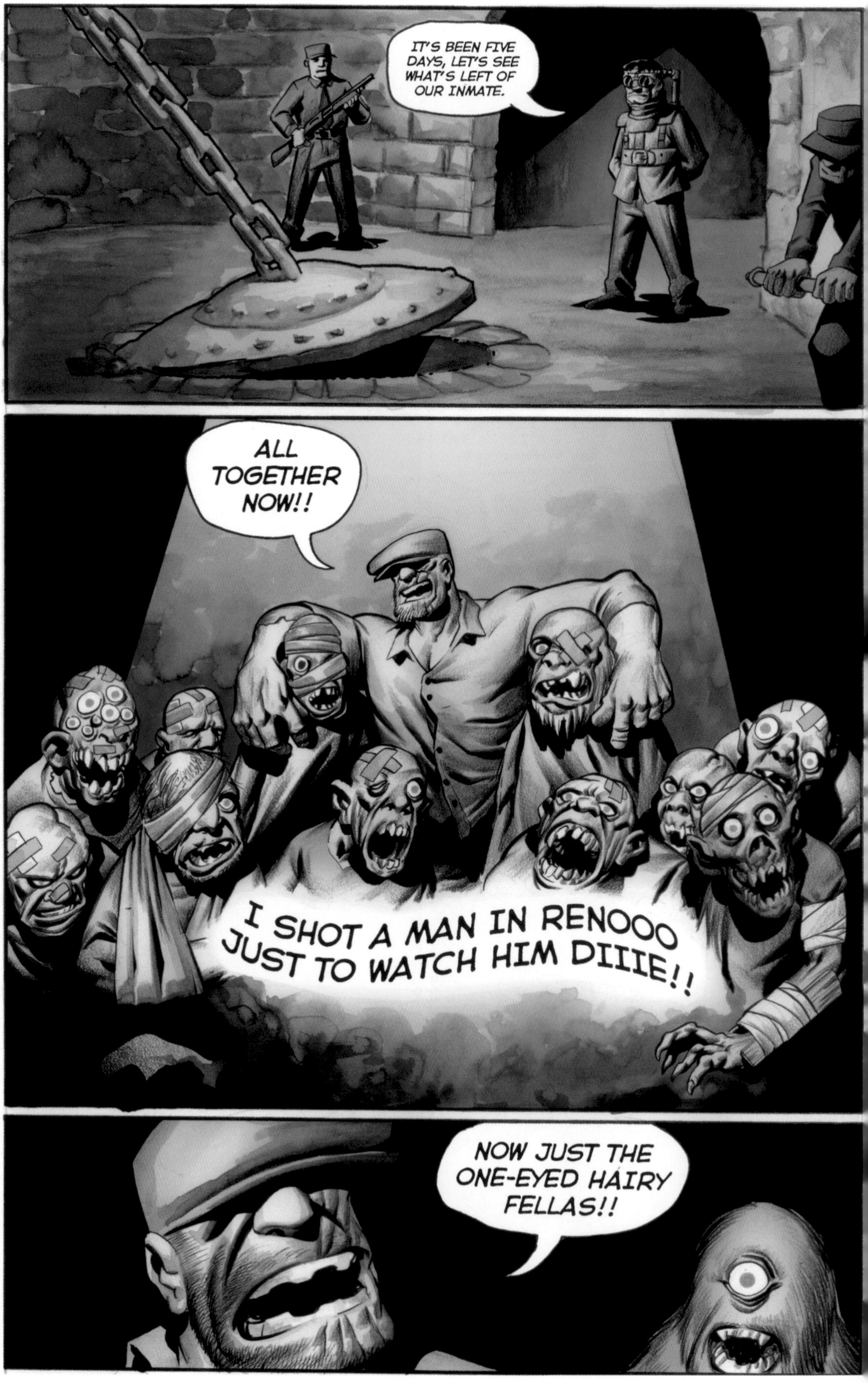
IT'S BEEN FIVE DAYS, LET'S SEE WHAT'S LEFT OF OUR INMATE.
ALL TOGETHER NOW!!
I SHOT A MAN IN RENOOO JUST TO WATCH HIM DIIIE!!
NOW JUST THE ONE-EYED HAIRY FELLAS!!

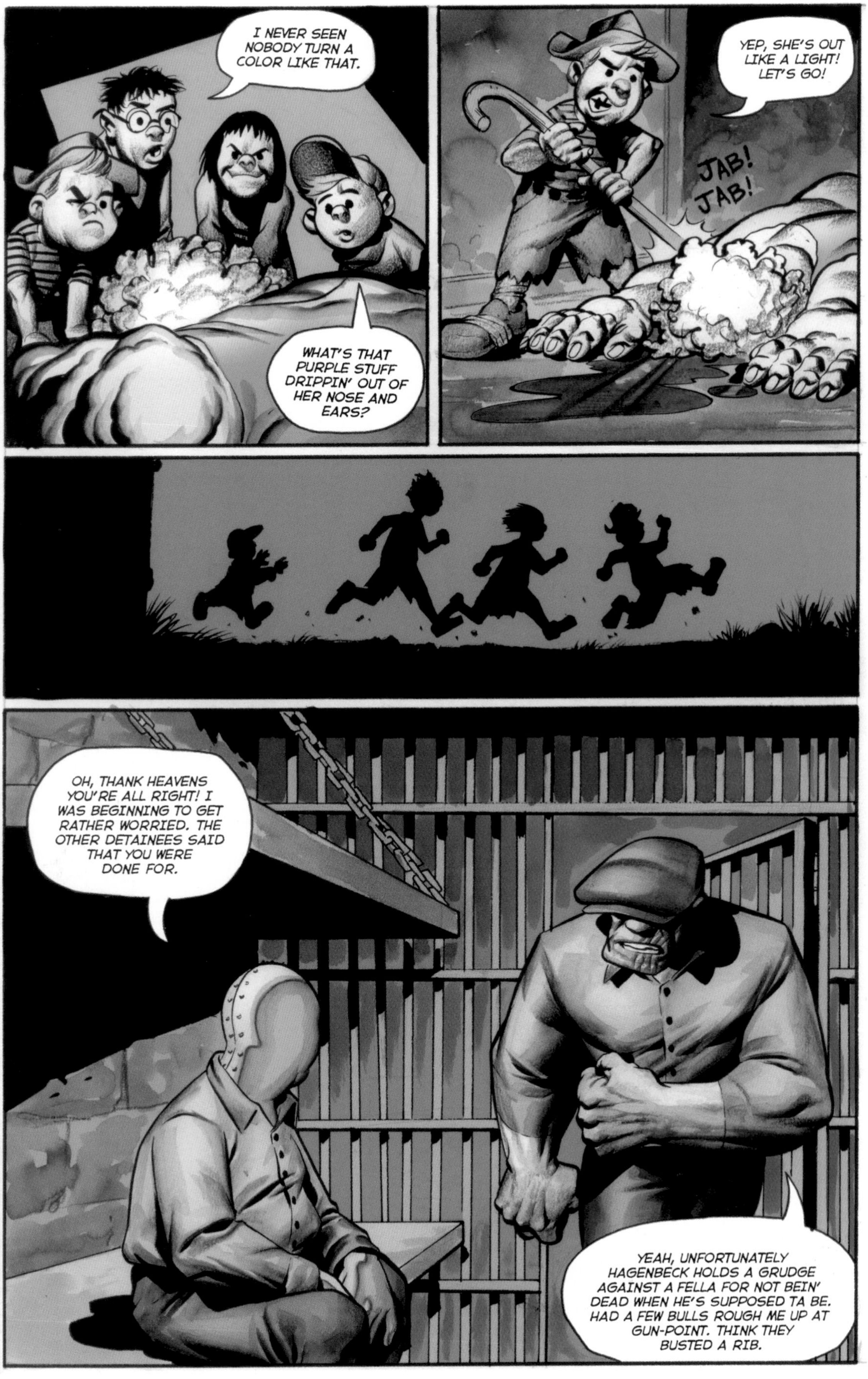

I NEVER SEEN NOBODY TURN A COLOR LIKE THAT.
WHAT'S THAT PURPLE STUFF DRIPPIN' OUT OF HER NOSE AND EARS?
YEP, SHE'S OUT LIKE A LIGHT! LET'S GO!
JAB! JAB!
OH, THANK HEAVENS YOU'RE ALL RIGHT! I WAS BEGINNING TO GET RATHER WORRIED. THE OTHER DETAINEES SAID THAT YOU WERE DONE FOR.
YEAH, UNFORTUNATELY HAGENBECK HOLDS A GRUDGE AGAINST A FELLA FOR NOT BEIN' DEAD WHEN HE'S SUPPOSED TA BE. HAD A FEW BULLS ROUGH ME UP AT GUN-POINT. THINK THEY BUSTED A RIB.

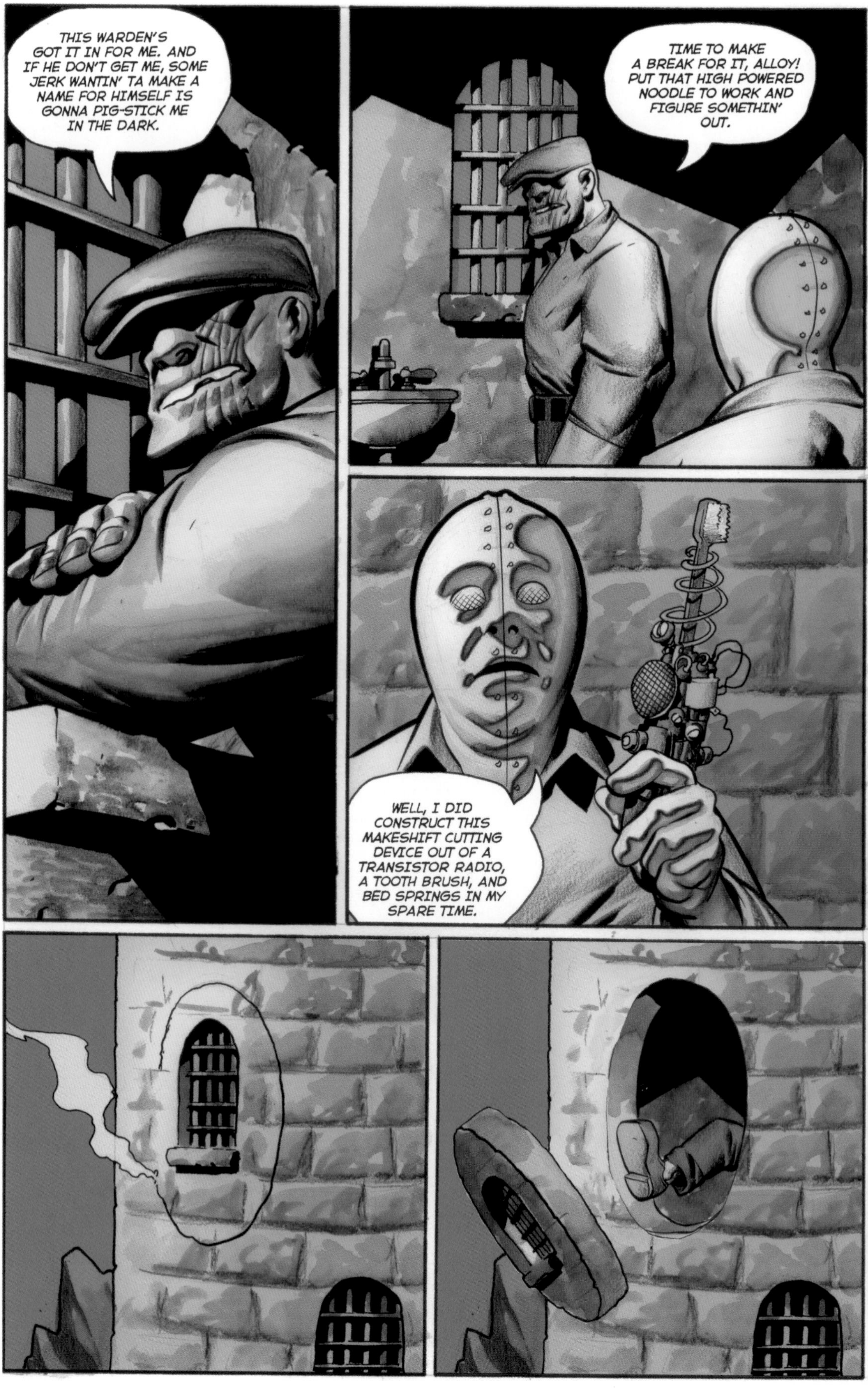
THIS WARDEN'S GOT IT IN FOR ME. AND IF HE DON'T GET ME, SOME JERK WANTIN' TA MAKE A NAME FOR HIMSELF IS GONNA PIG-STICK ME IN THE DARK.
TIME TO MAKE A BREAK FOR IT, ALLOY! PUT THAT HIGH POWERED NOODLE TO WORK AND FIGURE SOMETHIN' OUT.
WELL, I DID CONSTRUCT THIS MAKESHIFT CUTTING DEVICE OUT OF A TRANSISTOR RADIO, A TOOTH BRUSH, AND BED SPRINGS IN MY SPARE TIME.

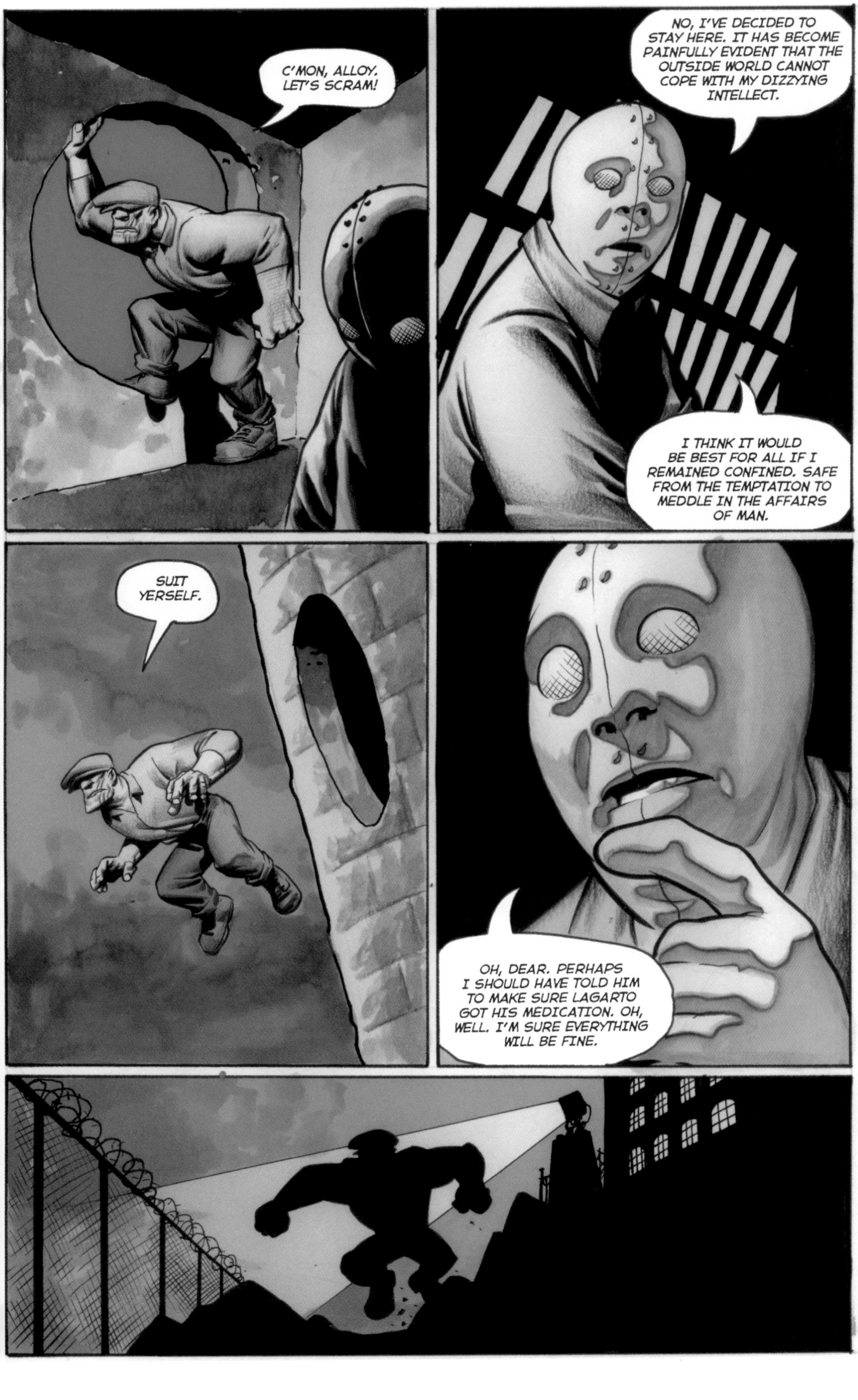
C'MON, ALLOY. LET'S SCRAM!
NO, I'VE DECIDED TO STAY HERE. IT HAS BECOME PAINFULLY EVIDENT THAT THE OUTSIDE WORLD CANNOT COPE WITH MY DIZZYING INTELLECT.
I THINK IT WOULD BE BEST FOR ALL IF I REMAINED CONFINED. SAFE FROM THE TEMPTATION TO MEDDLE IN THE AFFAIRS OF MAN.
SUIT YERSELF.
OH, DEAR. PERHAPS I SHOULD HAVE TOLD HIM TO MAKE SURE LAGARTO GOT HIS MEDICATION. OH, WELL. I'M SURE EVERYTHING WILL BE FINE.

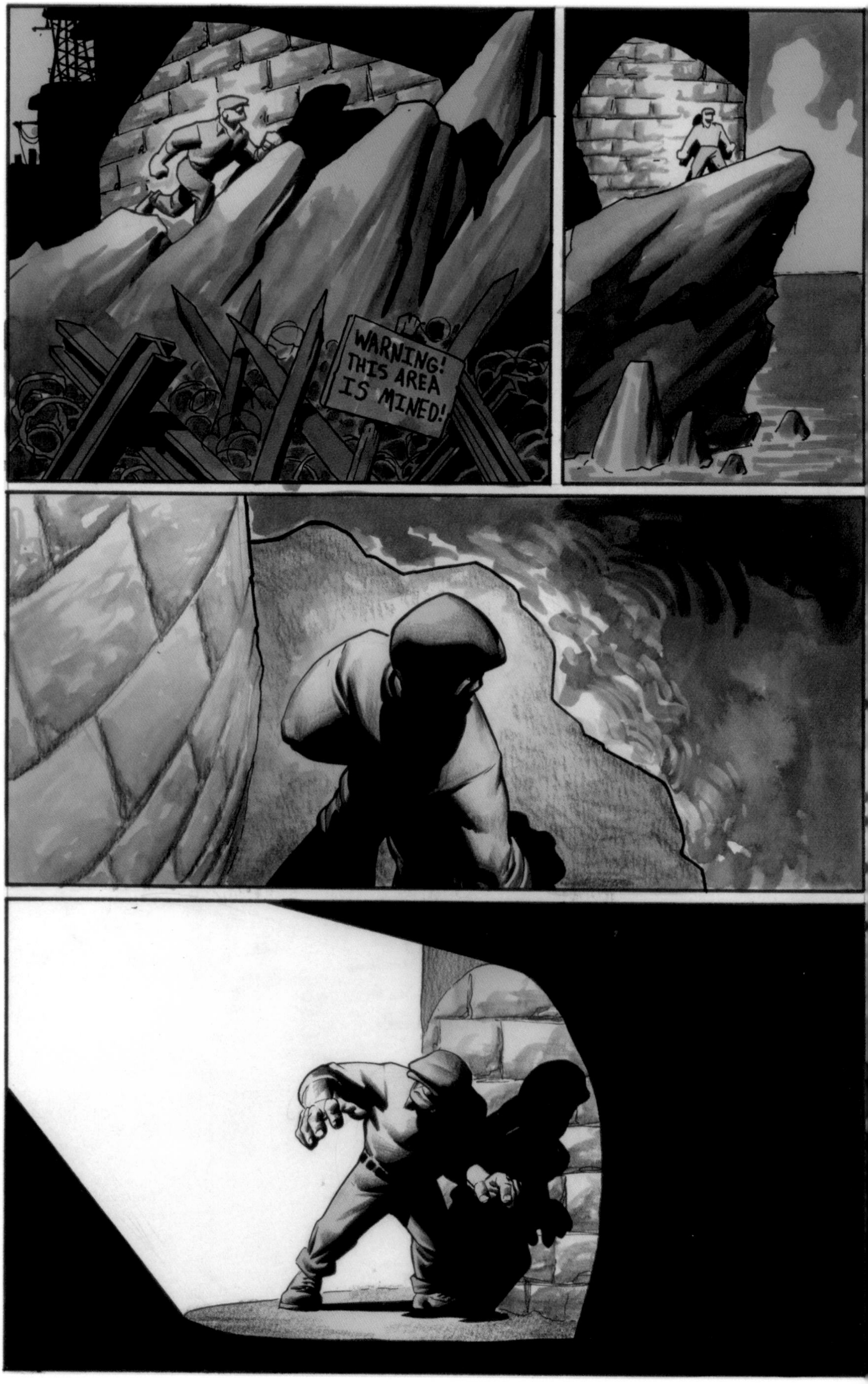
WARNING! THIS AREA IS MINED!

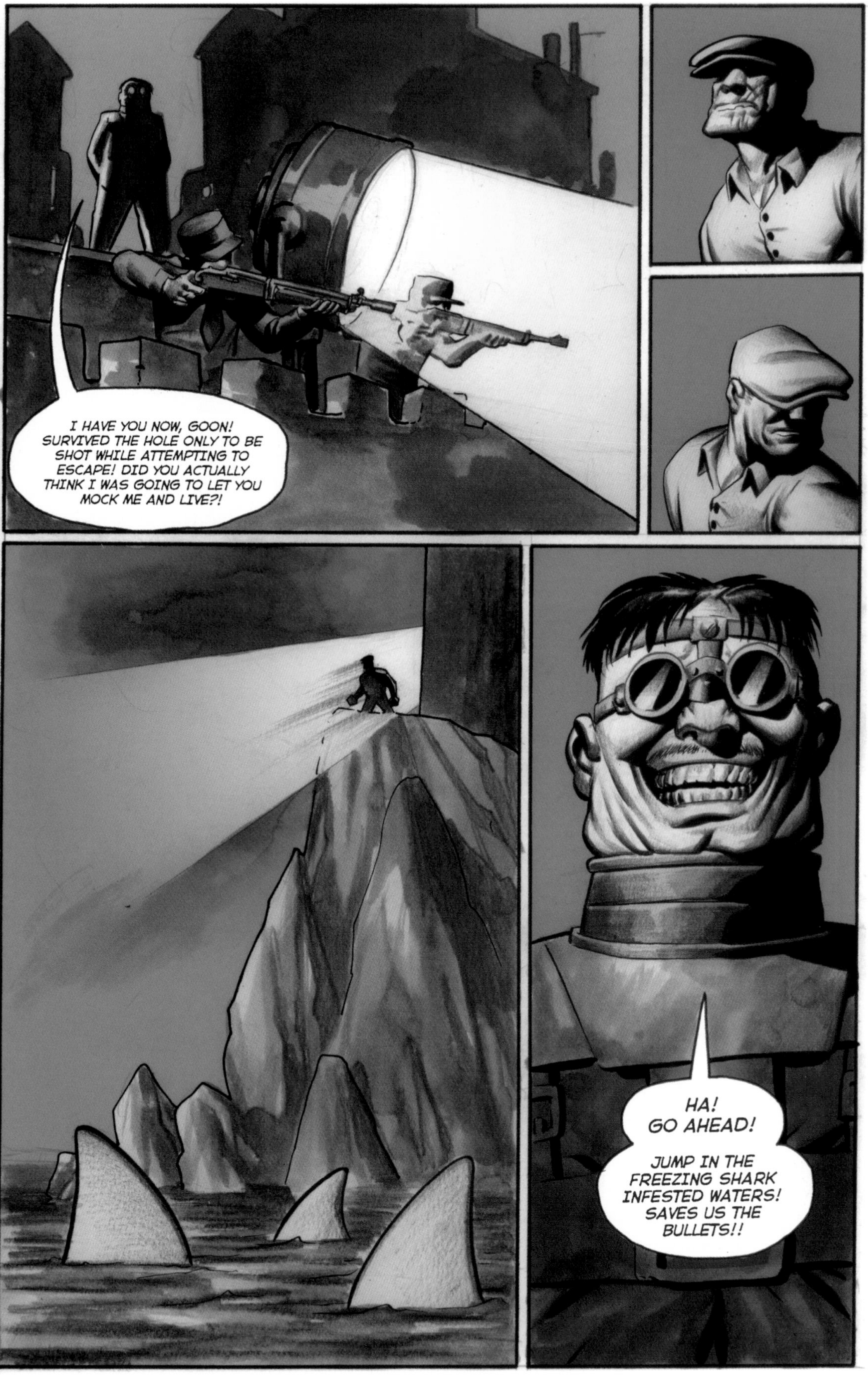
I HAVE YOU NOW, GOON! SURVIVED THE HOLE ONLY TO BE SHOT WHILE ATTEMPTING TO ESCAPE! DID YOU ACTUALLY THINK I WAS GOING TO LET YOU MOCK ME AND LIVE?!
HA! GO AHEAD!
JUMP IN THE FREEZING SHARK INFESTED WATERS! SAVES US THE BULLETS!!

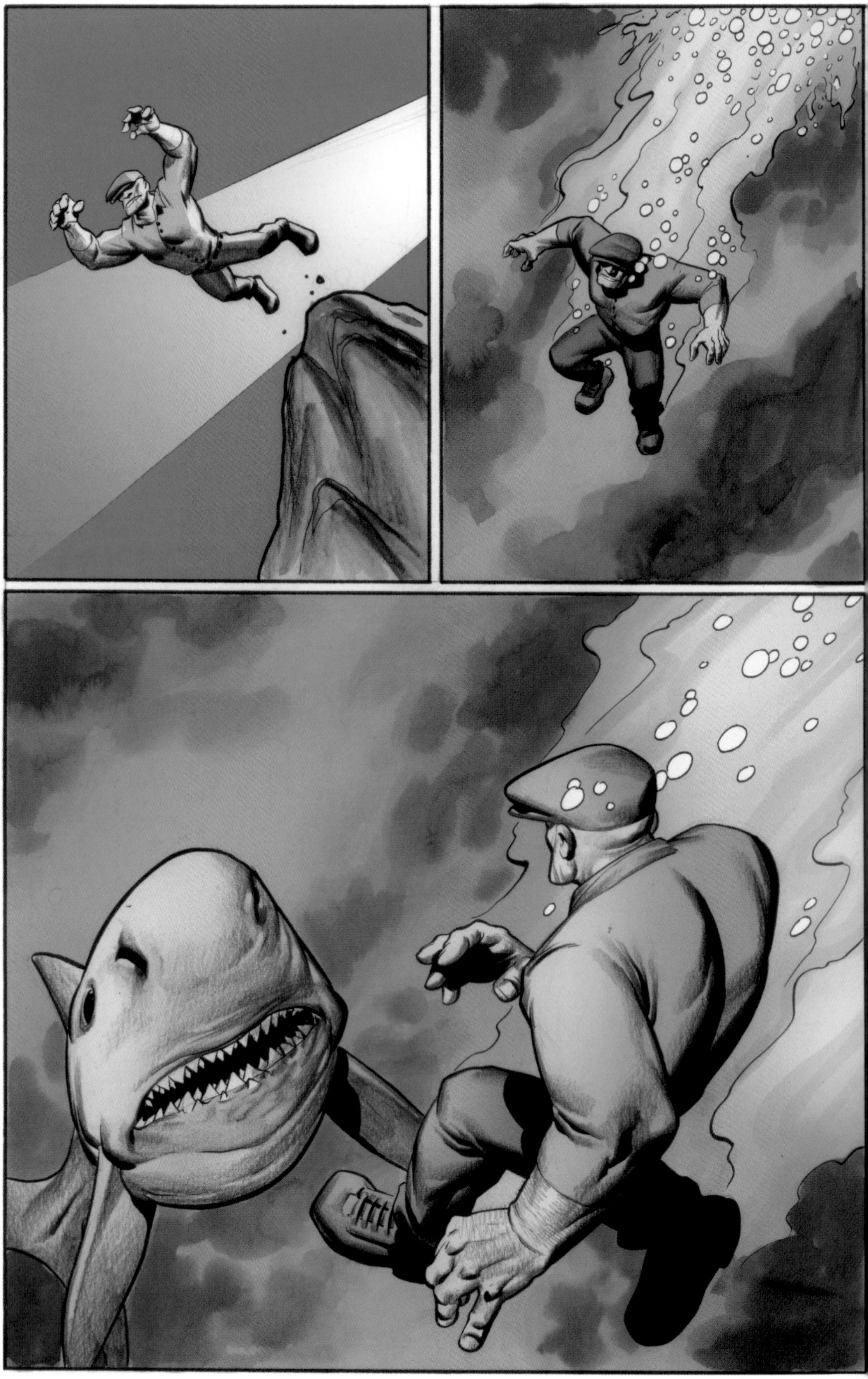

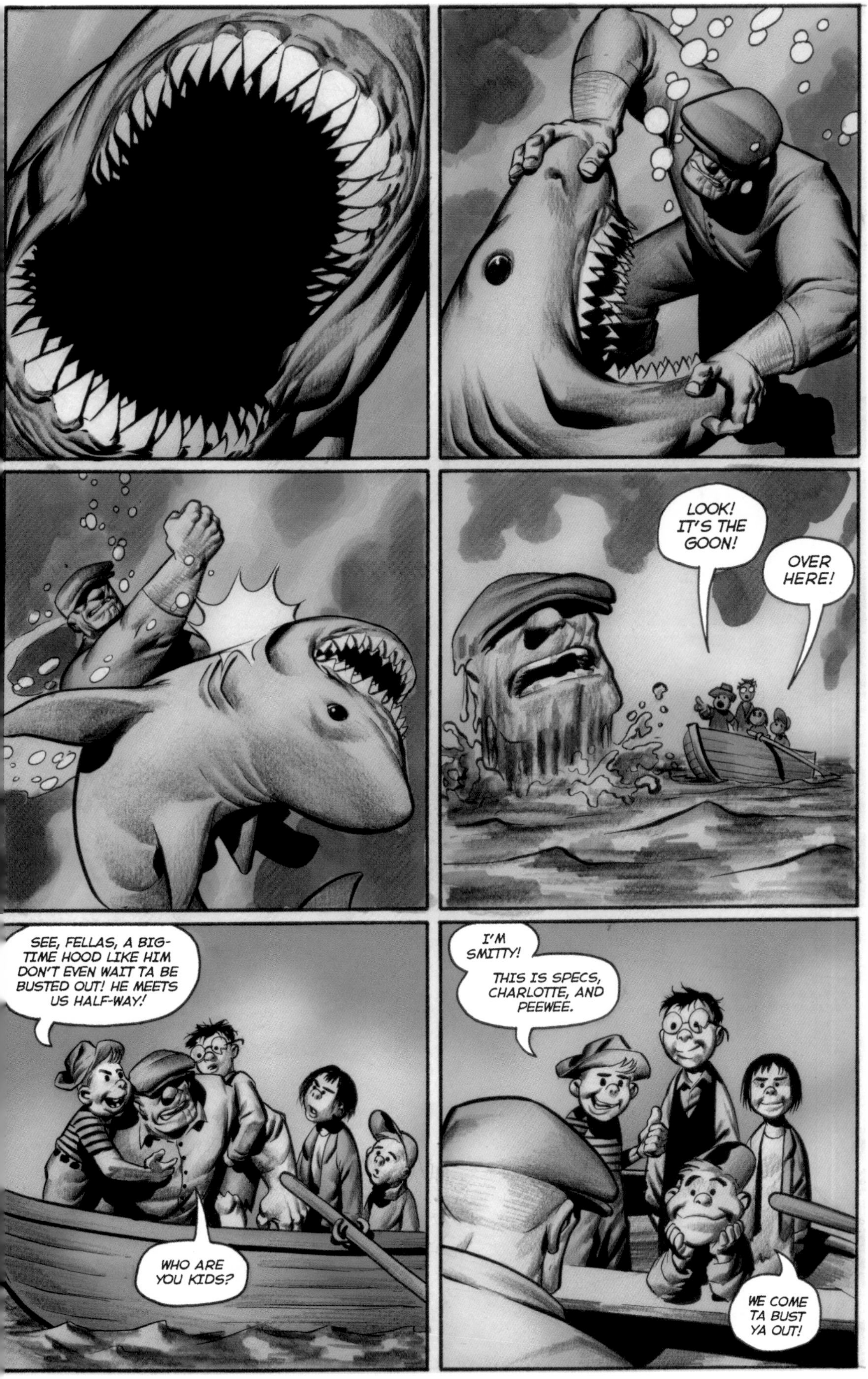
LOOK! IT'S THE GOON!
OVER HERE!
SEE, FELLAS, A BIG-TIME HOOD LIKE HIM DON'T EVEN WAIT TA BE BUSTED OUT! HE MEETS US HALF-WAY!
WHO ARE YOU KIDS?
I'M SMITTY!
THIS IS SPECS, CHARLOTTE, AND PEEWEE.
WE COME TA BUST YA OUT!

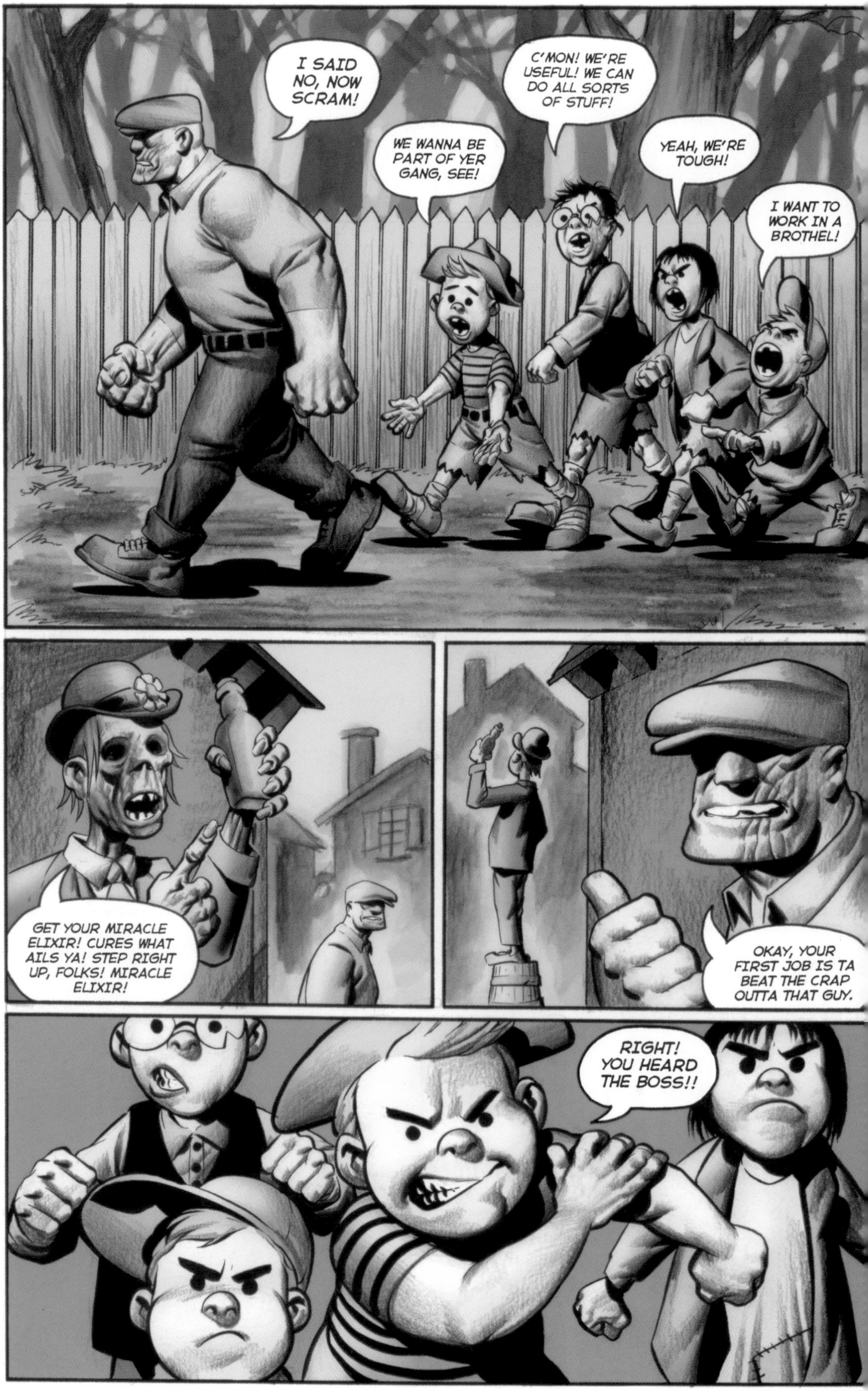

I SAID NO, NOW SCRAM!
WE WANNA BE PART OF YER GANG, SEE!
C'MON! WE'RE USEFUL! WE CAN DO ALL SORTS OF STUFF!
YEAH, WE'RE TOUGH!
I WANT TO WORK IN A BROTHEL!
GET YOUR MIRACLE ELIXIR! CURES WHAT AILS YA! STEP RIGHT UP, FOLKS! MIRACLE ELIXIR!
OKAY, YOUR FIRST JOB IS TA BEAT THE CRAP OUTTA THAT GUY.
RIGHT! YOU HEARD THE BOSS!!

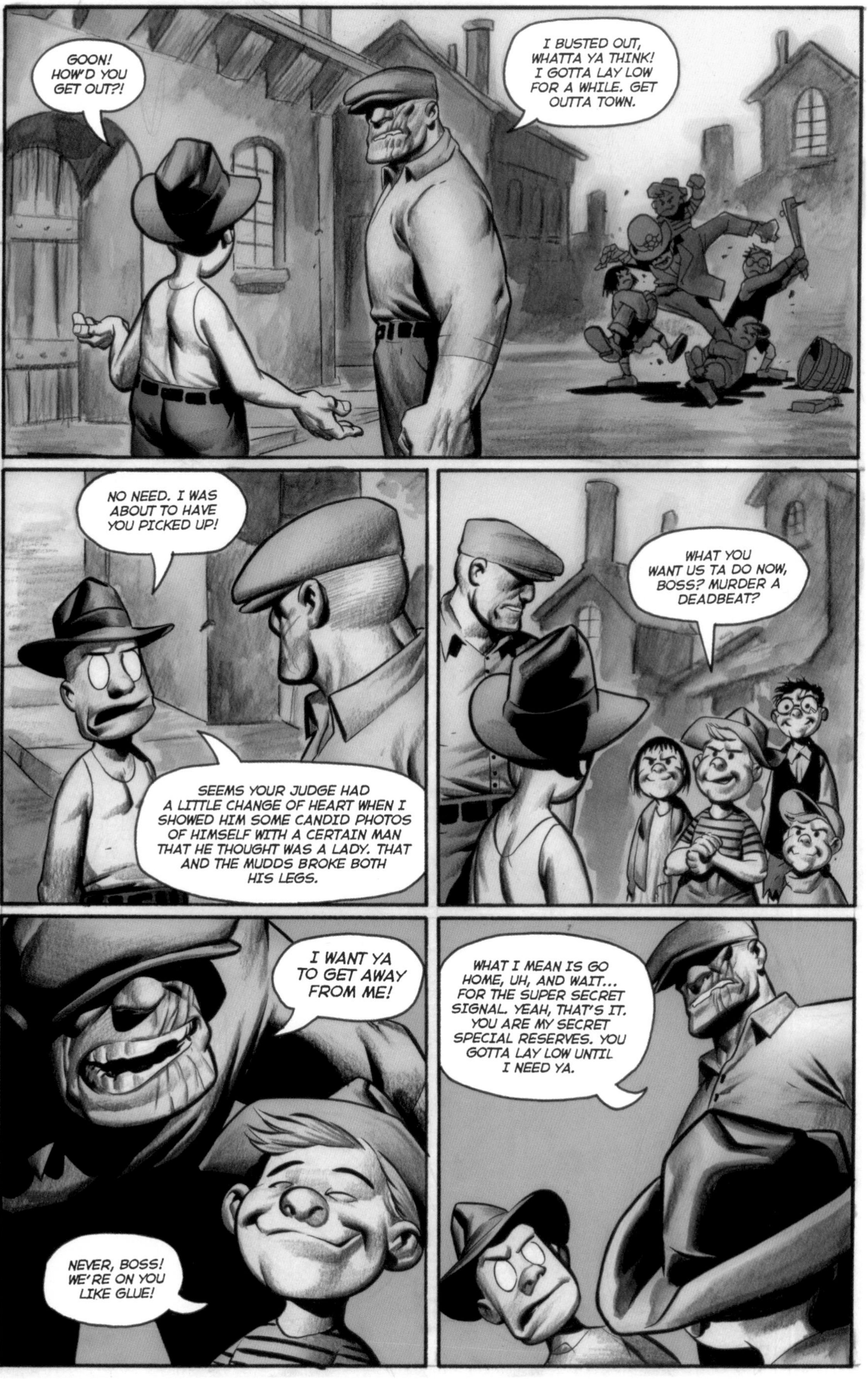
GOON! HOW'D YOU GET OUT?!
I BUSTED OUT, WHATTA YA THINK! I GOTTA LAY LOW FOR A WHILE. GET OUTTA TOWN.
NO NEED. I WAS ABOUT TO HAVE YOU PICKED UP!
SEEMS YOUR JUDGE HAD A LITTLE CHANGE OF HEART WHEN I SHOWED HIM SOME CANDID PHOTOS OF HIMSELF WITH A CERTAIN MAN THAT HE THOUGHT WAS A LADY. THAT AND THE MUDDS BROKE BOTH HIS LEGS.
WHAT YOU WANT US TA DO NOW, BOSS? MURDER A DEADBEAT?
I WANT YA TO GET AWAY FROM ME!
NEVER, BOSS! WE'RE ON YOU LIKE GLUE!
WHAT I MEAN IS GO HOME, UH, AND WAIT... FOR THE SUPER SECRET SIGNAL. YEAH, THAT'S IT. YOU ARE MY SECRET SPECIAL RESERVES. YOU GOTTA LAY LOW UNTIL I NEED YA.

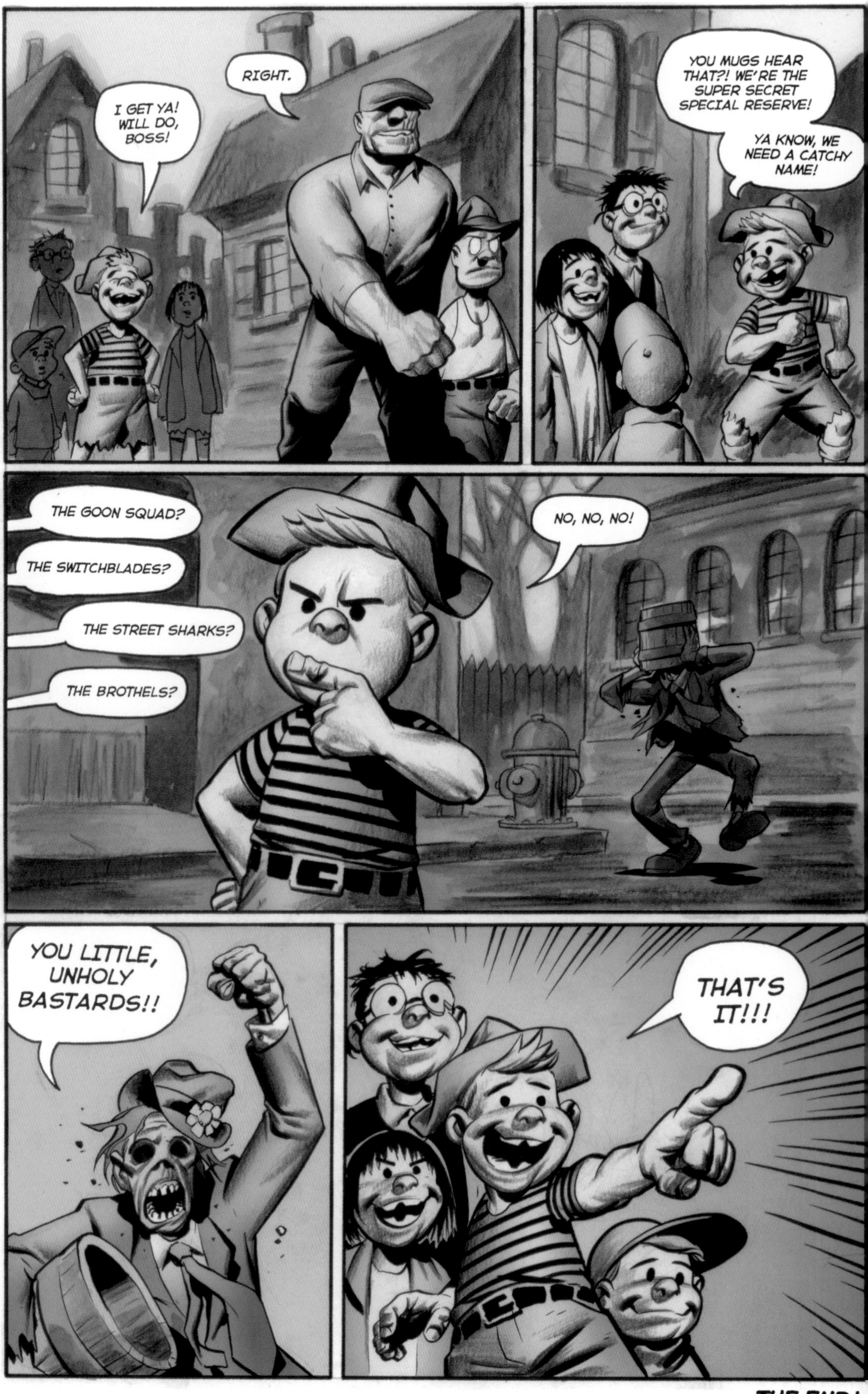

I GET YA! WILL DO, BOSS!
RIGHT.
YOU MUGS HEAR THAT?! WE'RE THE SUPER SECRET SPECIAL RESERVE!
YA KNOW, WE NEED A CATCHY NAME!
THE GOON SQUAD?
THE SWITCHBLADES?
THE STREET SHARKS?
THE BROTHELS?
NO, NO, NO!
YOU LITTLE, UNHOLY BASTARDS!!
THAT'S IT!!!

THE END!

Jimmy Turtle and the Legendary Boxcar of Well-Made Ladies Shoes

written by **Thomas Lennon**
illustrations by **Eric Powell**

When I asked Thomas Lennon to write a short Goon story, I was thinking more of a comic script that I could illustrate. But luckily for us he took it upon himself to write a fully fleshed-out prose story featuring Franky as the main character. When he sent over his first rough draft, I was thrilled. Well, after I read it and laughed my ass off, I was thrilled. Now, I think you have to hand it to this guy for two reasons. One, he has the guts to go on television as a somewhat feminine cop in short shorts. And two, he seems to be able to generate absurd comedy with relative ease. It was an honor to have him take a swing at my silly little world and to collaborate with him in a small way through my spot illustrations.

So here's to you, Tom! Thanks for a great story and sorry for breaking that chair over your back in San Diego. But that's another story all together.

—Eric Powell

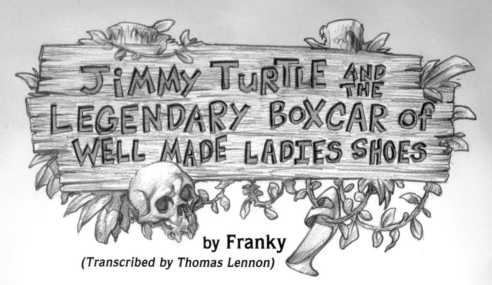

JIMMY TURTLE AND THE LEGENDARY BOXCAR of WELL MADE LADIES SHOES

by Franky

(Transcribed by Thomas Lennon)

I first heard about the legendary boxcar of well-made ladies shoes from a man who'd traveled amongst the boxcar hobos in their environs: Jimmy Turtle. Jimmy wasn't a hobo himself, but he was a chronic gasoline-rag huffer who had to move around a lot on account of a short con he'd run called "A Harp for the Lady."

This was one of Jimmy's best short cons. It worked like this: he'd arrive at the door of a spinster, dressed to the nines, and produce a catalogue of the finest harps made in Europe. He'd talk up the benefits of a harp in the home, get her to lay down some serious cabbage, then knock her over the head with a rock.

This was Jimmy's style. I was never sure why he didn't just skip the harp stuff and go straight to the rock, but he was a man of intrigue, and a chronic gasoline huffer. Maybe it's 'cause he already had the harp catalogue. Maybe it was just habit.

When I met Jimmy, he was in the middle of a nine-week huff bender, living in a roll of carpeting on Tresdale Avenue. I didn't know he was even in there 'til I took it home and started beatin' the carpet with a pipe. Out tumbles Jimmy, and we been friends since that day. It's also how come his left eye don't work right.

At first I thought we wouldn't be pals, but, as he emerged from his gas-rag haze, I could see that he was one of the most vicious sons a' bitches I ever met.

Jimmy bunked up with me 'til he could get back on his feet. It's hard to stand when you've been on the business end of a gas-soaked rag for nine weeks.

Pretty soon, Jimmy and I were running short and long cons together. Our best one was called "Parson and the Out-of-Town Gentleman." In this one, I played the Parson, while Jimmy was the Out-of-Town Gentleman. I'd work the bus depot,

in a full Parson get-up. I'd make
like I was lost, ask a good
samaritan for bus fare
to Kansas, then Jimmy
would saunter up—
dressed to the nines—
and hit 'em with a rock.

One night over ham-cake
and beans, Jimmy got to
telling me about his days
amongst the hobos.

"Them filthy bindle
toters?" I says.

"The same," says Jimmy. "You ever heard about the legendary boxcar of well-made
ladies shoes? A king's ransom in ladies shoes. Upwards of eight hundred dollars,
some say."

"You're full of it," I says.

"No, it's true," says Jimmy.

"Liar!" I says. And then I hit him with my good bean pan, and he passed out for
about a day.

We kept up "Parson and the Out-of-Town Gentleman" at the depot until the station
dick got wise. All the while, I was thinking about what Jimmy said about these
well-made shoes, and the kind of cabbage they might be worth to a fella that could
get his hands on 'em (apparently eight hundred bucks). One afternoon when we
had some free time in the cooler, I asked him about it again.

"So, you been to this boxcar?" I says.

"I ain't seen it," says Jimmy, "but I seen a map once. Belonged to a hobo named
Hobo John."

A voice chimed in, "You two taking that box car full of shoes? It's hooey. I've heard
the stories, too."

I turned and laid eyes on the ugliest spider I think I ever seen.

(This was before I was pals with Spider. He'd been pinched for a little misunder-
standing that the Feds were calling kidnapping. It was a fake kidnapping, but
once Spider and Charlie Noodles got nabbed—Charlie panicked, and didn't cop to
the fact that he was a voluntary hostage. They'd planned on making a quick fifty
from Charlie's uncle. Spider took the rap, pulled a short stint. Charlie made it up
to him later by cutting him in on a half gross of orchids he'd boosted. Charlie's
good people, ask anybody.)

Back to where I was:

"You're full of it!" I says to Jimmy as I broad-sided him with my shoe, as I didn't have a rock or my good bean pan.

That night, in the bunk under Spider, I had a dream. In the dream, I was sitting atop a mountain of well-made ladies shoes, and tiny little centaur people were worshipping me like a sultan, bringin' me cakes and splendid things.

I'm not sure what the centaur people meant, but I knew the other part was the hand of fate, telling me I had to get my mitts on these well-made shoes.

We got bounced in the morning, and we decided to set out in search of the legendary boxcar. I laid down two bits for an apple pie at Smeagle's and went out chumming for Hobo John.

The plan was to make nice with him by way of the pie, acquire the map, and then: rock to the head. The "make nice" part was plan A. Plan B *started* with the rock, and didn't involve making nice at all. In plan B, the pie would be consumed by us, in celebration of acquiring the map.

We headed to the train yard, which shoulda been lousy with hobos, but there was a particularly rough-lookin' Bull on patrol, and his billy club looked like it had played extra innings on the skulls of the hobo population. So we scrammed over to the spot behind the bridge with the broken sewer pipe that they call Hobo Falls.

A couple of winos were cookin' what used to be a cat on a spit—but no hobos. Jimmy let 'em have it with a rock until he got one of 'em to talking. (The wino was actually trying to talk the whole time, but when Jimmy was havin' at it with a rock, he was a regular John Henry.)

"Ain't you heard?" said the Li'lest Wino, through the blood and what was left of his teeth, "the hobos have all moved deep into the woods."

"The Hobo Jungul, they calls it," said a Slightly Larger Wino. "They're worshipping the Hobo King and livin' on the flesh of men."

If I had a nickel for every time somebody told me that something I was lookin' for was "holed up in the woods, livin' on the flesh of men," I'd be living in a palace made of rubies and candy.

"What about Hobo John?" I says.

"I'm Hobo John," says the Li'lest Wino.

"No you ain't, you's a wino," says Jimmy.

"I am now," says the Li'lest Wino (who now let's call Wino John).

"They call me Wino John now, on account of I ain't a hobo no more. You see a bindle on my shoulder?" he says.

He didn't have no bindle, and he was covered in his own filth and spilled hooch, and he was cookin' up a cat for lunch—solid wino credentials.

"Make with the map, Hobo John," I says.

"Wino John ... I just told you two seconds ago ..."

SCHRA-CRACK! Jimmy went with plan B to the head.

While the former Hobo John was taking a dirt nap, we shook 'em down. Sure enough, in his shoe, was a folded piece of paper with a crude drawing. It smelled like wino foot, but to me, it smelled like eight hundred clams worth of well-made shoes. And a little bit like wino foot.

The map had no words or names—most hobos can't hardly write for snot. But the pictures was pretty distinct:

1. A path leading Southeast from the Decaster place two miles into underbrush and a grove of elm trees.

2. A large elm, with branches that form what looks like an Indian Chief in profile, smoking a pipe.

3. A fork in the path, veering left with seventy-five paces marked out.

4. A double-headed dog, like the one they says guards the gate to hell.

5. A boxcar.

This was it—the legendary boxcar! The only thing that made me nervous was number 4, the double-headed dog, like the one they says guards the gates to hell. A couple a questions popped through my head:

Was this dog as big as it looked in the drawing?

Were those human skulls or animal skulls littered around its feet?

Did it for sure only have TWO heads, or did the drawer of the map just run outta steam and not draw *all* the heads?

Two headed hell dog—fine, I'm in. But start addin' heads, and the smart money starts movin' into the hell dog corner.

We went back to Norton's and started making plans. We knew we needed a couple of things: rope, a good flashlight, and anything that might kill a double-headed dog from the gates of hell. My thought on this was bullets.

Jimmy said regular bullets wouldn't do no good. If the dog had dug itself up from gates of hell, we'd need bullets that'd been blessed by a holy man. If it was just a mutated earth dog from a freak show, say, we'd just want something big gauge—something that could put a nice-sized window in it.

We decided to kill both birds with one stone and get our hands on some .45 shells with some holy elbow grease on 'em. The only catch was: how was we gonna get a holy man to bless our large gauge bullets. Killing things is often the sort of deal holy-types frown upon.

"We'll disguise the bullets as somethin' harmless. Somethin' that you wouldn't think twice about blessin'," I says. "Like frankfurters."

We picked up a half dozen frankfurter buns a Smeagle's, and loaded 'em up with our .45 shells. Then we covered the shells with kraut and relish. They looked pretty good.

We took 'em down to Our Lady of Persistent Sorrow. Father O'Brien was pitchin' pennies out back with Stella Johannsen's crippled brother Fred. Fred was good people, and everybody cut him slack on account of him being only a torso and head. I still feel bad about what was about to happen to him in a couple of seconds.

"Hey, Padre," I says, "how 'bout givin' a little blessing to these frankfurters Jimmy and I are about to eat?"

"Wait, you want me to bless frankfurters?" says the Padre with a suspicious-type look.

"Yeah—give 'em a little Hail Mary or something," I says.

"Somethin' to drive the devil out," says Jimmy, "something strong."

And now Padre O'Brien gets a real cross-eyed look, like we're speaking Swahili. And here's where things turned terrible for Stella Johannsen's crippled brother Fred.

"Looks like you've got an awful lot of frankfurters there, Francis," says the Padre, "more than two healthy boys can manage. How about donating one of those to God's humble servant?"

I was about to call it off, but it was too late: the thing that turns out so horrible for Fred Johannsen happened right then.

The Padre reaches out and takes one a Jimmy's frankfurters, and before you can say: "Wait, Padre, them wiener buns is fulla bullets," he bites in. BLAM!

His chompers musta hit right at the casing, 'cause next thing I know, Fred Johannsen is spoutin' blood like a maimed dolphin. I drop my frankfurters to help, but they must'a hit the pavement hard, 'cause two more rounds went off, creatin' a fountain of blood, relish, and kraut.

When the smoke cleared, Jimmy, the Padre, and myself were still standing. Fred Johanssen had taken four rounds to the face.

"That's impossible," I says. "I only heard three shots."

The Padre held up his hand—it was wrapped around a smoking .38 with a mother of pearl handle.

"Instinct," he says. "I'm a Jesuit."

The Padre lifted his tunic and slipped the .38 back into his ankle holster. We checked to see if Fred was alive, and tragically, he was.

(The rest of the Fred Johanssen story is for another day. He lived, but it suffices to say that with no limbs and four slugs in his kisser, he never ran for public office. Things was aggravated by the fact that three of the slugs was .45, one was .38, giving the scars a kinda uneven look, as if a dimwitted child had made a gingerbread man face right above Fred's own face. Later he grew a moustache to draw attention away from the bullet holes, but he ended up just looking like the guy Captain Weirdo fights in the one where he goes to the planet of the Potato Men.)

We got Fred patched up, and the Padre pulled us into his office. He wanted answers to a bunch of questions: Why were we trying to feed him bullets? This sorta thing. Yadda yadda.

We spilled our guts about the legendary boxcar, the well-made shoes—the whole caper. The Padre took a long look at us.

"I want in," he says.

"No dice," I says.

"Wait, Franky," says Jimmy, "if this dog with multiple heads is from hell, the Padre's exactly the kind of fella we want in our corner."

"Fine," I says, "but two conditions. The Padre's cut of the well-made shoes is fifteen percent or seventy-five pairs, whichever is less."

"Fine. What's the other?" says the Padre.

"Once the caper's over, we don't see each other for while. We divide the footwear, then until things cool off—we ain't friends, got it?"

"We're not friends now, Francis. I hardly know you, and what I know I don't like.

All I know is you're friends with The Goon." says the Padre.

"Good, then we won't have to practice avoidin' each other," I says.

We washed the kraut and relish off the rest of our ammo, and the Padre doused it all with water from a holy jar. Just for good measure he splashed a little on the rope and the flashlight, too.

The Padre insisted that we bow our heads, and pray for the success of the caper, and if possible, that Fred Johanssen would quietly die in his sleep that night, and not have to live the rest of his life as a bullet-riddled head and torso (which, as you know, he did).

It was around midnight when we set out for the Decaster place in the Padre's Packard. We pulled it off the road and covered the car with bramble brush so as to avoid suspicious lookie-loos. A couple lights were on in the Decaster place, and it sounded like somebody was sawing up a bathtub inside.

We scoured around in the brush 'til we found what looked sorta like it used to be a path. Jimmy was gettin' edgy. He'd been off the huff for a while now, and it didn't seem like reality was sittin' too well with him. He was twirlin' the flashlight real nervous like.

"You ever wonder how the boxcar woulda got all the way down here, Franky?" Jimmy asked, with a kinda jitter in his voice.

"Easy. A runaway, The Eastern Pacific used to run right along that ridge," I says, noddin' to the cliff above us. "Musta jumped the track just before the state line."

I was just startin' to think how hungry I was, and how I wish I'd kept a couple of them Smeagle's buns, when the ground beneath us trembled and a dog just like the one on the map came runnin' down the path. The head count was just right: two. His eyes were blazing with blue fire, and his cold breath felt like seein' a picture of somebody havin' a luau on your grave.

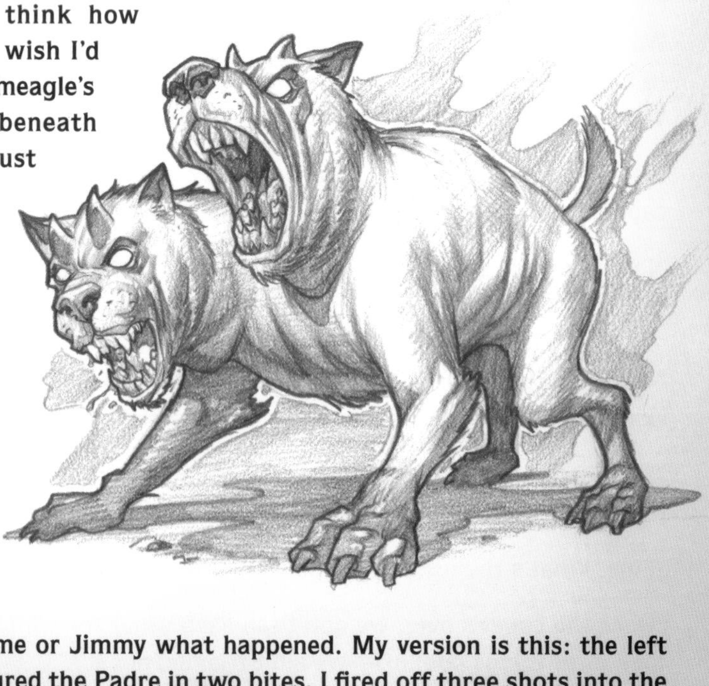

The details of what happened next differ depending on if you ask me or Jimmy what happened. My version is this: the left head is the one that devoured the Padre in two bites. I fired off three shots into the heart of the hell dog. The hell dog caught fire with the power of the holy bullets, growled with the voices of a thousand tortured souls, and then was sucked into a vortex, presumably back into hell.

Jimmy's version (which is wrong), goes like this: the dog comes runnin' up with the blue fire and whatnot. I panic and accidentally fire three shots into the Padre, who's then eaten (already dead) in two bites by the hell dog's right head. The dog catches fire, yadda yadda, and then hell vortex and whatnot.

In Jimmy's version, apparently EATING some holy bullets that are already inside a guy are enough to suck a dog back into hell. His version don't wash with me, and it's NOT the way it happened.

So, when the vortex cleared, we were down one Padre, but also down one hell dog, making the score about even. Our take of the shoes just shot up by fifteen percent, and there was a Packard in the bramble with no owner and the keys under the mat. Things were looking good.

This is when we should have turned back to Norton's for whiskey and pie in the late Padre's free Packard. But instead, we continued inching our way through the fog

and the tangled vines, with the sound of human or possibly animal skulls crunching beneath our feet.

We reached the deepest, darkest part of the gulley, and sure enough: the boxcar was there. It was lying on its side. The foliage had grown around it, making it look like some kinda jungle temple. We threw the rope over, and Jimmy hoisted me up top, to where the side door was (now it was more like the roof).

I started tuggin' on the door but it wouldn't do no good—the rust had sealed it shut. I fired off two rounds into the hinges, and the door popped off and fell inside the boxcar. Jimmy tossed up the flashlight and I shined it into the belly of the car.

(I now have one bullet, which will be important in a couple seconds.)

There was shoes alright. Hundreds of 'em. It was hard to tell how well-made they were, but they didn't look cheap, that's for sure. Even if they were pretty well-made, I was lookin' at a lot more than eight hundred clams worth of shoes. Maybe double that.

I jumped down in. The plan was that I'd toss 'em out to Jimmy, who would stack 'em, then we'd divide 'em up, based on quality and design.

As soon as I landed down in the shoes, I felt an awful chill crawl down my spine. That feeling got worse when I could see that something was moving under the shoes. Without waitin', I fired off my last holy bullet at whatever it was. But I musta missed, 'cause there was a rustling and then a thing that still haunts me to this day pulled itself up from the ladies shoes.

He was a hobo. Or he used to be. He looked more like what would happen if you sucked the air out of a hobo, dipped him in acid, then put the leftover bones and sinews back into his clothes and somehow stood him up. His eyes hung a couple inches out of their sockets like jingle bells. His cheeks had rotted away, so his tongue hung to one side. My flashlight shined right through his gelatinous body, casting a shadow of his skeleton on the wall behind him. He reached our his boney fingers at me.

"I thought you'd forgotten about me, Edgar," he said in the kind of voice you have when your cheeks have rotted away.

This was right about when I wished The Goon was with me and this undead hobo. He loves this sort of thing.

"I've been waiting … just like we planned," he says, "I stowed away and you were supposed to let me out when the train passed the state line, then we'd divide the shoes. That was the plan. How did you forget me this long? It's been so long, I had to eat whatever I could to survive."

I looked down, and sure enough—the undead ghost hobo had chewed off his own feet, he walked towards me on his pointy shin bones like some kind of horror flamingo.

"Imagine, eating your feet while trapped in a treasure trove of shoes," he says to me, as he's gettin' closer and closer, "I think the irony may have made me crazy, Edgar."

"Look pal," I says, "I ain't this Edgar who left you to rot in here. You got the wrong guy. I wasn't never in on your caper." But he wasn't listening, and his danglin' eyeballs were lookin' at my feet.

"I held up my end of the deal," he says, pulling out a huge rusty hobo fork, "but you didn't. Now I'll watch you eat your feet and then we'll be square."

At this point I really wished I had a couple more bullets.

"What's the hold up?" I hear Jimmy holler from up above.

Jimmy was lookin' right down at me, but on account of I pointed the flashlight up, he couldn't see the undead footless hobo who was about to cut my feet off as part of some kinda vengeance for an earlier failed plan to boost these same shoes.

"Toss me your heater!" I says to Jimmy, "Slackjaw hobo!"

"What?" says Jimmy, wasting valuable seconds that we would never get back.

Those seconds were just the time it took for googlie-eyes to pounce and plant that rusty fork in my ankle. I fall backwards and start spoutin' blood. The undead hobo's hackin' away at my feet, while his pointy shin bone stubs poke at my face like pool cues. I'm hammerin' at the side of his head with the butt of my .45, but all that's managing to do is push some of his brains out his left ear—which ain't slowing him down one bit.

From experience, I know that I need to calm down, get his heart away from the rest of his body, and bury it. It sounds easy, but this is a tall order when you're pinned and your adrenaline's kicking in.

Up above, Jimmy decides to start shooting.

Bullets in a contained metal box have a tendency to bounce around a whole bunch, and that's exactly what happened. The boxcar became a sort of popcorn machine, in which somebody had replaced the kernels with a whole bunch of bullets. This didn't help me too much.

With everything I had, I kicked the hobo's head. With a click, the head flew off, which was just the opening I was looking for.

(Zombies have for their heads a fascination along the lines of cats and yarn. Understandably, if you can be separated from your head and still be alive, you're gonna want to get it back ASAP.)

Jimmy threw the rope down and hoisted me up while the hobo head and the body scrambled for each other like blind man's bluff.

Me and Jimmy ran like squirrels back to the Packard.

As we drove back into town, we vowed never to return to that fateful boxcar (a vow that we honored for almost three weeks).

The next night at Norton's I was telling the story to The Goon, but I could tell he had something else on his mind that was eatin' him up. Jimmy couldn't believe that I'd made it up the rope without catching any lead. Later that night, I checked, and sure enough—I had. There was three bullets lodged in my leg and part of my back. I guess in all the brouhaha I just hadn't noticed. They're still there to this day. I don't feel 'em unless it rains a lot, then they get kinda itchy. I don't know if the holy elbow grease on 'em had some kind of magic effect, or if they just didn't hit any major arteries.

I like to think they're lucky. Maybe they is, maybe they ain't. Maybe they're what kept me on the sunny side of the dirt the time that me and Charlie Noodles had to set fire to that Spanish ghost ship.

But that is a story for another day.

THE GOON™

SKETCHBOOK

Eric Powell '05

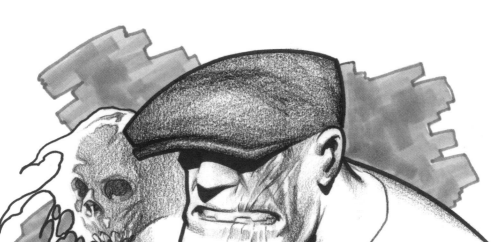

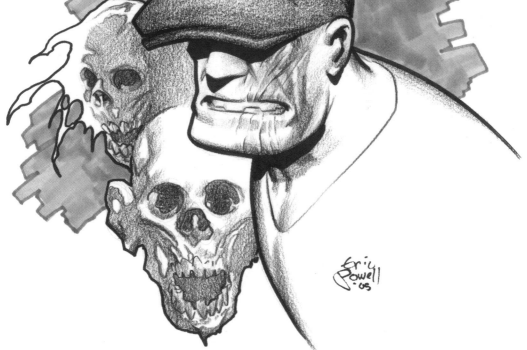

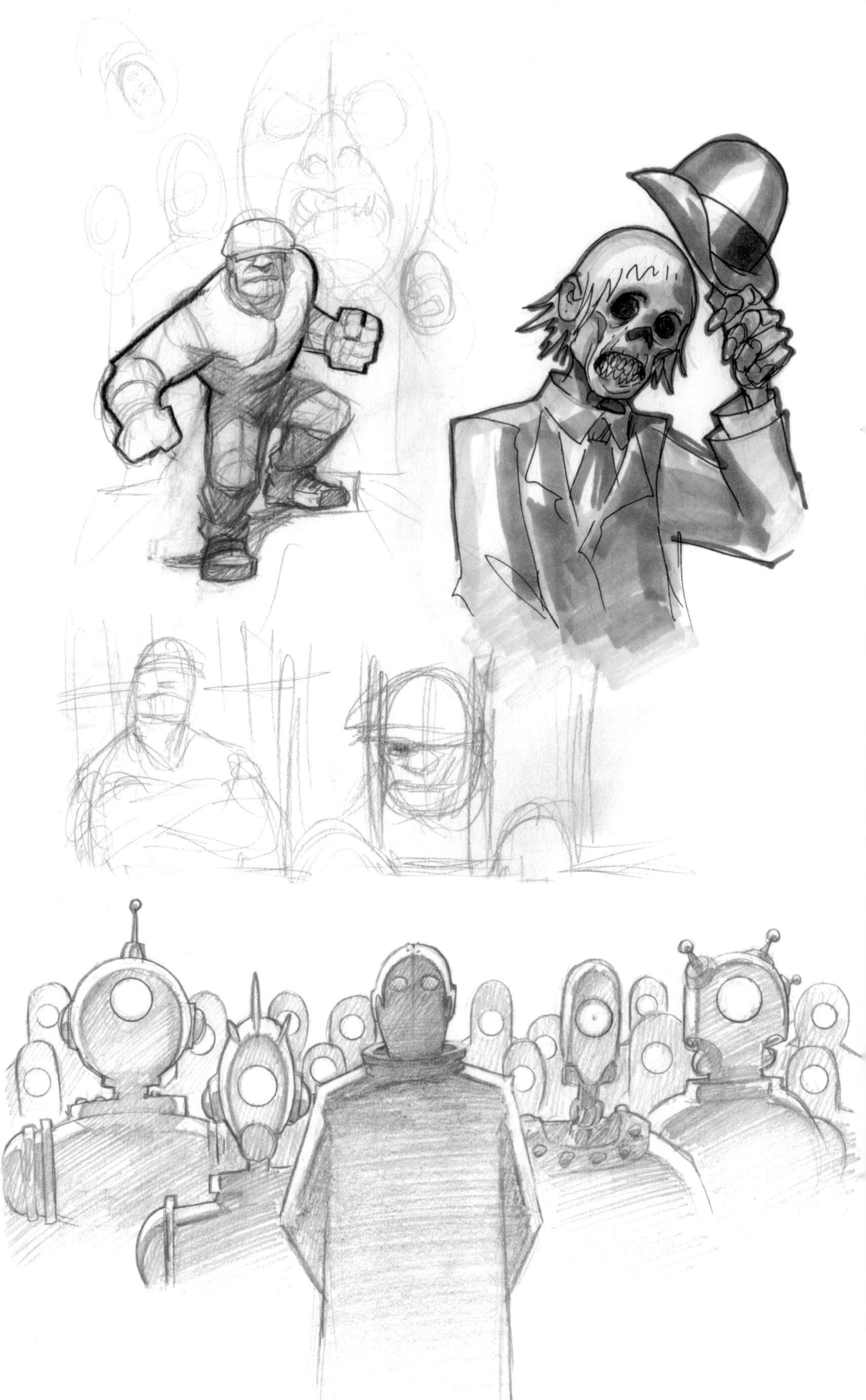

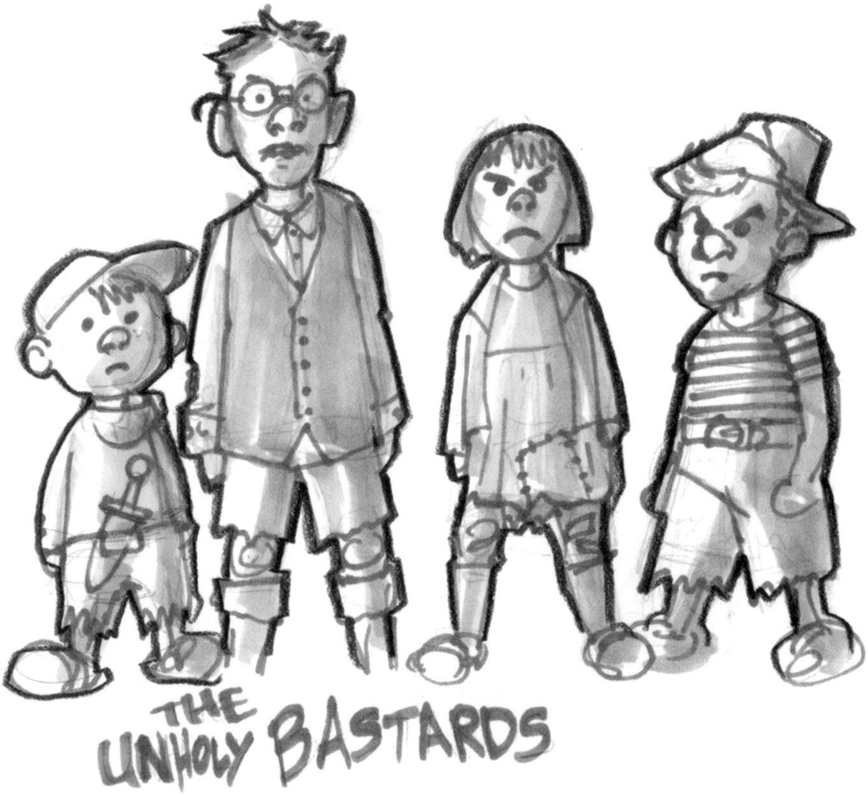
THE UNHOLY BASTARDS

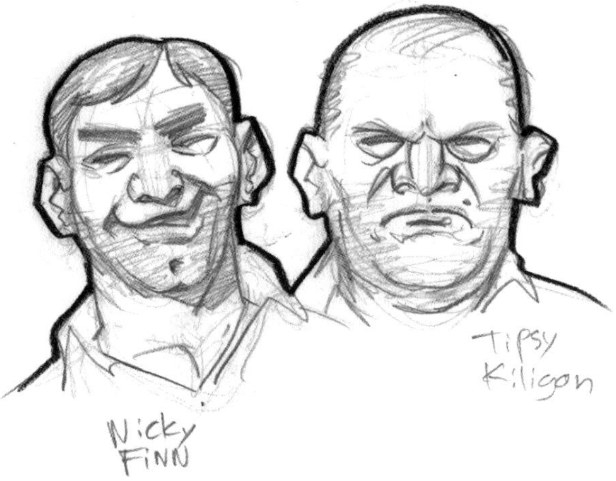
Tipsy Kiligan
Nicky FINN

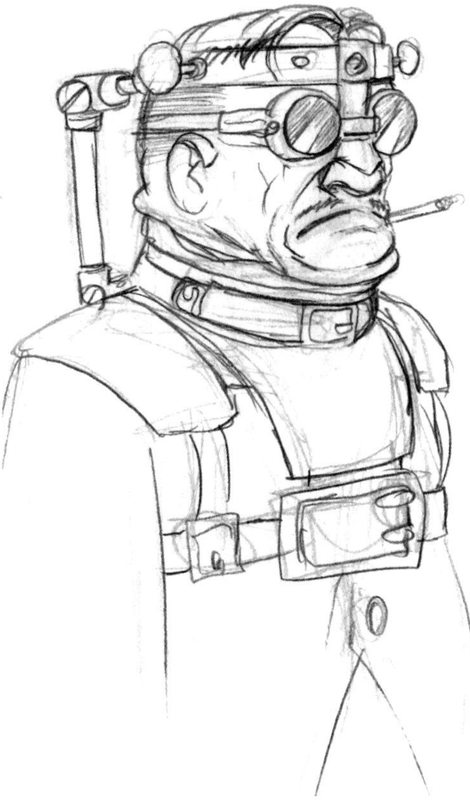

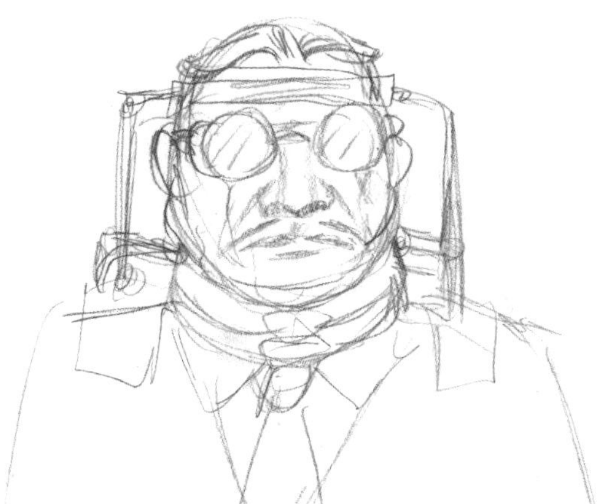

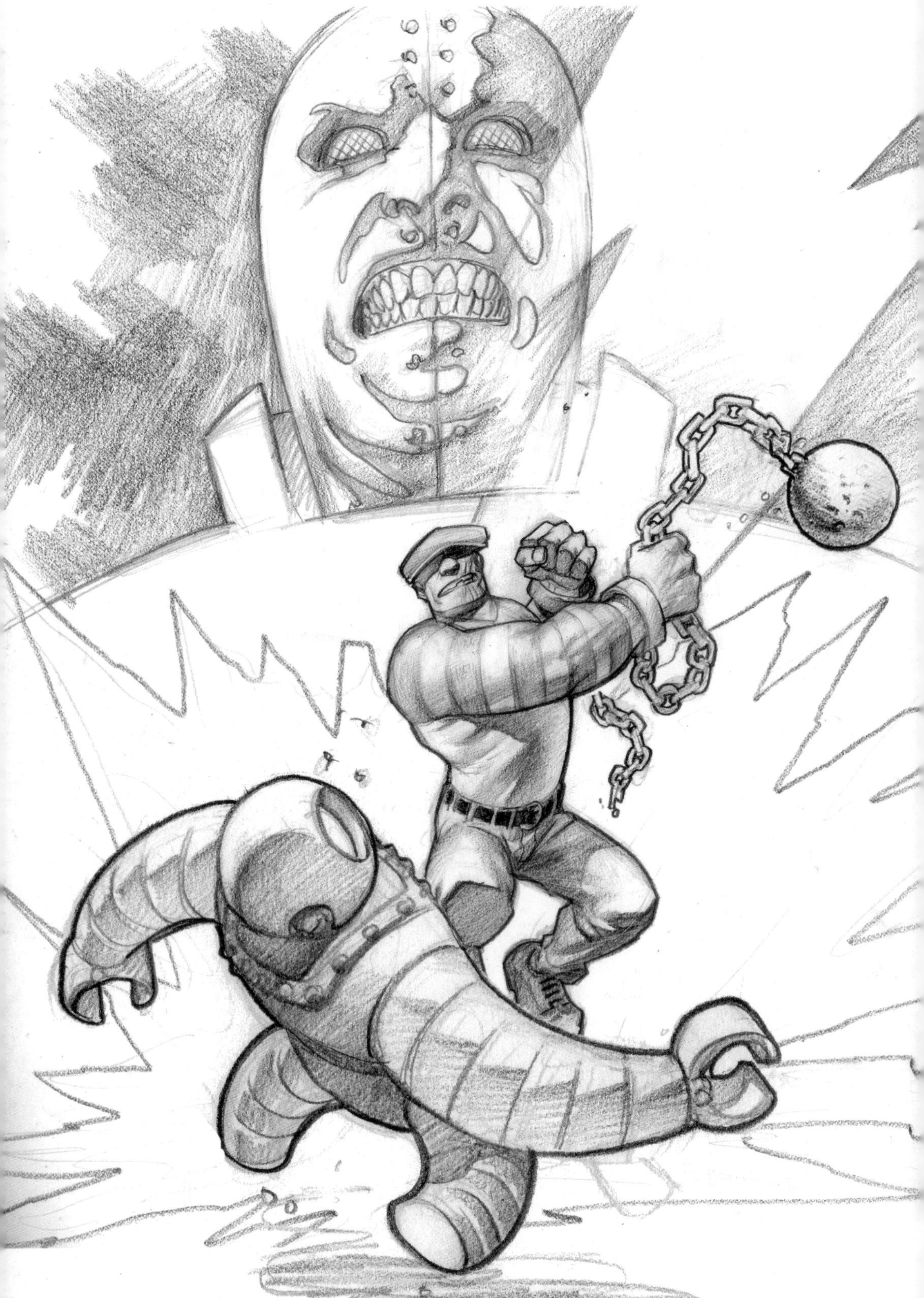

THE GOON

by Eric Powell

Volume 0:
ROUGH STUFF
ISBN: 1-59307-086-1 $12.95

Volume 1:
NOTHIN' BUT MISERY
ISBN: 1-56971-998-5 $15.95

Volume 2:
MY MURDEROUS CHILDHOOD
(AND OTHER GRIEVOUS YARNS)
ISBN: 1-59307-109-4 $13.95

Volume 3:
HEAPS OF RUINATION
ISBN: 1-59307-292-9 $12.95

_____

GOON HEAD SHOT T-SHIRT
M-XL $17.99   XXL $19.99

NORTON'S PUB T-SHIRT
M-XL $17.99   XXL $19.99

SQUID CAR T-SHIRT
M-XL $17.99   XXL $19.99

GOON ZIPPO LIGHTER
$29.99

GOON SHOT GLASS #1:
THE GOON
$5.99

GOON SHOT GLASS #2:
NORTON'S PUB
$5.99

GOON PVC SET
$14.99

ALSO FROM DARK HORSE BOOKS!

Mike Mignola
Jill Thompson
Evan Dorkin
Kelley Jones
Eric Powell
Gary Gianni
and others
The Dark Horse
BOOK OF THE DEAD

THE DARK HORSE BOOK OF THE DEAD

by Eric Powell, Mike Mignola, Evan Dorkin, Jill Thompson, Kelley Jones, Gary Gianni, and others

Mike Mignola presents a Hellboy yarn combining Shakespeare and graverobbing in this followup to Dark Horse's Eisner-nominated *Books of Hauntings* and *Witchcraft*. New additions for this volume include Goon creator Eric Powell, celebrated B.P.R.D. artist Guy Davis, and Kelley Jones. Plus a rare tale by Conan creator Robert E. Howard.

Hardcover, 96 pages, Full color
$14.95, ISBN: 1-59307-281-3

ZOMBIEWORLD
CHAMPION of the WORMS
MIKE MIGNOLA
PAT MCEOWN

ZOMBIEWORLD: CHAMPION OF THE WORMS

Mike Mignola and Pat McEown

A small-town museum is plagued by odd disturbances and missing persons — gifts from the new kid in town, Azzul Gotha, the 42,000-year-old Hyperborean mummy that just checked in. It's all-out zombie mayhem, complete with human sacrifice, a cemetery showdown, and the end of civilization.

Softcover, 80 pages, Full color
$8.95, ISBN: 1-59307-407-7

MAN WITH THE SCREAMING BRAIN
BRUCE CAMPBELL DAVID GOODMAN RICK REMENDER HILARY BARTA

MAN WITH THE SCREAMING BRAIN

by Bruce Campbell, David Goodman, Rick Remender, and Hilary Barta

Based on the film from B-movie mega star Bruce Campbell. An American industrialist is determined to exploit the crippled economy of a former Soviet state. But when he hits on the wrong gypsy girl, he soon finds himself in the grip of a mad scientist with a twisted brain-transplant scheme worthy of Dr. Frankenstein.

Softcover, 104 pages, Full color
$13.95, ISBN: 1-59307-397-6

damn nation
DAMN NATION
ANDREW COSBY
J. ALEXANDER

DAMN NATION

Andrew Cosby and J. Alexander

A vampire plague has spread from sea to shining sea and when a small holdout of scientists trapped outside of Buffalo, N.Y. discover a cure, it's up to a Special Ops team to go in and get it.

Softcover, 104 pages, Full color
$12.95, ISBN: 1-59307-389-5

AVAILABLE AT YOUR LOCAL COMICS SHOP OR BOOKSTORE
To find a comics shop in your area, call 1-888-266-4226
For more information or to order direct visit darkhorse.com or call 1-800-862-0052 • Mon.-Fri. 9 A.M. to 5 P.M. Pacific Time.
***Prices and availability subject to change without notice**

DARK HORSE COMICS™ *drawing on your nightmares*
darkhorse.com

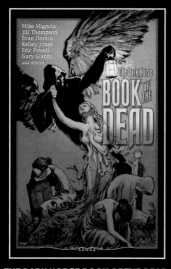

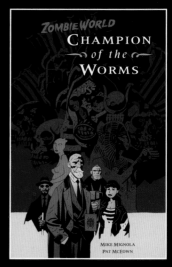

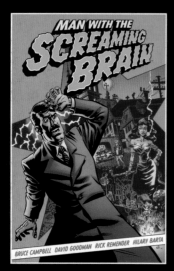

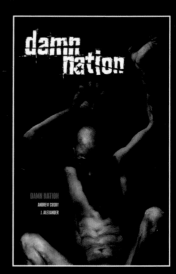